GRADE 7 CONTENTS

D0509148

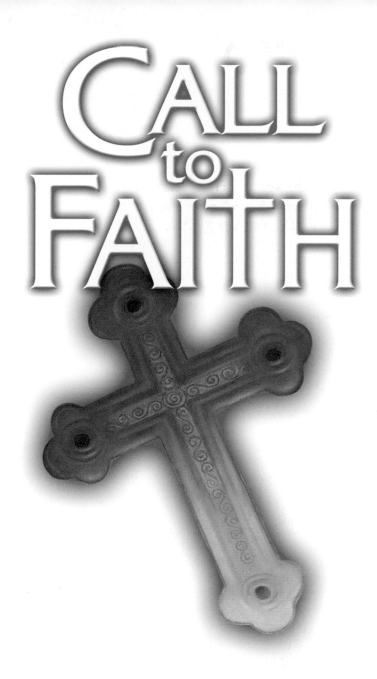

CALL to FAITH

GRADE 7

OSV

www.osvcurriculum.com

Nihil Obstat
Rev. Dr. Steven Olds, S.T.D.
Censor Librorum

Imprimatur
✠ Most Rev. Thomas Wenski
Bishop of Orlando
February 1, 2006

The Ad Hoc Committee to Oversee the Use of the Catechism, United States Conference of Catholic Bishops, has found this catechetical series, copyright 2007, to be in conformity with the *Catechism of the Catholic Church*.

The imprimatur is an official declaration that a book or pamphlet is free of doctrinal or moral error. No implication is contained therein that the person who granted the imprimatur agrees with the contents, opinions, or statements expressed.

Write:
Our Sunday Visitor Curriculum Division
Our Sunday Visitor, Inc.
200 Noll Plaza, Huntington, Indiana 46750

Call to Faith is a registered trademark of Our Sunday Visitor Curriculum Division, Our Sunday Visitor, 200 Noll Plaza, Huntington, Indiana 46750.

For permission to reprint copyrighted materials, grateful acknowledgment is made to the following sources:

Division of Christian Education of the National Council of the Churches of Christ in the U.S.A.: From the *New Revised Standard Version Bible: Catholic Edition*. Text copyright © 1993 and 1989 by the Division of Christian Education of the National Council of the Churches of Christ in the U.S.A.

GIA Publications, Inc.: Lyrics from "Take, O Take Me As I Am" by John L. Bell. Lyrics © 1994 by Iona Community. Lyrics from "Increase Our Faith" by David Haas. Lyrics © 1997 by GIA Publications, Inc. Lyrics from "We Choose Life" by David Haas. Lyrics © 1998 by GIA Publications, Inc. Lyrics from "We Praise You" by David Haas. Lyrics © 2002 by GIA Publications, Inc.

Excerpts from the English translation of *Rite of Penance* © 1974, International Commission on English in the Liturgy Corporation (ICEL); excerpts from *A Book of Prayers* © 1982, ICEL; excerpts from the English translation of *Rites of Ordination of a Bishop, of Priests, and of Deacons* © 2000, 2002, ICEL; excerpts from the English translation of *The Roman Missal* © 2010, ICEL; excerpts from the English translation of *The Order of Confirmation* © 2013, ICEL; excerpts from the English translation of *The Order of Baptism of Children* © 2017, ICEL. All rights reserved.

United States Conference of Catholic Bishops, Washington, D.C.: From the English translation of the *Catechism of the Catholic Church* for the United States of America. Translation copyright © 1994 by United States Catholic Conference, Inc.—Libreria Editrice Vaticana. From the English translation of the *Catechism of the Catholic Church: Modifications from the Editio Typica*. Translation copyright © 1997 by United States Catholic Conference, Inc.—Libreria Editrice Vaticana.

Call to Faith Grade 7 Student Edition
ISBN: 978-0-15-902280-1
Item Number: CU1376

8 9 10 11   000309 22 21 20
LSC Communications; Menasha, WI, USA; April 2020; Job #14357

ABOUT YOU

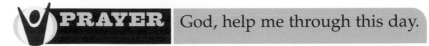

I can't believe it's time to start school again . . .
I wonder who's going to be in my class . . .
I wish I felt better about myself . . .

Did you ever look back at pictures of yourself as a child and wonder how you could ever have been that small, or that messy, or that funny looking? Have you ever read something you wrote last year in class or in your journal and wondered, "What was I thinking?" Sometimes it seems like we can grow into entirely new people in just one year!

Junior high is like that, maybe more than any other time in your life. You aren't a child anymore, but you can't drive a car yet. You have learned so much about yourself, but that person you see in the mirror still feels like a stranger sometimes. Well, hang on, because it's not over yet and things are about to get really interesting. By the time this year is over, you will definitely wonder who that person was that you saw in the mirror this very morning—the person you are as you read these words right now will seem like a little kid to you!

ACTIVITY

LET'S BEGIN How would you explain your day and why you do the things you do to someone who knows nothing about you and your world?

WHAT'S MY DAY LIKE:

WHAT I DO THAT'S REALLY IMPORTANT TO ME:

ABOUT YOUR FAITH

When everything is changing around you, there is one thing you can count on to remain the same: God never changes. His wisdom, his Church, and his love will always be there to help you make it through. We live in a world where everything changes all the time—and not always for the better. There are few things we can depend on to help us no matter what. That's why faith is so important. Things are different when you let God the Father, his Son, Jesus, and the Holy Spirit into your life.

This year you'll meet Jesus in a different and exciting way. You'll get to know him through the eyes of his closest friends and followers. You'll find out what was important to him and why it's important to us today. You'll get a chance to ask questions about topics that really matter to you, and discover what Jesus and the Church have to say about them.

ACTIVITY

SHARE YOUR FAITH List 3 things you want to find out about who Jesus is and what it means to follow him.

1. _____

2. _____

3. _____

▶ Now, partner with someone you don't know well. Share your questions with each other and then find out what others in the group are wondering about.

ABOUT YOUR BOOK

When people say you shouldn't judge a book by its cover, that's about not judging people by the way they look. You've got to get to know them. You may think you know what's in this book after looking at the cover—and you might be right. But take another look and think about it for a minute. In addition to the stories of today, the scripture stories, the Catholic teachings, and the activities, here are some of the extra features you should look for as you read.

GO TO THE SOURCE sends you directly to the Bible to find out more about the scripture passage or story explained in your book.

WHERE IT HAPPENED is just that. A mini-tour of where biblical or Church events took place and where the saints lived their extraordinary lives.

GLOBAL DATA gives you interesting facts and statistics about various countries and regions of the world as well as about the Church in different locations.

CATHOLICS TODAY offers a view into the way people live out their faith by the ways they pray, the stands they take, and the choices they make. This is about how Catholics from all over put their faith into action, and how you do, too.

CHECK THIS OUT! points out different faith facts and bits of information that connect to the main topics you are learning.

Words of Faith define core Catholic teachings and help you to understand the "what" and "why" of your faith.

PEOPLE OF FAITH puts the whole message of the Good News into real-life circumstances by presenting biographical sketches of ordinary and extraordinary people who responded to Christ's call to follow him.

ACTIVITY

CONNECT YOUR FAITH Choose one of the features and find out how it's used in the first unit of your book. What new bit of information or insight did you gain from the feature?

A CALL TO FAITH

PRAYER

Leader: Let us take time, here and now, to gather
for prayer,
in the name of the one who call us to
"come and follow."

Jesus said, "I am the light of the world. Whoever
follows me will never walk in darkness but will
have the light of life" (*John 8:12*).

Reader 1: Lord Jesus, I want to follow!
Help me to trust you and know you will show
me how to love.
Let your light shine in me for friends who are searching,
and for all who are lost and can't find the way.

All: **We are called to love tenderly.**

Leader: Jesus called to Peter and Andrew as they sat in their boats,
"Follow me and I will make you fishers for people" (*Mark 1:17*).

Reader 2: Lord Jesus, I want to follow!
Let me be ready when you cast your net!
Send me in search of the others you call to.
Help me to lead all the lost ones to you.

All: **We are called to serve one another.**

Leader: Jesus said, "Whoever serves me must follow me . . ." (*John 12:26*).

Reader 3: Lord Jesus, I want to follow!
Help me to stand by the things that I say.
Remind me that actions speak louder than words.
Give me a mission to go out and serve all that I can.
Send me as a witness to all your good news.

All: **We are called to act with justice.**

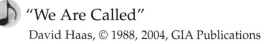 "We Are Called"
David Haas, © 1988, 2004, GIA Publications

1 GOD Our Creator

PRAYER You have given us so much, Creator.

Pretty incredible—the stars and planets, life on Earth
The whole universe works together.
How did we get here—and why are we here?

Ryan held up a photo of a recently discovered planet for his science class that he'd downloaded from the Hubble Telescope Web site. "They say it's the most earthlike planet they have ever seen outside of our own solar system," he told them.

Mona wondered, "Do you think it's possible that God created another planet like the one we live on?" But her face blushed red when Brandon laughed out loud.

"What does God have to do with it? We've just been learning all about the 'big bang' and how these planets and stars evolved. Didn't you listen?"

After some thought, Mona answered, "I can't imagine that these beautiful stars and planets could come into existence on their own—how could it really be just a random accident?"

"Science book," Brandon said as he held his up in the air. "Explains it real clearly."

Mona turned from Brandon to her good friend Ryan, who still had the space pictures in his hand. "What do you think?"

"I don't know. Why does it have to be a choice between believing either science books or faith? Maybe they're both right somehow." Then, after a pause, he added, "Whatever. There's no way either of you can prove you're right. The only thing we know for sure is how amazing it all looks in these pictures—no matter how it all got there!"

ACTIVITY

LET'S BEGIN What is the conflict between Brandon and Mona? With whom do you identify most in this story: Brandon, Mona, or Ryan? Why?

▶ **How do you think the universe and our planet began?**

▶ **Think of a time when you stared at the stars on a clear night. What thoughts came to your mind?**

_____

_____

_____

_____

_____

THE MYSTERY OF GOD

Focus How do we come to know who God is?

Most people can't help but have a sense of awe and wonder at the beauty and order of the stars, planets, and galaxies, especially when they look at some amazing satellite images. Looking at pictures of the universe can sometimes make us aware of how human beings are a part of "the big picture." And at some point in our lives, most of us ask ourselves what's the reason for it all and what role do we play in that bigger picture.

✠ SCRIPTURE

GO TO THE SOURCE
Read **Genesis 1:1–2:4** to find out more about why God created the world and humans.

✠ SCRIPTURE

"In the beginning when God created the heavens and the earth, the earth was a formless void . . ."

—*Genesis 1:1–2*

The stories of creation in the Book of Genesis show something wonderful: Even though humans are a small part of the universe, they have a special place in the eyes of God. And God shows that he wants all humans to know and love him.

Seeing God in the Works of Creation
From the beginning of our time on earth, the natural world has helped humans recognize and acknowledge God. People felt God's power in the forces of wind, fire, and water. They saw God's beauty in the trees and flowers. They got a sense of God's generosity as he gave them the responsibility to be caretakers of his many gifts of creation.

The first humans were able to see these aspects of God because he had given them the gift of human reason. Like all of us, they were given an intellect—the ability to think and make connections. With the gift of intellect, we can grow in knowledge and search for the meaning of the things we experience. With human reason, we discover the power and presence of God even in the most basic and simple parts of his created world.

? Thunder, a sunset, mountains, the ocean, a baby . . . what aspect of nature helps you see God as the Creator?

? How do you experience God's presence in the world?

Beyond Words The works of creation are not the only way through which people can learn about God. We can discover who God is through the ways he acts in our lives. In creating Adam and Eve, the first man and woman, God showed his great generosity and love. He made them in his image so that they could be like him, free to think and choose, able to love and experience friendship. Out of love God made himself known to them.

Although he shows himself in so many ways through creation and through his relationship with people, God cannot be fully or completely known. Whether God is seen in creation or in relation to a human person, each revelation of God is only a small aspect of who God is.

This is why God is called a **mystery**, because the depth of who God is cannot be seen or understood by humans. Human expressions of God are limited because we are human. We will never know all about God's nature while on earth. We will only know God completely in heaven.

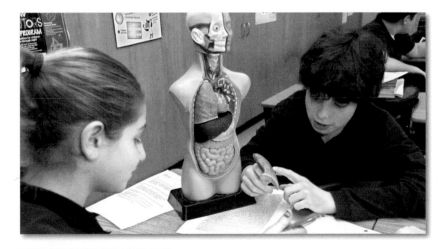

mystery

eternal

CATHOLICS TODAY

The stories of creation in Genesis reveal a number of truths. God:

▶ created the world from its beginning

▶ created man and woman, breathing into them his divine Spirit

▶ created the human family to live in harmony

▶ gave humans a prime role in overseeing the gifts of creation

The faith of the Church does not describe *how* God carried out this creation, and Catholics are free to explore scientific theories, like evolution, that describe how the world developed. Theories can be compatible with faith when they acknowledge that God is the creator and agent of that movement, and he directly creates each human soul.

ACTIVITY

SHARE YOUR FAITH List some ways you get to know God.

▶ **What are some questions you have about God and creation?**

▶ **Who or what do you think can help you answer your questions?**

GOD'S PLAN FOR US

Focus How do humans fit into God's plan?

The first humans reflected the goodness and glory of God. They were created in harmony with one another and with God. And when they freely chose to turn from God and to sin, God did not abandon them. Humans did not completely lose what made them like God—their ability to be good, to love, to be holy, to think, and to be free. Human nature remained basically good, but weakened, often inclined to sin. God remained with humans and promised to restore, or bring back, the human family to its original glory so that all can once again share life fully with him.

The stories of Genesis show that God wanted to lead all people to know his love.

▶ With Noah, God made a lasting covenant, or binding agreement, to bring all creation back to the harmony he had originally intended it to have. (See *Genesis 9:1–17.*)

▶ God made Abraham the "father of all nations" and promised that through Abraham's descendants all nations would be blessed. (See *Genesis 15:1–21.*)

▶ In spite of her old age, God blessed Sarah with a son; she and her husband Abraham shared in God's blessing and promise. (See *Genesis 17:15–19*; *21:1–3.*)

God planned from the beginning of creation to give his only Son, Jesus Christ, to the world. Through his Son Jesus, God the Father wanted to reconcile all of his creation to himself so that the human race would be restored to the place that they enjoyed originally. The promise of salvation was planted in the hearts of the Israelites, God's Chosen People. This hope gave them the courage to face hardship and even exile.

WHERE IT HAPPENED

THOUGH NO physical evidence has been found, archaeologists suspect that the garden described in the creation story was located somewhere between the Tigris and Euphrates rivers, in what is now modern-day Iraq. (See *Genesis 2:10–14.*)

Euphrates River
Tigris River
ASSYRIA
• Nineveh
Damascus
BABYLON
• Babylon
ISRAEL
• Jerusalem

Garden of Eden

The story of God's relationship with his Chosen People is recorded in the Old Testament. Throughout their history, God's Chosen People had hints of the salvation that would one day be brought into the world by Christ. For example, when the Israelites fled from slavery in Egypt, God helped them navigate their way across the Red Sea. (See *Exodus 14:21–31*.) This liberation was an example and preview of the freedom that Christ would bring us, helping us navigate our way toward the plan God the Father has for all humans. We see in this example how the Jewish faith, unlike other non-Christian faiths, is a response to God's revelation in the old convenant.

What do you think God's plan has to do with you?

What signs of God's plan exist in the world?

CHECK THIS OUT!

The bishops of the Appalachian mountain region of the United States recognized that the works of creation help us to know who God is. When they spoke about the need for economic justice for the poor of that region, they observed that those who live in the Appalachian Mountains "experience

▶ in their height, God's majesty,

▶ in their weight, God's strength,

▶ in their hollows, God's embrace,

▶ in their waters, God's cleansing,

▶ in their haze, God's mystery.

These mountains are truly a holy place."

ACTIVITY

CONNECT YOUR FAITH When and how do you sense the presence of God in your life, in others, in nature, or in current events?

IN YOUR LIFE

IN NATURE

IN OTHERS

IN CURRENT EVENTS

KNOWING GOD

Focus What are some of the things that we know about God?

Because of the way humans think, it's hard to understand anything that does not have an explainable beginning or origin. Yet, the story of creation shows us that "God is" and "has always been," even before the beginning of time, and will be forever. This is what it means to say that God is **eternal**.

God alone created the heavens and the earth. He didn't need to create anything at all, not the heavens and earth or any human persons. He is complete in himself— he isn't lonely. Yet God chose freely to show himself by creating out of nothing all that we see around us today.

God Is Truth God is Truth itself. God will never deceive us or lead us in the wrong direction. Whatever God makes known about himself is true, and the words that he speaks are always true. God is faithful to his word. So, his promise to bring salvation to all people is a promise that we can count on.

✝ SCRIPTURE

GO TO THE SOURCE
Read **1 John 1:5** and **1 John 4:6** to see how John speaks about God, who is Truth and Love.

? When have you counted on someone to tell you the truth— and they did? When has someone counted on you to tell them the truth—and you did?

? What does all this tell you about the power of the Truth?

God Is Love Have you ever been hurt and felt like getting back at someone to "punish" that person? This natural reaction is part of what it means to be a human being who is imperfect. But we strive to grow more like God. One of the reasons people stand in awe of God is because God is strong and consistent in showing love for his people. God's love is perfect.

In the Old Testament, we find a God who never stops showing his love to the Israelites in powerful ways. When his people were in Egyptian captivity, he led them to freedom. When they grumbled in the desert, he fed them and gave them water. Over and over, the people who belonged to God would fail to act like it, but God's response would always be the same: a forgiving and compassionate love.

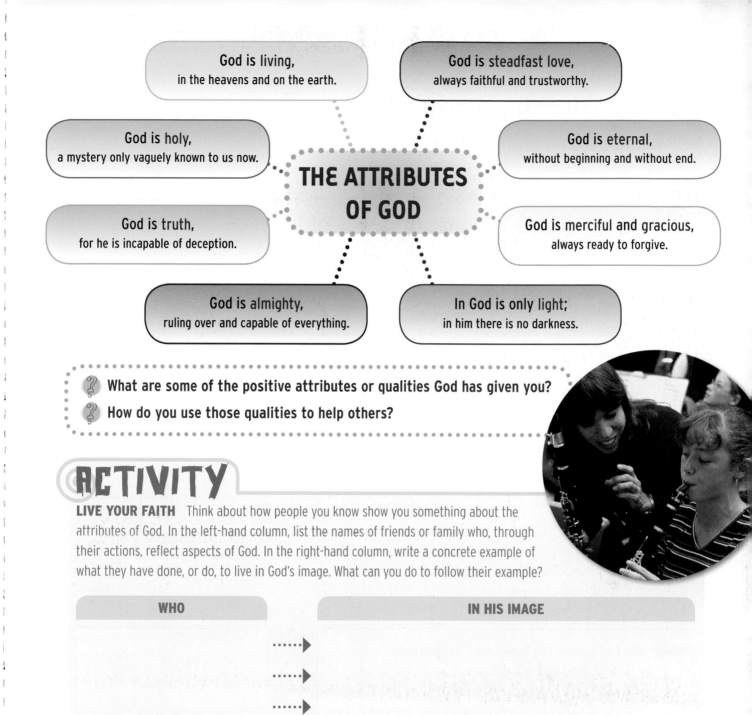

THE ATTRIBUTES OF GOD

God is living, in the heavens and on the earth.

God is steadfast love, always faithful and trustworthy.

God is holy, a mystery only vaguely known to us now.

God is eternal, without beginning and without end.

God is truth, for he is incapable of deception.

God is merciful and gracious, always ready to forgive.

God is almighty, ruling over and capable of everything.

In God is only light; in him there is no darkness.

? What are some of the positive attributes or qualities God has given you?

? How do you use those qualities to help others?

ACTIVITY

LIVE YOUR FAITH Think about how people you know show you something about the attributes of God. In the left-hand column, list the names of friends or family who, through their actions, reflect aspects of God. In the right-hand column, write a concrete example of what they have done, or do, to live in God's image. What can you do to follow their example?

WHO	IN HIS IMAGE
·····▶	
·····▶	
·····▶	

IN SUMMARY

CATHOLICS BELIEVE

We can come to know God through all that he has created and through human reason.

▶ Out of nothing, God created the heavens and the earth, and made humans in his image and likeness, making it possible to know him and share in his divine qualities.

▶ God promised to restore the human race to the harmony and perfection for which he originally created us, and throughout history he has shown himself and his plan in many ways.

▶ From the Genesis creation accounts and the world around us, we get a sense of the attributes of God—eternal, almighty, truth, love, merciful, holy, living.

CELEBRATION OF THE WORD

Leader: Our God is an amazing and awesome God,
beyond our understanding,
but here right now—here in our midst.
Let us prepare to hear God's word to us about his creation.

A reading from the Book of Genesis.
Read Genesis 1:1–31.

The Word of the Lord.

All: Thanks be to God.

Leader: There is a single and wonderful source of life.
Let us turn in prayer to God the Creator.

Respond to each petition with these words:
Hear us, O Lord.

Reader 1: O God, you have created the earth and the heavens,
And in your goodness, you created us.
Help us treasure and respect all you have created.

All: Hear us, O Lord.

Reader 2: O God, at times it is hard to imagine
that there is a creator who could envision
all the beauty we see around us.
We thank you for all you have given to us.

All: Hear us, O Lord.

Reader 3: O God, with love and generosity
you created all we see.
Help us to accept the love you have for us,
And to share that love in the way we live.

All: Hear us, O Lord.

Leader: O God, in your infinite wisdom
you have given us life.
In the wonders of nature,
through the seasons of the year
and the seasons of our lives,
we offer you thanksgiving
with every breath we take.

All: Amen.

♪ "Over My Head"
Traditional Spiritual

14

REVIEW

A **Work with Words** Circle the letter of the choice that best completes the sentence.

1. Because God's complete identity cannot be seen or understood by humans, God is _____.
   - **a.** a mystery
   - **b.** a spirit
   - **c.** Trinity
   - **d.** eternal

2. Because God was, is, and always will be, he is _____.
   - **a.** spirit
   - **b.** love
   - **c.** eternal
   - **d.** truth

3. Because God is _____, we can count on his promise to bring salvation to all people.
   - **a.** faithful
   - **b.** holy
   - **c.** eternal
   - **d.** spirit

4. Genesis tells the story of _____.
   - **a.** salvation through Christ
   - **b.** Israel's exodus from Egypt
   - **c.** God's creation
   - **d.** evolution

B **Check Understanding** Complete each sentence with the correct term from the word bank at right.

5. The first humans were able to see the reflections of God through his creation because he gave them the gift of _____.

6. God's relationship with his Chosen People is told in the _____.

7. The exodus of the Israelites from slavery in Egypt is a preview of the _____ that Christ would bring.

8. We will only fully understand God when we are in _____.

9. Even when we disobey him, God shows us _____.

10. Love, truth, and mystery are examples of _____.

Word Bank

- compassionate love
- God's attributes
- theological virtues
- heaven
- human reason
- original sin
- Old Testament
- salvation
- communion

C **Make Connections: Cause and Effect** Write a one-paragraph response to the question.

How has God's creation affected you? How have you experienced God through his creation?

OUR CATHOLIC FAITH

WHAT NOW?

★ Show your appreciation for nature in how you use the gifts of creation.

★ Do something to restore the beauty of creation where it has been harmed or abused.

★ Look at what is beautiful in your own life and how it can help connect you to God.

★ Be a person who speaks the truth, stands up for the truth, and seeks the truth.

★ Show love and acknowledge love whenever you see it. It is your way of recognizing God in you and in the world.

ACTIVITY

LIVE YOUR FAITH In the spaces below, examine how you live in God's creation.

▶ **NOTICE**—How do you pay attention to the world around you? Name two things that surprise you as being signs of God's presence or remind you of what he is like.

▶ **CONNECT**—What could you do with your friends, class, or family to connect to what you've noticed, such as taking care, showing other people, using it?

▶ **PRAY**—What do you want to say to or ask from God because of this? What questions do you have? What thoughts do you want to share?

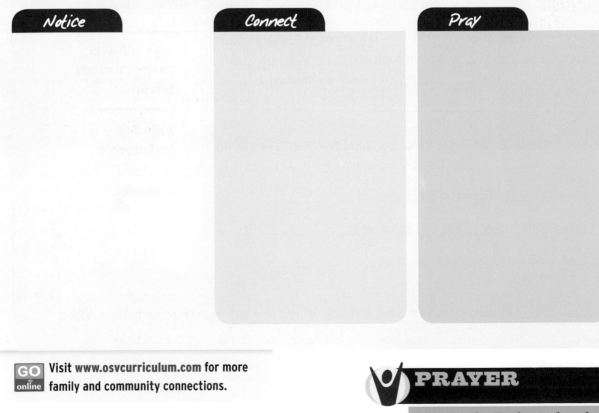

Notice	Connect	Pray

GO online Visit www.osvcurriculum.com for more family and community connections.

PRAYER

Heavenly Father, thank you for the beauty of creation and the beauty of my life.

Saint Kateri Tekakwitha

▲ **Saint Kateri Tekakwitha, 1656–1680**

Kateri Tekakwitha (Gah-dah-LEE Degh-agh-WEEdtha) is known as the "Lily of the Mohawk." But during her life, she was not known for an outward beauty. God gave her something greater than physical beauty; he gave her a spiritual beauty that came from her purity and faith. Kateri is the first Native American to be named a Saint. She is patroness of the environment and ecology. Her feast day is July 14. Many Native American ministries in Catholic churches in the United States and Canada were established because of Kateri Tekakwitha.

Tekakwitha was born near the town of Auriesville, New York, in 1656. Her mother was a Christian Algonquin. Her father was a Mohawk. Sadly, in 1660 Tekakwitha lost her mother and father to smallpox. Tekakwitha almost died, too. Her face was scarred for life, and her eyes were badly affected. Tekakwitha's uncle and two aunts took her in. In 1667, three Jesuit missionaries visited the Mohawks. Tekakwitha helped care for these men. She took note of their kindness and holiness. She worked in the fields, and she would go into the woods to pray to God. She would make crosses and place them throughout the woods to remind her to take time to pray during her chores.

Over the years, Tekakwitha's family tried to make her marry. Again and again, she refused. Tekakwitha had set her heart on following the religious life. So in 1675, when Father Jacques de Lamberville visited, she asked to be baptized. The young Native American girl was given the name Kateri.

Kateri's family was very angry about her new life. Some even said they would kill her. Father Lamberville told her to pray and to seek safety. Kateri fled to a Christian village of Native Americans in Sault Sainte-Marie, Canada.

Kateri gave her life to prayer, penitence, and care of the sick and elderly. Many said Kateri's prayers for them were answered.

Kateri had always been in poor health. In 1680, she became very ill. She died at the age of 24, speaking the names of Jesus and Mary. After her death, people noticed that the scars on Kateri's face cleared. It was a miracle. Her face now reflected the inner beauty she had been given by the Creator.

GLOBAL DATA

Ontario, Canada

- Ontario has a population of 13,210,700.

- Ontario is home to approximately 4 million Catholics.

- Ontario is larger than France and Spain put together.

- Ontario has about 250,000 lakes. The Iroquois word "Kanadario" means "the land of shining waters."

- Ontario was first settled 10,000 years ago by Algonquian and Iroquois tribes.

CHAPTER 2 Knowing GOD Through Scripture

PRAYER God, I want to know you better.

How can I learn more about myself?
How can I learn more about others?
How can I learn about God?

Lisa sat alone on the bus, staring at the empty seat next to her and thinking about her best friend, Tyra. Why did she have to move away? Okay, her father had a new job—Lisa knew that meant moving. But it just seemed so wrong that Tyra wasn't sitting next to her or walking into school with her today. It had taken time and work for them to become friends. What good was there in making friends with people if they were going to move away? It just didn't seem like it was worth the risk. She opened her class planner and scribbled a note that read: *Promise to self—NO MORE new friends!*

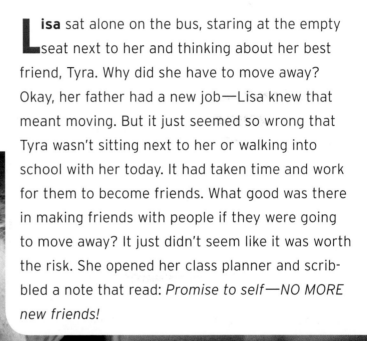

So Lisa wasn't very happy when she showed up for class and realized she was going to have a new science lab partner. When she walked into class and saw a new boy sitting in Tyra's seat, she felt angry that Tyra had been "replaced" by this shabby and unfriendly looking guy.

The teacher confirmed Lisa's fear by announcing that Jason would now be her lab partner. Jason's first words surprised her. "Thanks for being so nice about this. It must be hard to get a new partner in the middle of the school year," he said.

"No problem," she faked with a shrug. Trying to actually *be* nice instead of grumpy, she asked, "Where are you from?"

He told her about himself and his family. He talked about growing up in the city and how difficult the moving was because of the friends he left behind. Then she told him about Tyra, and he listened to what she said about missing her best friend. She could tell he understood how she felt.

After listening to him talk about his life a little, Lisa realized that Jason was okay, not weird or unfriendly. At the end of class, Lisa opened her planner to write down the homework assignment. She laughed at herself when she saw the note she had written just before class. She'd already broken the silly *"Promise to self"* and it wasn't even lunch yet!

ACTIVITY

LET'S BEGIN What was the key in helping Lisa move forward? What might have happened if Jason hadn't been willing to talk about himself with Lisa? What might have happened if Lisa's negative judgment had kept her from listening to Jason?

▶ **How did you get to know your best friends?**

▶ **What did you do so that they could know you better?**

GOD SPEAKS IN HUMAN WORDS

 Focus What are some of the ways in which God speaks to us?

When we meet someone for the first time, our ideas about the way the person talks or looks can sometimes get in the way of understanding him or her. But once we start to hear the person's story, we have a better understanding of him or her. If we are open, we can become friends. In much the same way, once we get to know God's story, our friendship with him grows.

God Inspires God wanted humans to get to know him, so he chose to speak to them with human words. Although no word can capture everything about God, these words do tell us about who God is and his hopes for us. Sacred Scripture, also called the **Bible**, is God's word to us written by humans acting under God's direction and guidance. God's **inspiration** is the divine foundation for the stories and texts of the Bible. Scripture records the story of the relationship between God and his people and the important communications that God had with them through history. By the Holy Spirit's action, the writers faithfully wrote the stories about God and the truth about God's plan for us.

? When has someone asked you to speak for him or her to others? What is it like to speak or act in someone else's name?

Interpreting Scripture The Old Testament tells the story of God's relationship with Abraham and his descendants. It includes the laws, history, and stories of the Israelites. After Jesus' Resurrection, many different people wrote about his life and ministry. The Church identified a set number of books as being truly inspired by God. This body of sacred texts is called the **canon** of Scripture. It includes forty-six books in the Old Testament and twenty-seven books in the New Testament. The Gospels tell us about Jesus' ministry and teachings. The early Christian community learned about Jesus through letters written by Saint Paul and his followers. "The Old Testament prepares for the New and the New Testament fulfills the Old; the two shed light on each other; both are true Word of God" (*Catechism of the Catholic Church*, #140).

▼ *St. Luke Writing*, from a Book of Hours by Jean Bourdichon (1457–1521)

Because God is the author of Scripture, the interpretation of Scripture should help us understand what he intends to tell us in the biblical text and what he desires for us. The Holy Spirit helps us to interpret Scripture.

The Bible contains a variety of literary forms. A literary form is the way something is written. Knowing the literary form helps us to understand the meaning of what is being said. The Bible includes some of these forms.

CHAPTER
Words
of Faith

Bible

inspiration

canon

evangelists

conscience

Literary Forms

▶ **Narrative stories** recall in a straightforward way something about God's relationship with the world. (See *Matthew 2:1–12.*)

▶ **Parables** make people look at ordinary events with a startling twist that opens them up to the surprising way God works. (See *Mark 4:1–20.*)

▶ **Teaching** enlightens people to understand how to live the Christian life. (See *Luke 6:20–36.*)

▶ **Miracle stories** teach how God's power and healing transform the world. (See *John 4:46–54.*)

▶ **Laws** portray the rules of conduct that God has set for us in living a good life. (See *Mark 12:28–34.* See also the Books of Exodus, Leviticus, Numbers, and Deuteronomy.)

▶ **Hymns and psalms** show the joy and struggle of being in relationship with God. (Choose any psalm from the Book of Psalms for reflection.)

▶ **Proverbs** are short sentences of wisdom. (See the Book of Proverbs.)

▶ **Apocalyptic literature** reflects the expectation of decisive intervention of God in history, especially at the end of the world. (See the Books of Daniel and Revelation.)

ACTIVITY

SHARE YOUR FAITH Working with a partner, create an outline of *The Story of God and His People.* The story must span from creation to the present time. Choose what you believe are the main points.

THE IMPORTANCE OF THE GOSPELS

 Focus How do the senses of Scripture help us understand the message?

Scripture is so rich in expressing divine truth that there are many senses, or layers, of Scripture. Two layers of meaning that can be seen in Scripture are the literal sense and the spiritual sense.

The *literal sense* of Scripture refers to the actual words that have been recorded. Understanding the literal sense involves studying the culture in which the words were written—the meaning of those words in the time they were written.

The *spiritual sense* of Scripture builds on the literal sense, and it includes three dimensions:

▶ The *allegorical sense* shows how certain events pointed to Jesus, even before his birth. The crossing of the Red Sea, for example, is a sign of his victory over death.

▶ The *moral sense* of Scripture explains how to live justly and humbly before God.

▶ The *anagogical sense* shows how human events and realities are signs of our heavenly future. The Church, for example, is understood as leading to the new Jerusalem of heaven.

Christ the Good News The four Gospels according to Matthew, Mark, Luke, and John have the central place in Scripture because they present Jesus' life, ministry, and teaching. And we revere the Old Testament, too, because the events recorded in it point to the salvation that God would bring when he sent his only Son to become man.

When the author of John's Gospel wrote that the Word was with God and the Word was God, he meant the living Word that is Jesus Christ. (See *John 1:1*.) Jesus Christ is the single Word through whom all the other words in Scripture have their meaning. Because Jesus himself is the living Word from God, the Gospels present the ultimate truth of revelation. Jesus is the fulfillment of God's word and of God's promise.

✝ **SCRIPTURE**

GO TO THE SOURCE
Read **John 1:1–14**. In what way is Jesus the Word of God? What is given to those who believe the Word?

A Different Emphasis Although all four Gospel writers center on Jesus Christ, they each emphasize different aspects of him.

▶ Matthew addresses a Jewish audience and wants to show them that Jesus is the fulfillment of the Old Testament stories and promises of a Messiah.

▶ Mark, in a brief but detailed way, stresses the announcement of God's Kingdom. Mark shows how the disciples did not always understand Jesus and only gradually came to know who he is. When they did, they were ready to proclaim him to the world.

▶ Luke focuses more on practical and ordinary things so that people will be open to Jesus' message of salvation in their life. He emphasizes Jesus as a Savior who helps us overcome the evil of sin, suffering, and death. He often shows Jesus in prayer.

▶ John focuses more on spiritual things so that the readers will see they are entering into an intimate relationship of love with God. Throughout John's Gospel, Jesus is shown answering questions that people pose to him. When they misunderstand his answers, he tells them more so that they can understand his truth.

Think of a time when you heard a single story told by more than one person. Why do you think there is a difference in the way two people tell the same story?

LOOKING BACK

The Gospels were not put into their written form until some time after Jesus' Resurrection. They were probably written between A.D. 65 and 100.

1. The first part of the Gospels that was developed centered around the life and teachings of Jesus. People were not necessarily keeping record of what they saw Jesus say and do. They did not yet know of his importance.

2. The second part that was developed were the stories people passed on by word of mouth. After the Ascension the disciples passed on everything they had witnessed and learned about Jesus.

3. In the third stage, the authors of the Gospels, called **evangelists**, put into writing other aspects and features of Jesus' ministry.

▶ The Dead Sea Scrolls date from 300 B.C. to A.D. 68 and include all of the books of the Bible except Esther. This is a portion from the Book of Psalms.

ACTIVITY

CONNECT YOUR FAITH In a small group, read a Gospel passage. Write about what it means to you. Then, as a group, discuss what it means.

▶ What do you learn about God's word when you see the way different people respond to it?

CONVERSATION WITH GOD

Focus How does God speak to us today?

To this very day, God continues to speak to his people. When the word of God is proclaimed at Mass, it is the voice of God that the assembly hears. This Word proclaimed from the Scriptures is Jesus Christ, a living Word. Even though human readers proclaim this word, God speaks through them.

The proclamation of the Scriptures at Mass takes place during the Liturgy of the Word. This is one way in which Catholics today dialogue with God. Through psalm responses, the homily, and silent reflection, they respond to God and commit themselves to follow God's word. The prayer life of Christians relies on God's word, the worship of the Church, and growth in Christian virtue that Jesus models for us.

The Word as Light When the prophet Isaiah spoke of God's goodness to the Hebrew people, he said that a people in darkness had seen a great light. In a similar way, Jesus explained that people who walk in the darkness will stumble because people in darkness cannot see where they are going. This is why the word of God is a light to all people.

CATHOLICS TODAY

Scripture has an important role in our lives:

▶ We proclaim and reflect upon it in communal worship.

▶ We discover more about Jesus and his message as we read it by ourselves and in religious education classes.

▶ We discuss its message for us today in Bible study.

▶ We pray with it personally and with our families.

▶ We turn to it for wisdom and for guidance.

Following the Light By listening to the word of God, you develop a **conscience**—the ability to know right from wrong—that makes it possible to live a right and just life. A conscience formed by God's word:

▶ Challenges us to live a good life and avoid evil

▶ Helps us judge between choices that are right or wrong, good or bad

▶ Strengthens us to put God's word into action and to be signs of his goodness

God speaks to followers of Jesus Christ through their conscience and the teachings of the Church. He gives us the confidence we need to live with faith.

ACTIVITY

LIVE YOUR FAITH Ask an adult you admire how Scripture affects his or her decision making.

_____

_____

▶ **Think about the last time you had to make a difficult choice. How did you go about making that choice? Ask yourself how that process would be helped next time if you use Scripture to guide you.**

Difficult choice: _____

_____

How would Scripture help: _____

_____

IN SUMMARY

CATHOLICS BELIEVE

God speaks to us and tells us about himself and his plan for us.

▶ God is the author and inspiration of the sacred words of Scripture that humans have recorded under his guidance and direction.

▶ The four Gospels, which developed over the course of time after Jesus' Resurrection, are the center of the Bible because they record the truth of the life and ministry of Jesus.

▶ God continues to speak to us today through the Scriptures, as we proclaim them at Mass, reflect on them personally, rely on them for making choices, and study them to learn more about the life and teachings of Jesus.

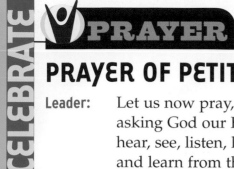

PRAYER OF PETITION

Leader: Let us now pray,
asking God our Father to help us
hear, see, listen, live,
and learn from the wisdom of Scripture.

Reader: A reading from the holy Gospel according to Luke.
Read Luke 4:16–22.

The Gospel of the Lord.

All: Praise to you, Lord Jesus Christ.

Side 1: God of love,
open our ears to always
hear your voice—fill us with your Word.

All: Fill us with your Word.

Side 2: God of light,
open our eyes to always
see your path—fill us with your Word.

All: Fill us with your Word.

Side 1: God of wisdom,
open our hearts to always
act as we should—fill us with your Word.

All: Fill us with your Word.

Side 2: God of goodness,
open our hands to
always reach out and serve—fill us with your Word.

All: Fill us with your Word.

Leader: Loving Father,
You alone have the words of everlasting life.
Send us your Spirit and give us the grace so that we
always welcome your word,
your wisdom and guidance,
and your love.
May the gifts we have received
be gifts we freely share with others.
We ask this through your Son,
who is Jesus Christ, our friend and brother.

All: Amen.

♪ "Make Us Worthy"
Michael Mahler, © 2003, GIA Publications, Inc.

REVIEW

A **Work with Words** Complete each sentence with the correct term from the word bank at right.

Word Bank

- the Bible
- canon
- Tradition
- evangelists
- Apostles
- the Gospels
- inspiration
- proverbs

1. _____ records the story of the relationship between God and his people.

2. This body of sacred texts chosen by the Church as inspired by God is called the _____ of Scripture.

3. The authors of the Gospels, called _____, wrote about Jesus' life and ministry.

4. As a literary form, _____ are short sentences containing great wisdom.

5. _____ present Jesus' life, ministry, and teachings.

B **Check Understanding** Indicate whether the following statements are true or false. Then rewrite false statements to make them true.

_____ 6. Even though the Bible was written by humans, God is the principle author because he inspired the writers.

_____

_____ 7. When John writes in his Gospel that the Word was God, he is referring to the Holy Spirit.

_____

_____ 8. The primary sense of Scripture refers to the actual words that have been recorded.

_____

_____ 9. The spiritual sense of Scripture includes the allegorical sense, showing how certain events pointed to Christ.

_____

_____ 10. The Letters of Paul are the central books of Scripture because they present Jesus' life, ministry, and teaching.

_____

C **Make Connections: Evaluate** Write a one-paragraph response to the question.

Each Gospel emphasizes a different aspect of Jesus. How does each Gospel fulfill Jesus' command to spread the Good News?

OUR CATHOLIC FAITH

ACTIVITY

LIVE YOUR FAITH Choose three of your favorite Scripture passages. Look through the Bible if necessary.

▶ List each passage and, in the center box, briefly write what the Scripture is about, or what it means to you. In the right-hand box, write how it can help you in your everyday life. (Some examples are relating to a new person, choosing values you want to live by, dealing with conflicts, and so forth.)

SCRIPTURE	WHAT DOES IT MEAN?	HOW DOES IT AFFECT MY LIFE?
1.		
2.		
3.		

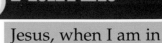

GO online Visit www.osvcurriculum.com for more family and community connections.

PRAYER

Jesus, when I am in need, please let it be you that I turn to.

Saint Matthew

▲ Saint Matthew

Eyewitnesses—the people who were there with front-row seats to see events unfold—give the best accounts of history. The disciples lived day in and day out with Jesus for three years. They ate with him, walked with him, and learned from him. So who could be better to tell the story of Jesus' life?

Matthew 9:9 tells the story of how Matthew first met Jesus: "As Jesus passed on from there, he saw a man named Matthew sitting at the customs post. He said to him, 'Follow me.' And he got up and followed him." As a tax collector, Matthew worked for the Roman governor, the enemy of the Jewish people. Fellow Jews saw Matthew as a traitor, among the lowest of the low. But Jesus saw in him an Apostle and called him to be among his closest friends. Matthew goes on to write about a party he gave for Jesus in his home.

"And as he sat at dinner in the house, many tax collectors and sinners came and were sitting with him and his disciples. When the Pharisees saw this, they said to his disciples, 'Why does your teacher eat with tax collectors and sinners?' But when he heard this, he said, 'Those who are well have no need of a physician, but those who are sick. Go and learn what this means, 'I desire mercy, not sacrifice.' For I have come to call not the righteous but sinners.'" (*Matthew 9:10–13*) This truth would change Matthew's life forever.

While Matthew spent those three years with Jesus, he watched the everyday things Jesus did—eating, sleeping, praying, laughing, and talking. He also saw the miracles Jesus performed and witnessed his Resurrection and Ascension. Matthew wrote about it all in the Gospel according to Matthew. The book was written to convince Jews that Jesus was the promised Messiah. God had set up a spiritual kingdom for his Son rather than the earthly kingdom the Jews expected, so the writings of Matthew explained what that meant. Although the exact date of the Gospel is not known, we do know it was written before the Romans destroyed the Temple in A.D. 70.

As an Apostle, Matthew preached among the Jews in the area of Palestine for fifteen years. The details of Matthew's later life are not certain. Most ancient writers believe that he preached to the Jews in Ethiopia to the south of the Caspian Sea (not Ethiopia in Africa) and places in the East. Some believe that he died a martyr's death.

GLOBAL DATA

Palestine

- Palestine today refers to Palestinian territories that include the West Bank and the Gaza Strip.

- Palestine has a population of over 4 million people.

- Palestine is home to Roman Catholics as well as several churches of the Eastern Catholic Tradition, including the Armenian Catholic Church, the Coptic Catholic Church, the Maronite Catholic Church, the Syrian Catholic Church, and the Melkite Greek Catholic Church.

- Palestine is located on the eastern coast of the Mediterranean Sea in southwest Asia.

- Palestine shares the holy city of Jerusalem with Israel. Jerusalem is holy to Christians, Muslims, and Jews.

JESUS Sign of God's Love

Nothing's better than love. I believe that.
And there's nothing worse than losing it.
Sometimes I'm not sure it's worth it.
Especially when it's gone.

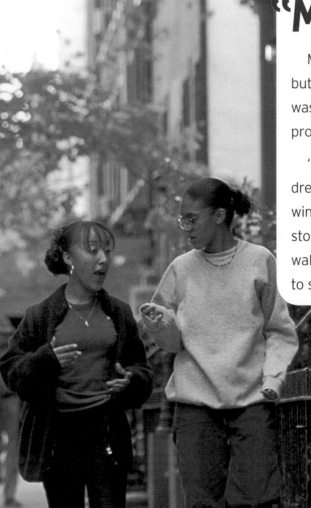

"Megan, you don't look so good."

Megan started to shoot Kirsten a dirty look, but stopped. She sighed. She knew her best friend was right. The dark circles under her eyes were proof enough.

"I'm not sleeping much. I keep having this awful dream. I find myself standing at my bedroom window. It's pitch black outside, and there's a crazy storm. For some reason there's a huge hole in the wall next to the window, so I grab a blanket and try to spread it across the hole."

"Does it help?" Kirsten asked.

"No," Megan went on. "The wind is howling, and the wind and rain are pouring through the hole. I turn my head over my shoulder and yell as loud as I can, 'Mom! Help!'"

Kirsten shivered. "That's some dream." She knew that Megan's mom had passed away three years ago.

"Maybe the hole in the window is me," Megan said.

"How?" Kirsten asked.

"Well, it was bad enough when my mother died. I just knew that no one would love me like she did. My father didn't have much time for me, and he was so sad I didn't want to bother him with my problems. Then he seemed to get better, especially when he met Janet. Now he's so caught up with having a new wife that he doesn't have any time for us kids. Plus Janet wants me to call her 'Mom,' but she hardly knows me, and I don't think I can get used to her. I really miss my real mom and the way she loved me."

"So you think that maybe the hole in the wall is like a hole in your heart?" Kirsten asked.

"Yeah. I do. I miss my mom so much. Janet is nice, but she isn't my mom. It's just not the same."

ACTIVITY

LET'S BEGIN What do you think is the best way for Kirsten to help Megan? How could Janet help her? What advice would you give Megan?

▶ **Revisit the thoughts that come before the story. What's your opinion?**

_____

_____

_____

_____

_____

JESUS: GOD'S OWN LOVE

Focus How does God show his love for us?

Being loved is great, but sometimes it can be complicated. Sometimes people will show their love only if we behave in a certain way. At other times, people do love us, but they have a hard time expressing it. Plus, we have to build up trust and friendship with new people in our lives before we get to the point where we love them.

With God it is different, because God loves us without any conditions. God showed how much he loved us by sending his only and much-loved Son into the world.

Jesus: The Way to God The relationship between God the Father and God the Son is the most intimate and loving relationship possible. But God the Father did not keep his Son for himself. Instead, he chose to share him with the world.

In Jesus Christ, God showed us everything he could about himself. What God told us about himself first through creation and history, and then through his Chosen People, the Jews in the Old Testament, he revealed in the most perfect way in Jesus Christ. With the coming of Jesus, there is no further revelation. In Jesus Christ God has taught us everything that there is to be revealed.

Even though God has fully revealed himself in Christ, our understanding continues to grow as we discover new things about what God has shared with us. Our limited human minds cannot understand God the first time we learn about him. It takes years of growing into understanding. New experiences and continually being taught more about God help us come to know him more and more, but we'll never fully understand God because he is mystery.

❓ How many times have you heard a story, or seen a movie, twice and realized you missed something the first time?

Jesus: Given to Us As many passages of the Old Testament testify, God made a covenant with his people and said he would never forget his promise. A **covenant** is a binding agreement, in this case, a promise to remain in a relationship of love together.

✝ SCRIPTURE God showed the depth of his love when he made a new covenant in Jesus Christ, a covenant that would last forever. At the Last Supper, Jesus and the Apostles were celebrating God's original covenant when Jesus explained that now he was going to be the Father's new covenant. God the Father made that covenant present in the world through the gift of Jesus' own Body and Blood. In Luke 22:20 we read, "This cup that is poured out for you is the new covenant in my blood." By pouring out his blood Jesus offered forgiveness for sins so that all people would be reconciled with God. The Gospels of Matthew, Mark, and John also record the Last Supper.

❓ Imagine that you were asked to give away—or say goodbye to—the person you love the most. How hard would that be for you? Could you do it?

✝ **SCRIPTURE**

GO TO THE SOURCE
Read **Matthew 26:26–30**. What does Jesus give us to celebrate and commit ourselves to the new covenant with God?

▼ *The Last Supper*, by Frans Pourbus the Elder (1545–1581)

SHARE YOUR FAITH What's one of the hardest sacrifices you've ever made because of your love for a family member, friend, or God?

JESUS SHOWS US THE FATHER

Focus How do we see God through Jesus Christ?

Sometimes we meet people who say all the right things, but we might wonder if they live the way they talk. With Jesus, there is no doubt that everything about his life is true. He not only talked about God the Father, but he also showed us who God is in the way he lived. He did this because he is God. We can call Jesus *God*, like we call *God* the Father God and God the Holy Spirit *God*.

One with the Father It always feels good when someone remembers our name when we haven't seen that person for a long time. On the other hand, people are sometimes embarrassed when they can't remember the name of someone they should know. In the Hebrew tradition, knowing a person's name implied a close relationship between the two people.

The Hebrew people thought of themselves as being unworthy to utter God's name. This is why they were shocked when they heard Jesus address God in the most intimate of ways. When he taught the disciples the Lord's Prayer, he began with the Aramaic word ***abba***. (See *Luke 11:2–4*.) The English equivalent of this word is "daddy" or "papa."

Jesus invited his disciples to address God in the same way, as we do today when we pray "Our Father." By being baptized in Christ, Christians share that close relationship with God. We become adopted children of God, sons and daughters who can count on God's love at all times. (See *Galatians 4:6*.)

What are some ways you call on God?

CHECK THIS OUT!

The many titles of Jesus show his closeness to God and to all people:

- ▶ Son of God
- ▶ Son of David
- ▶ Savior
- ▶ Son of Man
- ▶ Rabbi (Teacher)
- ▶ Lamb of God
- ▶ The Only Begotten Son
- ▶ Bread of Life
- ▶ Son of Mary
- ▶ Messiah

◀ **Christ, the Good Shepherd**

What We Learn from Jesus

In every way, Jesus Christ is the fulfillment of God's own revelation. Everything about Jesus points to God and the coming of his heavenly kingdom on earth.

▶ In prayer, Jesus shows us how trustworthy God is, how God listens and cares for each of us.

▶ In miracles, Jesus shows us God's desire to make us whole and help us change our lives for the good.

▶ In his love for the poor, for children, and for sinners, Jesus reveals that God cares for every single human being.

▶ By accepting death on the cross, Jesus shows that following God's plan is the best plan, even when it involves sacrifice.

▶ In the Resurrection, Jesus makes it known that God's heavenly reign and divine life can be a part of our human existence.

What does Jesus show you about God's love?

CONNECT YOUR FAITH Read the Lord's Prayer. (See *Luke 11:2–4*.) Describe several personal ways by which you address God in your own prayers. How do your names for God show how you feel about him?

_____

_____

_____

_____

_____

LAWS THAT POINT TO GOD

Focus How do laws lead us to God?

When we study the world and the universe, we find a marvelous order to it in the movement of the heavenly bodies, in the cycle of time and seasons, in the fruitfulness of all creation, in the cycle of birth and death, in the relationship of man and woman, and in the laws that are inscribed in our hearts.

This order is created by God. The laws of nature are like building blocks that form the foundation for all life. **Natural law**, or natural moral law, consists of universal practical judgments that all people can understand through their common sense. Natural law requires us to do good and avoid evil. Natural law is part of God's eternal law, which he shares with us to keep his order.

> What are some other positive natural laws that you can think of?

God's Revealed Law Besides the natural moral law, God has revealed ways that help us live in covenant relationship with God. God's revealed law was evident when he gave us the **Ten Commandments** through Moses. (See *Exodus 20:1–17*.) These laws helped to make clear God's hope for the way the Jewish people (and all people) are to live in relationship with him and with one another. But this was not the end of God's revealed law. It continued in the Old Testament and led to the Gospels and the fulfillment of God's revealed law in Christ.

✝ SCRIPTURE

GO TO THE SOURCE
Read **Exodus 20:1–17** and **Deuteronomy 5:6–21**. How are they alike? Are there any differences? How do they help you live?

Jesus, the New Law Not only did Jesus shock people by his close relationship with God the Father, but he also surprised them in the way he spoke of the law. He did not want them to follow God's law only because they feared punishment. Instead, he wanted them to live their lives by relying on the love of God that had been planted within their hearts.

He explained it all in the Sermon on the Mount, where he said that those who would be blessed are the poor, those who mourn, the meek, the merciful, and the peacemakers. He showed the positive side of the law.

Jesus gave his followers a new law—to love one another as he has loved them. We try to do this because Christ poured out his life for us, and his Holy Spirit dwells within us. God's Spirit within us deepens whenever Catholics gather to pray and celebrate the sacraments of the Church. Believers in Christ are called to live holy lives, not primarily because of external laws, but because of the law of love that exists within our hearts.

How is it different when you are doing something because you were told to, and when you are doing something because, in your heart, you know it is right?

ACTIVITY

LIVE YOUR FAITH What are other signs of God's love? Write them in the cross, and describe how you can be a sign of God's love.

IN SUMMARY

CATHOLICS BELIEVE

Jesus is the fulfillment of the law and he perfectly reveals God the Father to us.

▶ We know God through Jesus Christ and recognize Christ as the sign of God's love.

▶ Jesus has a close and intimate relationship with the Father, and he invites us to share in that relationship as God's sons and daughters.

▶ The natural and revealed law help us choose what is good and live as God's people; by pouring out the Holy Spirit, Jesus plants within our hearts a new law of love.

PRAYER

PRAYER OF ADORATION

Leader: Let us pray.

Reader 1: Father, you gave us your greatest gift—
your Son, Jesus,
who lived and experienced
the same joys and heartaches that
we experience.

All: Your love is never ending.

Reader 2: You sent Jesus to teach us
how to live,
to grow, to learn,
and to know the happiness
that comes from belonging to you.

All: Your love is never ending.

Reader 3: You had Jesus show us the way
to be a servant;
he washed our feet,
he opened his hands,
and offered his life for us.

All: Your love is never ending.

Reader 4: You raised him up again to new life,
showing us all
that we too can share in your life,
and become who you want us to be.

All: Your love is never ending.

Leader: Loving Father,
Help us to remember your love always.
We ask this in the name of your Son Jesus,
who is your everlasting love.

All: Amen.

♪ "Your Love Is Never Ending"
Marty Haugen, © 1987, GIA Publications, Inc.

REVIEW

A **Work with Words** Circle the letter of the choice that best completes the sentence.

1. God's _____ is a promise to remain in a relationship of love with his people.

   a. law   **b.** covenant   **c.** word   **d.** spirit

2. The Aramaic word _____ can be translated as "daddy" in English.

   a. Yahweh   **b.** papa   **c.** padre   **d.** *abba*

3. The order in the universe created by God is called _____.

   a. cycle of seasons   **b.** cycle of time   **c.** creation   **d.** none of the above

4. _____ requires us to do good and avoid evil.

   a. Universal law   **b.** Natural law   **c.** Original law   **d.** Laws of nature

B **Check Understanding** Indicate whether the following statements are true or false. Then rewrite false statements to make them true.

_____ **5.** God's law of nature is evident in the Ten Commandments.

_____

_____ **6.** Jesus wants people to follow God's law because we are afraid not to.

_____

_____ **7.** Through Jesus' miracles we see God's desire to make us whole.

_____

_____ **8.** Jesus gives us a new law—to love one another as he loves us.

_____

_____ **9.** God's revealed law is manifested only in the Ten Commandments.

_____

_____ **10.** Believers in Christ live holy lives when they voluntarily live by the law of love that dwells within our hearts.

_____

C **Make Connections: Infer** Write a one-paragraph response to the questions below.

How was Jesus' relationship to God the Father surprising to people of the time? What new law did Jesus give us to help live out that relationship here on earth?

OUR CATHOLIC FAITH

WHAT NOW?

★ Think of ways, even small ones, that you can show your love for someone.

★ Discover ways to become a friend with Jesus, such as

- reading some of the stories of Jesus and thinking about how they apply to you

- naming the kinds of things you do that reflect Jesus for others

- thinking of the people you know who live in a Christian way

- talking with someone about what friendship with Jesus means

★ Learn how to accept love from others.

★ Be outwardly thankful for the love that people show to you.

ACTIVITY

LIVE YOUR FAITH Consider who shows you love and how. Then complete the chart.

	Who shows God's love to you?	How?
At home		
At school		
In clubs or sports teams		
In the world		

GO online Visit www.osvcurriculum.com for more family and community connections.

PRAYER

May your life, Jesus, teach me to be your friend, and guide me in being a friend to others.

40

Saint Mary MacKillop

Jesus loved the weak, the poor, and the powerless. He loved sinners, even when he told them the truth about sin. He loved everyone the same—without putting conditions on how much he would love. He said we should love as he did—that we should care for children, for the poor, for the least, and for the lost. One Australian woman, Mary MacKillop, took Jesus at his word. Like Jesus, she loved the forgotten. The homeless, the poor, the prostitutes, and the prisoners all received her love unconditionally.

Mary Helen MacKillop was born in Melbourne, Australia, on January 15, 1842. Her father had studied in Rome to be a priest. But due to poor health, he returned to Australia and was not ordained. Mary attended private schools and was tutored by her father, but her family was poor—and sometimes even homeless.

Mary went to work at age sixteen as a governess, then a clerk, and a teacher. When she met Father Julian Tenison Woods, he asked for Mary's help. He wanted to give poor children a free Catholic education. In 1866, Mary and Father Woods opened the first Saint Joseph's School in an old stable. Soon she was responsible for seventeen schools.

Mary traveled through England, Scotland, and Ireland to raise money for her schools. She attracted many young women who felt called to help, so the Sisters of St. Joseph began. In 1867, her groups of Sisters moved to small outback towns and large cities around Australia and New Zealand. Over time, they moved—to Peru, Brazil, and the refugee camps of Uganda and Thailand. Mary and these Sisters helped shape Catholic education. They also opened orphanages and cared for the homeless and poor. They took in ex-prisoners and ex-prostitutes to make a new start in life.

Mary was often ill. She died on August 8, 1909. Since her death, the number of Sisters has grown to about 1,200. They work mainly in Australia and New Zealand. The "Brown Joeys," as they are called, serve the "little ones" of God.

Pope Saint John Paul II beatified Mary on January 19, 1995, and she was canonized by Pope Benedict XVI on October 17, 2010. Mary is the first person born in Australia to be beatified and recognized by the Roman Catholic Church as a saint. Her unconditional love and care for those in need gave hope and help to many. Today, her Sisters continue in that same spirit.

▲ **Saint Mary MacKillop, 1842–1909**

GLOBAL DATA

Australia

- Almost 5.1 million, or approximately 26 percent of Australians, are Catholic.

- Australia is slightly smaller than the forty-eight contiguous United States.

- Australia includes the Great Barrier Reef, the largest coral reef in the world.

- Australia is the world's smallest continent, but the sixth-largest country.

- Australia is the driest inhabited continent on earth.

- Australia is home to one of the world's longest surviving cultures: Aboriginal culture goes back at least 50,000 years.

Faith in Action!

CATHOLIC SOCIAL TEACHING

DISCOVER | Catholic Social Teaching:
Care for God's Creation

IN THIS UNIT you have learned how we can find God in creation and how creation shows us a lot about who God is—wise and generous, the source of all goodness and beauty. And we are part of the goodness and beauty of God's creation. Yes, our God is an awesome God!

Care for Creation

Our response to God's sharing all this goodness and beauty with us involves several steps. First, God wants us to enjoy it. God invites us to pause every day to notice the beauty around us and just enjoy it—see it, smell it, touch it, listen to it, taste it. It could be a sunset, a flower, a creek, a bird, a mountain, a sky full of stars, a baby. Just enjoy them! Second, God wants us to realize that he is right there in all that beauty and to say "thank you, God." Yes, we are made to live in communion with God in the midst of his "garden of paradise" on earth. This is real happiness. Third, God wants us to take care of this garden, to make it even more beautiful, and to share it with others. In the Book of Genesis, God tells us to "have dominion" over the earth. This doesn't mean we can do anything we want to the earth. Even if something is "our property," we are not free to destroy

it or harm it. We have to take care of the beauty and resources of the earth for future generations and to share it with others now. God made it for everyone.

Because God meant his creation to be for everyone doesn't mean we have the right to take property from someone else. That would be stealing, which is against the Seventh Commandment. But it means that if we see that someone has been kept from enjoying God's blessings, either because their property has been stolen or because they have been unfairly kept from having anything, we should try to help them. God calls us to be generous and fair. He wants us to make a difference in the way the world operates by speaking up for others and helping all people to enjoy his blessings together.

How do you say "thank you, God" when you enjoy his gifts of beauty?

CARING FOR CREATION can be done in a variety of ways. Let's look at what one St. Louis school accomplished.

BRING PEACE
TAKING ACTION MATTERS

"Be the Peace" was the 2004–2005 theme for St. Joan of Arc School in St. Louis, Missouri, and the "Shalom Club" took the lead. The Shalom Club is an international effort of the School Sisters of Notre Dame to help children "develop a worldwide look at important peace and justice issues affecting the lives of children and creation and take action to make a difference."

The Shalom Club at St. Joan of Arc was made up of two delegates from each homeroom in grades four through eight. The first half of the year focused on poverty, but their biggest event was Earth Day. One Shalom Club team developed ideas for a "trash-free" lunch. Letters were sent home asking parents to help pack simple, "trash-free" lunches in reusable containers. A second Shalom Club team developed creative games to be played while the other half of the student body was eating their "trash-free" lunches.

A third team worked on a prayer service to celebrate creation. During the service, the Shalom Club presented the Native American legend "The Story of the Rainbow" as they created a colorful rainbow at the altar steps. A representative from each homeroom placed a symbol or gift of creation around the rainbow, while Shalom members led a poetic litany of thanks. Students extended their hands in blessing toward a large blue and white earth, which was circled with creative dance by delegates bearing tall blue vigil candles. The earth bearer then led a candlelight procession as everyone sang "All the Ends of the Earth."

To build toward Earth Day, the seventh-grade religion class displayed two large panels they created to depict each section of the Earth Charter. The fifth-grade classes took responsibility for recycling in the school. And the Student Council joined with the Shalom Club in raising $2,500 for the victims of the tsunami that hit Southeast Asia right after Christmas. The Shalom Club is fulfilling its mission—" . . . to take action to make a difference."

❓ **What is your school doing year-round to care for God's creation?**

❓ **If there was a Shalom Club at your school, would you join? Why or why not?**

SERVE **Your Community**

A BEAUTY TRIP

① Take a trip around your neighborhood (or a special place in your community) and make a list of the different forms of natural beauty you find.

② Choose your favorite and spend ten minutes enjoying it with all your senses.

③ Say a prayer of thanks to God for this beauty.

④ Decide what you can do to protect or enhance this beauty.

⑤ Take a photo and send it to a friend, or make it the screen saver on the family computer.

my favorite place . . .

my prayer . . .

my action . . .

MAKE A DIFFERENCE IN YOUR SCHOOL NEIGHBORHOOD

Discuss with your classmates different ways that your school could improve its recycling program (or that the area around your school or neighborhood could be made more beautiful) and create a plan for doing it.

Project Planning Sheet

Equipment needed

Others who should be asked to help

How to publicize your project

Other specific tasks

Your specific task(s)

Calendar for completing the project

Why do you think most people don't stop during their day to enjoy the beauty of God's creation? What keeps you from doing this more often?

_____

_____

_____

What makes you the happiest? How do you feel about your relationship with God here and now?

_____

_____

_____

What do you think God wants you to do about all the harm that humans are doing to his creation?

_____

_____

_____

What did you learn about yourself in taking your "Beauty Trip"?

_____

_____

_____

What did you learn about yourself and about caring for creation when you did your part in the class project?

_____

_____

_____

What did you learn about God and about your faith in doing each of these activities?

_____

_____

_____

List one thing that may have changed about the way you see creation since you started this project.

_____

_____

REVIEW

A **Work with Words** Match the words on the left with the correct definitions or descriptions on the right.

_____ **1.** allegorical

_____ **2.** inspiration

_____ **3.** canon

_____ **4.** evangelist

_____ **5.** covenant

_____ **6.** *abba*

_____ **7.** natural law

_____ **8.** revealed law

A. the body of sacred texts identified by the Church as being the truly inspired word of God

B. God's intent fulfilled in Christ

C. an author of a Gospel

D. Aramaic word that means "daddy"

E. spiritual sense of Scripture that shows how certain events point to Christ

F. order of the universe created by God

G. God's promise to remain in a loving relationship with his people

H. God's divine guidance in the books of the Bible

B **Check Understanding** Complete each sentence with the correct term from the word bank at right.

9. God gave us the gift of _____, which allows us to grow in knowledge and search for meaning.

10. The Old Testament tells of God's relationship with

_____.

11. The freeing of the Israelites from slavery in Egypt that is described in the book of Exodus previews the _____ that Christ would bring us.

12. When John writes in the Gospel that the Word was God, he is referring to _____ as "the Word."

13. As a literary form, _____ contain(s) wisdom in short sentences and sayings.

14. Understanding the _____ of Scripture, which refers to the actual words recorded, requires an understanding of the time in which it was written.

Word Bank

- literal sense
- love
- moral sense
- Jesus
- word
- salvation
- proverbs
- Chosen People
- human reason
- Gospels
- Ten Commandments
- eternal law

15. The _____ are the most central books of Scripture because they present Jesus' life, ministry, and teaching.

16. When God gave Moses the _____, he was giving us evidence of his revealed law.

17. Jesus wants us to follow God's law out of _____, not out of fear.

18. Natural law and revealed law are part of God's _____.

C Make Connections Write a short answer to the following questions.

19. Infer. Which story about Jesus from the Gospels is your favorite, and why? What does this story reveal to you about God?

_____

_____

_____

_____

20. Compare. How, in your life today, are you like the Israelites in the desert? In light of how God responded to the Israelites, how do you think God responds to you?

_____

_____

_____

_____

CHAPTER 4 GOD Is Trinity

What is God like?
How can I understand God?

Mark's dinner plate slowly rotated in the microwave. Coach's words had been turning around and around in his head the same way ever since his mom had driven him home from baseball practice. He wasn't quick enough. He wasn't paying attention. The coach had picked on one thing after another in front of the whole team as they slogged through the field in the drizzling rain.

Mom and his sister, Cesseli, were cleaning up the kitchen together while having some tense discussion about a note from one of her teachers. "I have to call Cesseli's teacher before it

gets too late," Mom apologized, and gave him a hug as they left the room. "We can all have dessert in the family room together afterward, okay?"

Yeah, great, Mark thought, not in a mood for cake or talking. Slowly chewing his mushy leftovers, Mark stared into the den where his dad was working at the computer. His eyes fell on the family portrait hanging there. It had been taken at his grandparents' anniversary party last summer. Everyone was smiling that day. Mom was looking at Dad with a special look that said she was both proud and relieved at how well everything had turned out.

Mark remembered how excited Dad had been to plan just the right celebration together. Mom had spent hours cooking and creating decorations. They had asked Mark to put together a slideshow telling the story of his grandparents' lives and how much their marriage meant to everyone. The portrait now made him think about how his family had always been there and would always be there for each other.

As he put his plate in the sink, Mark saw that his dad had left the den to join his mom and sister on the sofa. They were relaxed now that Mom's phone call with Cesseli's teacher had cleared things up. Mark smiled and then tossed his soggy baseball glove on the stairs and joined them.

ACTIVITY

LET'S BEGIN Discuss the relationships in this story. Beyond worries and stresses, what keeps Mark's family going? How do they manage? What draws Mark to join his parents and sister?

▶ **What are some different items in your home that show your family and its history? Why are these items on display? How does having a history together make a difference?**

GOD IS ALWAYS THERE

Focus How do we get to know God?

Have you ever ended up with a problem turning around and around in your head, not sure what to do about it? With so much going on, you might not think of turning to a family member. You might wonder how others could even understand what you are feeling, much less help you. Sometimes family and friends can help. Different individuals within a family relate to each other in love—over time and through difficult times.

God is always there, even when you don't think family and friends can help much. The sure guide through the ups and downs of life is our faith in his presence and in his words.

God Takes the First Step God created the universe and keeps it going through Jesus Christ, the Word who has existed forever, and through the Holy Spirit, the giver of all life and goodness. We know God because he chooses to show himself to us. If it were left totally up to us, we could never really know the true God, because he is a mystery beyond our own comprehension. Only with faith can we begin to know God.

Fortunately, God doesn't wait for us to make the first move. He has been there from the beginning of time and he is with us from the first day of our life. He understands us, even when we don't understand him. On our own, we would be stuck in misunderstanding and confusion. We would never get close enough to God to understand the truth. But he loves us so much he wants us to know the way. God the Father sent us his Son and the Holy Spirit to help us find our way to him. Whenever God sends his Son to us, he also sends his Spirit.

WHERE IT HAPPENED

WHERE DID the disciples think Jesus was sending them? Peter traveled from Jerusalem after Pentecost to Lydda, Joppa, and Caesarea. He lived in Antioch for a while, and in Rome, where he preached the message before being martyred.

The disciple Paul traveled widely to proclaim the Good News. On his first journey, Paul sailed from Antioch to Cyprus and regions that are now in Turkey. On his second and third journeys, he traveled through Asia Minor and Greece, eventually returning to Jerusalem.

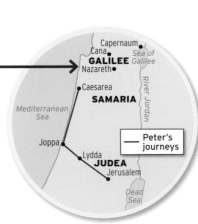

Help from Heaven The Son of God came down from heaven to show us the way to God the Father and to bring salvation to all.

✝ **SCRIPTURE** When his earthly mission was accomplished, Jesus returned to his heavenly Father. Before he left, Jesus told his Apostles to continue his work, sharing his message of hope and new life to people everywhere. He instructed them, "Go therefore and make disciples of all nations. . ." (*Matthew 28:19*). Jesus told them to baptize new disciples in the name of the Father, and of the Son, and of the Holy Spirit. He promised his friends he would always be with them.

Jesus is always with us, too. When we are baptized, we become members of God's family, the Church, and receive the gift of faith. Through faith, we can believe in and rely on God, even though we don't completely understand.

So help from heaven does not stop with Jesus' time on earth, his public ministry, and his Ascension. Through the Apostles, Christ established the Church. He sent the Holy Spirit as a guide and counselor to the Church. Since the time of Jesus and the Apostles, believers have proclaimed God as Father, Son, and Holy Spirit.

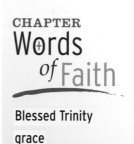

Words of Faith

Blessed Trinity

grace

✝ **SCRIPTURE**

GO TO THE SOURCE
To get the full story of Jesus' commissioning of the Apostles, read **Matthew 28:16–20**. This gathering took place soon after Jesus' Resurrection. How do you think the Apostles felt about Jesus' words? If you had been with Jesus in this story, what would you have asked him? How do Jesus' words speak to you as a member of the Church?

▼ *The Disciples Attempt to Fish in Lake Tiberias without Success*, **from the Predis Codex by Cristoforo de Predis (mid-1400s)**

ACTIVITY

SHARE YOUR FAITH Think about the following questions and share your thoughts with a partner.

▶ **Who or what helps you maintain your relationship with God? When have you felt closest to God in the last six months?**

51

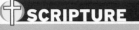

THREE DIVINE PERSONS IN ONE GOD

Focus How can we understand a mystery?

At the beginning of every Mass, we make the Sign of the Cross and say, "In the name of the Father, and of the Son, and of the Holy Spirit." Our belief in three Persons in one God is the center of our celebration. When we pray at Mass, we pray in the name of our Trinitarian God. We base our faith on this central belief.

Christians use a special description for God. We describe God as the **Blessed Trinity**, which means that there is only *one* God in three divine Persons.

▶ The Father is God, the first Person of the Trinity, who brings everything into existence by the Son through the Holy Spirit.

▶ Jesus Christ the Son is God, the second Person of the Trinity, who was sent by the Father and became man.

▶ The Holy Spirit is also God, the third Person of the Trinity, who comes from the Father and the Son.

It's somewhat like your family. You and your dad and mom are unique individuals, but are inseperable as one family. The three members of the Blessed Trinity are distinct from one another, so we can talk about them as Father, Son, and Holy Spirit, but are inseparable in what they do. Each member of the Trinity is fully God and has the same divine nature. There is only one God in three divine Persons.

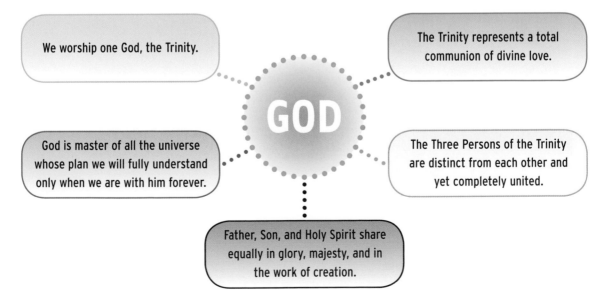

We worship one God, the Trinity.

The Trinity represents a total communion of divine love.

God is master of all the universe whose plan we will fully understand only when we are with him forever.

GOD

The Three Persons of the Trinity are distinct from each other and yet completely united.

Father, Son, and Holy Spirit share equally in glory, majesty, and in the work of creation.

How Can This Be? The Blessed Trinity is a mystery. We are never going to understand this mystery until we meet God face-to-face in heaven. Meanwhile, the gift of faith assures us that what Christians know about the Blessed Trinity is true.

Being human, we still ask questions and search for answers. As people of faith, we often are guided in our relationships by our heart, not only by our head. Despite his hard times as a baseball player, Mark remembered the joy his family felt in planning the anniversary party for his grandparents. He recognized that the love they felt for each other grew and spread throughout his family. This love made his family stronger than they could be individually.

Our relationship with God is something like this, too. When we sense God's presence and respond to him in our lives, he responds back with love. When we place our trust in his love, we feel it in our heart, and we come to believe in it and know it with our mind.

Love is *the* answer to the mystery of the Trinity. The truth is that the Son loves the Father and the Father loves the Son. The Holy Spirit shares his exact same love with both the Father and the Son.

This love between the Father, Son, and Holy Spirit is a model for the connections, affection, and bonds we can make with one another. Human communities such as families, schools, and groups of friends can mirror the unity of the Trinity.

When have you felt really loved by God? Out of touch with his love?

CHECK THIS OUT!

We use comparisons from our life experience to talk about and describe God. However, our comparisons are limited. They do not capture the true mystery of God. So, God is *like* a human parent, a strong father, a loving mother, someone who has our best interests at heart, someone who makes sacrifices for our benefit. But God is also different from a parent. Even though we speak of God as "Father," the mystery of God goes beyond any human experience or worldly images we use.

ACTIVITY

CONNECT YOUR FAITH Think of three friends or family members. Write something about your friendship with each person, including how that friendship differs from the other two. Is your faith a part of any of these friendships? If so, how? If not, how can you share your beliefs with your friends?

To be in relationship with God means I should know and obey his laws. But there are lots of other rules from other sources. What about my parents' rules? What about the laws of our country and our state?

The authority of our parents comes from God's authority, so parents and children need to honor their relationship in a loving way, as the Fourth Commandment tells us. Civil authority (the authority of our government) also comes from God's authority and his care for all people. Those who govern us do it as a service for the good of all. Those in charge of governments should uphold the rights and dignity of all citizens and should also promote justice and peace.

GOD'S PLAN FOR US

Focus How does the Trinity work?

The three Persons of the Blessed Trinity work together through their relationship with each other something like the way a loving family works together for the same goals. The Father sent the Son on his mission of salvation. The Son acted in obedience to the Father to set humanity free from sin. The Holy Spirit comes to help us be part of a loving relationship as members of the Church.

The work of all three relates to God's plan of loving goodness. God does have a plan for all his children. He wants us to know and share in his love, to bring his goodness and love to others. He desires us to become like him, and so he cares for us and guides us with his wisdom and love. The Father works through the Son, his Holy Spirit, the Church, and the actions of people to help us. God doesn't give up on us. He continues to show his care and act on our behalf.

The unity, love, and goodness within the Blessed Trinity radiate outward toward all. This outpouring reaches its peak when the Trinity shares his own life and special helps with us. We call this sharing of divine life **grace**. God offers us this free, undeserved gift so we can become his adopted children. Sometimes we do not feel God's love, even though it's there. Our own actions and stubbornness may block God out or make it difficult to feel his presence. But God's grace is still available to us—if we trust in him and his hopes for us. Then, our lives can get back on course, going in the right direction.

Home Is Where the Heart Is The gift of faith is like a compass that points us in the right direction. If we stay directed by faith, then our actions will build up God's kingdom. Our lives will show Gospel values such as justice, peace, and love.

This is why it is so important to learn and remember what we believe. The teachings of our Catholic faith help us understand and strengthen our relationships with God and others. We are to give our minds, hearts, and lives to God in love and for love. As long as your life is moving in God's direction in that relationship with him, you will be journeying into deeper truth, wisdom, and love. You will be on your way home.

❓ Imagine that your life is a story in a book. In what ways is the story of your life following God's love and the teachings of faith?

❓ What would you like to change about the way you are living in order to follow the guidance of faith more closely?

LOOKING BACK

In the Middle Ages, most people couldn't read. Churches used stained-glass windows and architecture to teach important truths of faith such as the Blessed Trinity. The doorways below are an example. The single triangular arch holds within it three interlocking circular arches. In the same way, God the Father, God the Son, and God the Holy Spirit are three in one.

ACTIVITY

LIVE YOUR FAITH If you give your mind, heart, and life to God, you are journeying into a deeper truth, wisdom, and love. Reflect on what these ideas mean by answering the questions below.

1. What does it mean to you to give your mind to God?

2. What is one way you have given your heart to God?

3. Who is someone you know who gives his or her life to God? How do you see that he or she has done this?

IN SUMMARY

CATHOLICS BELIEVE

As Catholics, believing in the Blessed Trinity is central to our faith.

▶ The Trinity is a mystery that can never be totally understood by the human mind, but can be approached through faith. The Father sent the Son and the Holy Spirit to help us know him and to guide us to him.

▶ The love that the Father, the Son, and the Holy Spirit have for each other shows us what our own relationships should be like.

▶ God has a plan of loving goodness for all his people and offers the gift of grace so that we can become more like him. This sharing in divine life helps us trust in God, have faith in him, and work for his kingdom.

CELEBRATE

MEDITATION ON PRAISING THE TRINITY

Leader: We gather here this day
in the name of the Father,
and of the Son,
and of the Holy Spirit, Amen.

Prepare yourselves to be in Jesus' presence.
Close your eyes and focus on opening your mind and heart to God.
Take a deep, relaxing breath, and enter into the meditation:
(read the following, slowly and meditatively)

Reader 1:   O God, our Father,
creator,
and maker of all creation,
we praise you, and we bless you! *(pause)*

We thank you for this good earth,
the air we breathe,
the rain that cools our nights,
the sun that warms our days,
and the life you give to each and every one of us. *(pause)*

Reader 2:   O God the Son,
our brother, teacher,
and Savior,
we praise you, and we bless you! *(pause)*

We thank you for showing us the way to live,
to trust in the Father and to love one another,
to serve our sisters and brothers,
and to take care of the poor and those in need. *(pause)*

Reader 3:   O God the Spirit,
Our Holy guide,
and friend for the journey,
we praise you, and we bless you!

We thank you for walking with us,
in our struggles,
our choosing,
our playing, and in our praying. *(pause)*

Open your eyes and let us pray together, in song.

 "We Praise You"
David Haas, © 2002, GIA Publications, Inc.

56

REVIEW

A **Work with Words** Complete each sentence with the correct term.

Word Bank

- Blessed Trinity
- disciples
- miracles
- Holy Spirit
- counselor
- Father
- Gospel
- Church

1. Jesus gave the disciples a command to go and make _____ of all nations.

2. Christ established the _____ through the Apostles.

3. God the Father sends his Son to us; he also sends the _____.

4. The Holy Spirit is a _____ to the Church.

5. The love in the _____ is a model for the connections and love we can have with others.

B **Check Understanding** Circle the letter of the choice that best completes the sentence.

6. Christians describe God as the _____, meaning one God in three Persons.
   - **a.** Father
   - **b.** Holy Spirit
   - **c.** Blessed Trinity
   - **d.** a and b

7. The Persons of the Blessed Trinity are _____.
   - **a.** Father, Son, and Holy Spirit
   - **b.** Jesus and the Holy Spirit
   - **c.** Matthew, Mark, and Luke
   - **d.** Paul, Silas, and Timothy

8. Through _____, the free, undeserved gift of God's love and life, we can become God's children.
   - **a.** faith
   - **b.** grace
   - **c.** hope
   - **d.** baptism

9. _____ is the second Person of the Trinity.
   - **a.** God, the Father
   - **b.** God, the Son
   - **c.** The Holy Spirit
   - **d.** all of the above

10. Through the sacrament of _____, we become members of God's Church.
    - **a.** the Eucharist
    - **b.** Confirmation
    - **c.** the Holy Spirit
    - **d.** Baptism

C **Make Connections: Draw Conclusions** Write a one-paragraph response to the questions.

What is God's plan of goodness and love? How does grace fit into God's plan of loving goodness?

OUR CATHOLIC FAITH

WHAT NOW?

★ Think about how you treat others.

★ Resolve to show others the love and interest God shows you.

★ When you make the Sign of the Cross, think about what the words and gestures mean.

★ Reflect on what your image of God is.

ACTIVITY

LIVE YOUR FAITH Think of a dilemma you faced recently. How do you see that God showed his care for you in the solution to your problem?

_____

_____

_____

Write one descriptive word for each Person in the Trinity. Then list a circumstance when you would pray to that Person.

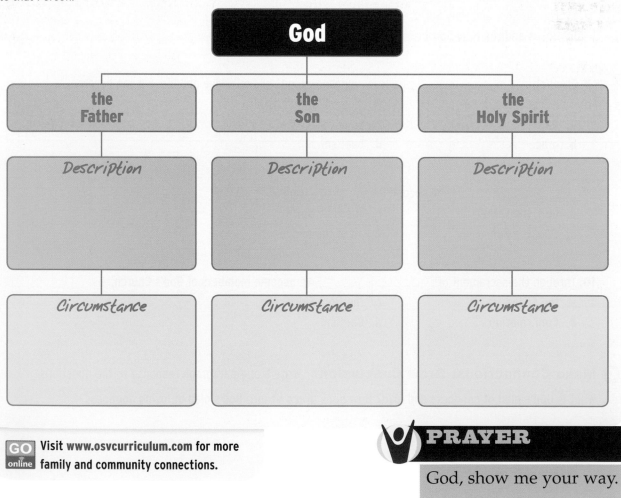

God

the Father	the Son	the Holy Spirit
Description	Description	Description
Circumstance	Circumstance	Circumstance

PRAYER

God, show me your way.

Saint Frances of Rome

Starting when she was just eleven years old, St. Frances of Rome had a very special three-way relationship with God and with the Roman people she served by her good deeds. You could think of her as a living example of the Trinity of God.

Frances was born in Rome in 1384 to a wealthy, noble family. She learned to have a peaceful personality and a serious devotion to God from her mother. From her father, however, she inherited a strong will. That will gave her the strength to devote her life to helping people less fortunate than herself.

On the orders of her father, she married Lorenzo Ponziani at the age of thirteen. He was noble and wealthy, and he loved her very much. Her mother-in-law pressured Frances to entertain as part of Rome's social scene, but her heart was with the city's poor people.

Frances and her sister-in-law Vannozza became close friends, and prayed together. They visited prisons to give comfort and served in hospitals. It was not fashionable for noblewomen to help the poor, and people gossiped about two girls out alone. However, Lorenzo supported his wife's efforts and did not try to stop her from doing the work of God.

In the early 1400s, a flood brought disease and famine to Rome. Frances and Vannozza went out to the poor with corn, wine, oil, and clothing from their family's possessions. Her father-in-law tried to stop her, but a miracle happened. The family's empty corn loft suddenly filled with corn and their empty wine cask was full. These incidents completely converted Lorenzo and his father.

With her husband's and father-in-law's blessings, Frances sold her jewels and clothes and distributed money to the needy. When civil war came to Rome, Frances' house was destroyed. She was able to fix it up, and she turned it into a hospital and a homeless shelter.

After the war was over, Frances started a lay order of women attached to the Benedictines called the Oblates of Mary. The women lived in the world but pledged to offer themselves to God and to serve the poor. They bought a house where the widowed members could live in community.

After Lorenzo's death, Frances moved into the house with the other Oblates and was made mother superior. At the age of fifty-two, she fulfilled her lifelong dream of becoming a nun. She died four years later. Her last words were, "The angel has finished his task—he beckons me to follow him."

▲ *Madonna and Child with Saint Frances of Rome,* by Orazio Gentileschi (1563–1639)

GLOBAL DATA

Rome

- Rome is the capital of Italy and its third largest city.
- Rome is the home of the Roman Catholic Church and the pope.
- Rome is built on seven hills overlooking the Tiber River.
- Rome was once the center of a vast empire stretching from England to the Middle East.

5 JESUS Word of God

⊻ PRAYER O God, let your Word be alive in me.

People can be so shallow and judgmental!
Do I judge people too quickly?
How do I know what someone is really like?
How can someone know the real me?

"**She** hates me." Maria's voice sounded harsh. Maria saw red—literally. She glared at the sea of red marks Mrs. Monroe had made on her essay. "Look, you're not special," Jenn said. "She shreds everybody's papers." "Whatever," Maria muttered under her breath.

Maria knew that Jenn was right: Mrs. Monroe had a reputation as a demanding teacher. And that's why Maria had been working extra hard in Mrs. Monroe's class. An "A" from her really meant something. She wanted an "A" so badly she could taste it.

As she changed her clothes for volleyball practice, Maria thought, "Forget her." But then she made an angry promise to herself to give Mrs. Monroe a hard time in class the next day as a "payback."

The next day, on her way to join Jenn and their friends in study hall, Maria frowned as she saw Mrs. Monroe walking toward her. Then she noticed Mrs. Monroe was talking to a freshman girl who was crying. She had her arm around the girl's shoulders. Her face was lowered, speaking quietly, keeping her back to the hallway, so passing students couldn't see the girl crying.

Sitting with her friends, Maria unwrapped a grape sourball Jenn had given her. She told her friends what she had just seen, how Mrs. Monroe had comforted the girl. "Wow. That was cool of Mrs. Monroe," Jenn replied. "I don't care what she did," Maria said. "She's still awful to me." But the harsh words rang in Maria's ears later. She felt more confused than angry now that she had seen another side of her teacher. "What would people think of me if all they saw and heard was what I did in class?" she wondered.

That night, while she listened to her mp3 mix and studied science, Maria thought about Mrs. Monroe. How could she be so mean as an English teacher and so nice as a person? She snatched up the paper and forced herself to read the comments. As she read, Maria began to see the weak areas in her writing. She had to admit that the comments were probably true. If she took them as advice instead of criticism, her paper would be better. Maybe I misjudged her, Maria thought to herself. "I wonder what I'd think of her if I came to her for advice and wasn't worried about my grade?"

ACTIVITY

LET'S BEGIN Discuss what could happen in this story. What does Maria discover about Mrs. Monroe and about herself? How do you show different parts of yourself when you're in different roles, for example, as a son or daughter, a big brother or sister, a student or an athlete? Are any of these *not* the real you or are they *all* the real you?

▶ **How do *you* remain true to who *you* are? When you're getting to know someone else, how do you get to know the authentic, or real, person?**

THE ETERNAL WORD

Focus What is the "eternal Word"?

As humans, we are called by God to be authentic, which means to be true to who we really are. But our personalities have many different dimensions. We are complex. Sometimes, we are not easy to understand. So God the Father sent Jesus as our model of being authentic. He was always true to who he was, even when there was a cost.

It takes time to see the complexity of a person, especially someone you want to be friends with. So it is with Jesus. He too was complex. He was fully human and fully divine at the same time. Getting to know the true nature of Jesus takes time and study. The Bible holds the information we need.

✝ SCRIPTURE

GO TO THE SOURCE
Read **John 1:1–14**. Why do you think Jesus is called "the Word"? What does that symbol mean to you?

✝ SCRIPTURE

The Son of God The Gospel according to John begins differently than the Gospels according to Matthew, Mark, and Luke. Instead of starting with the birth of Jesus or with his ministry on earth, it goes back to the beginning of time to tell us about Jesus before the world began. That is a side of Jesus we might not think of at first.

> In the beginning was the Word, and the Word was with God, and the Word was God. He was in the beginning with God.
>
> —*John 1:1–2*

Jesus is the Word. He was with God the Father before creation. Then the Son of God became human, like us. What had been invisible, existing above and before all else, became visible. God's loving presence was now in the flesh. Jesus Christ, the only Son of God, is the eternal (everlasting) Word.

? We say "Jesus *is* the Word," not "Jesus *was* the Word." Why do you think we write about Jesus in the present tense?

◀ **Madonna and Child**

The Wonder of the Incarnation The **Incarnation** is what we call the mystery that the Son of God took on a human nature. This word literally means "in the flesh" and shows our understanding that Jesus Christ has two different natures—human and divine—united together in one divine person. Jesus is like us in all things but sin.

Jesus is the only begotten Son of God. Only Jesus has this unique relationship with God the Father. The Son of God not only has the same divine nature as his heavenly Father, but also shares in our human nature. Jesus is both truly God and truly man.

Words of Faith

Incarnation

Annunciation

miracle

— What's in a Name? —

The name *Jesus* literally means "God saves" (see *Matthew 1:21*). Jesus entered the world to bring salvation to all people. Being Christian means believing that Jesus is not just some wise prophet or miracle worker, but that he is the only Son of God. That is why we call him "Lord."

In the Gospel according to John, we find Jesus using many "I am" statements that teach us about who he is and how he relates to his Father and to us.

"I am the bread of life" John 6:35	We are fed by Jesus in the Eucharist.
"I am the light of the world" John 8:12	With Jesus, we never have to walk in darkness or confusion.
"I am the gate" John 10:7	We must go through Jesus to be with God.
"I am the good shepherd" John 10:11	Jesus watches out for us and risks himself for us.
"I am the vine, you are the branches" John 15:5	We must remain attached to Jesus to live.

ACTIVITY

SHARE YOUR FAITH Look at the "I am" statements in the table above. Which of the images of Jesus do you like the most? What other images of Jesus can you think of from Bible stories you've heard or read?

GOD IS WITH US

Focus How did Jesus change our relationship with God?

Long before the birth of Jesus, God used the prophets to speak to his people. Then, in an ancient promise God made to the prophet Isaiah, the Lord said: "'Look, the virgin shall conceive and bear a son, and they shall name him Emmanuel', which means, 'God is with us'" (*Matthew 1:23*). God fulfilled that promise of closeness to his people through the Incarnation of his Son, Jesus Christ.

The Incarnation is amazing news for us. It means that God is not at all distant or removed from our daily lives. In the wonder of the Incarnation, God the Father speaks directly to us in his Son Jesus. Christ lives among us and invites us to follow him, to make our lives like his own in love.

God the Son became human to lead us back into a friendship with the Father and harmony with one another, to restore God's creation. He comes to bring back all things to himself in love. But how does this great mystery of the Incarnation happen? How can it be that the almighty God who existed first and forever is revealed in Jesus?

Why do you think it was in God's plan to become human in Jesus?

▼ *Annunciation*, **by Lorenzo di Credi (c. 1459–1537)**

The Holy Spirit Prepares Jesus is God and shares in the divine nature. But Jesus came from somewhere—he didn't just show up, already made. He entered the world much like any other human being: He was born. However, Jesus' conception is very different from ours.

First, Mary was visited by the angel Gabriel, the messenger from heaven, who announced to her that she would be the Mother of God and give birth to the Savior. We call the angel's visit to Mary the **Annunciation**. All of human history hinged on Mary's reply. Because she said "yes" to God's plan, she became the most important woman in history. In conceiving Jesus, Mary helped in God's plan to turn his people back to the good ways he had always intended for us.

Second, Mary became the Mother of God because God the Holy Spirit made it possible. From before Mary was born, the Holy Spirit was acting in her so that through her the Son of God could become man. By the power of the Holy Spirit, not by human means, Mary became pregnant. Jesus Christ was born to Mary and the world at the right time, through the power of God.

✝ **SCRIPTURE**

GO TO THE SOURCE
Read **Matthew 1:18–23**. What did God want from Joseph? How did Joseph respond to God's call?

❓ **Who do you know of who has a great devotion to Mary, the Mother of God? How does this devotion seem to be helpful to this person?**

Mary—Mother of God and Our Mother

By cooperating with God's plan, Mary was already helping her son, Jesus, in his work as Savior. Before he started his ministry of preaching and healing among the people, Mary became her Son's first and foremost disciple. By saying "yes," Mary anticipated and took part in all the things her Son would do for us.

Mary, Mother of God, is *our* spiritual mother, too. She received the Lord in her heart before he was conceived in her womb. And, when he was on the cross, Jesus gave Mary to his beloved disciple and all of us. Just like any mother, she shows us the way to live by her example. Her life shows us the way to Jesus.

CHECK THIS OUT!

Mary responded with a joyous song after the angel Gabriel's Annunciation to her that she would become the mother of the Son of God. This great hymn is commonly called the Magnificat (from the Latin for the opening words, "My soul magnifies the Lord"). (See *Luke 1:46–55*.) When we sing it at Evening Prayer, or vespers, we hear the Lord's call to stand with the poor and oppressed, as Mary did.

ACTIVITY

CONNECT YOUR FAITH What are some ways we, as Christians, have been asked to be the disciples of Jesus? Create a poster showing ways you can follow Mary's example and say "yes" to God.

SIGNS OF BEING GOD

Focus How did Jesus' actions show he was the Son of God?

In his public ministry, Jesus worked miracles. A **miracle** is a sign, wonder, or action that can only take place through the power of God. When Jesus worked miracles, it was obvious something extraordinary was happening through him. People experienced God's power in amazing ways that changed their lives and led many of them to believe in Jesus and have faith in him as the Son of God.

Jesus healed people of their diseases. He cast out demons. He restored the dead to life. All four Gospels record this miraculous power in Jesus. For example:

▶ Jesus gave sight to a man who had been blind from birth. Because he did so, the man came to believe that Jesus is Lord. He "saw" Jesus for who he truly is and bowed down before him in worship. (See *John 9:1–41.*)

▶ Jesus restored the ability to walk in a paralyzed man. As he did so, he performed an even greater healing. He forgave the man's sins. To prove that he has this power to forgive sins, the Lord commanded the man to walk—which the man did. The crowd gave glory to God. (See *Luke 5:17–26.*)

▶ Jesus raised a widow's dead son to life again. The Lord stopped the funeral procession on its way out of the city gates and commanded the young man to rise. The man sat up and began to speak. At first the crowd was fearful; then, they praised God's power, saying "God has looked favorably on his people." (See *Luke 7:11–17.*)

These miracles, and others like them, show us the awesome divinity of Jesus. At the same time, they show us the human nature of the Son of God. How? Many of these accounts of Jesus' miracles also tell us about his emotions, like compassion or pity (See *Matthew 20:34, Mark 6:34*), anger (See *John 11:33*), and tears (See *John 11:35*).

Which do you think was easier: to believe in Jesus after *seeing* his miracles or after *hearing* about them from others who saw them? Do you agree that seeing is believing?

CATHOLICS TODAY

We profess faith in Jesus' divinity and in the Blessed Trinity by reciting together the words of the Nicene Creed every time we gather for Sunday Mass or on Holy Days. There are three major sections to the Creed. Each one pertains to a specific Person of the Blessed Trinity: God the Father, God the Son, and God the Holy Spirit. The Creed has been translated into almost 1,300 languages all around the world. The language in the Nicene Creed was revised when we began to implement the English translation of the Third Edition of the *Roman Missal* in the first week of Advent in November 2011. The revisions, including changes to the Nicene Creed and the Apostles' Creed, were made to correspond with the wording of the Third Edition of the *Roman Missal* in Latin (2002).

The Two Natures of Jesus Christ: Divine & Human

Jesus Who Worked Miracles
(See *Luke 5:1–11*)

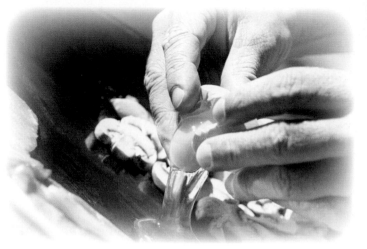

Jesus Who Provided Breakfast for His Disciples
(See *John 21:7–13*)

How do each of these images symbolize the nature of Jesus?

ACTIVITY

LIVE YOUR FAITH Think of a problem that you are facing now. Brainstorm some solutions that Jesus could offer you. Think of ways he could help you solve the problem from his human nature. Think of other ways he could help you from his divine nature.

IN SUMMARY

CATHOLICS BELIEVE

Because Jesus is the Son of God, truly divine and truly human, he saves us and brings us back into relationship with God the Father.

▶ The Son of God has existed for all time, and through the Incarnation, became fully man while remaining fully God.

▶ Through the work of the Holy Spirit, the Son of God was born to Mary, who is a model of trust and discipleship for all of us. Her acceptance of God's will brought Jesus into the world.

▶ Jesus showed that he was divine in many ways, particularly through the working of miracles, which also gives us a glimpse into his human nature and emotions.

LITANY OF THE HOLY NAME OF JESUS

Leader: We gather here this day
in the name of the Father,
and of the Son,
and of the Holy Spirit.

All: Amen.

Leader: Jesus, Son of the living God . . . have mercy on us.
Jesus, splendour of the Father . . . have mercy on us.
Jesus, brightness of eternal light . . . have mercy on us.
Jesus, king of glory . . . have mercy on us.
Jesus, Son of justice . . . have mercy on us.
Jesus, mighty God . . . have mercy on us.
Jesus, most powerful . . . have mercy on us.
Jesus, most patient . . . have mercy on us.
Jesus, most obedient . . . have mercy on us.
Jesus, author of life . . . have mercy on us.
Jesus, good shepherd . . . have mercy on us.
Jesus, eternal wisdom . . . have mercy on us.
Jesus, our way and our life . . . have mercy on us.
Jesus, teacher of the Apostles . . . have mercy on us.
Jesus, strength of martyrs . . . have mercy on us.

Let us pray,
Lord Jesus Christ, . . . mercifully listen to our prayers
and grant us the gift of your divine mercy
that we may ever love you with our whole heart
and never cease from praising you and glorifying your holy name.

All: Amen.

♪ "Pentitential Litany"
Rory Cooney and Gary Daigle, © 1999, GIA Publications, Inc.

REVIEW

A **Work with Words** Circle the letter of the choice that best completes the sentence.

1. The _____ is the mystery of the Son of God taking on a human nature.

  a. Blessed Trinity   **c.** Word

  b. Annunciation   **d.** Incarnation

2. The word *incarnation* literally means _____.

  a. son of man   **c.** in the beginning

  b. in the flesh   **d.** creation

3. At the _____, Gabriel announced to Mary that she would be the Mother of God.

  a. Incarnation   **c.** Resurrection

  b. Annunciation   **d.** creation

4. A(n) _____ is a sign, wonder, or action that can only take place through the power of God.

  a. incarnation   **c.** act of faith

  b. annunciation   **d.** miracle

B **Check Understanding** Complete each sentence with the correct term from the word bank at right.

> ### Word Bank
> Word
> authentic
> spiritual mother
> God
> man
> Jesus
> Magnificat
> Mary
> hope

5. Jesus is our model of being _____ because he is always true to who he is, even when there is a cost.

6. In the first chapter of the Gospel of John, Jesus is called the _____.

7. Jesus is both true God and true _____.

8. The name _____ literally means "God saves."

9. Mary sang the _____ after Gabriel's visit, beginning with the words "My soul proclaims the greatness of the Lord."

10. Mary is our _____ because when Jesus was on the cross he gave her to us.

C **Make Connections: Predict** Write a one-paragraph response to the question.

Identify an area in your life where you need to say "yes" to God as Mary did. If you said "yes," how might your life be different?

OUR CATHOLIC FAITH

WHAT NOW?

★ For one week, look for new aspects of your friends' personalities.

★ Ask Jesus to help you to be true to yourself.

★ Name your favorite Scripture passage that shows Jesus as both divine and human.

★ Speak to an adult who has said "yes" to God as Mary did.

ACTIVITY

LIVE YOUR FAITH What is your definition of the word "authentic"?

▶ Write your name in the center space of the web diagram below. In the surrounding spaces, write "I am" statements that are authentic to yourself and show ways you are living a Christian life.

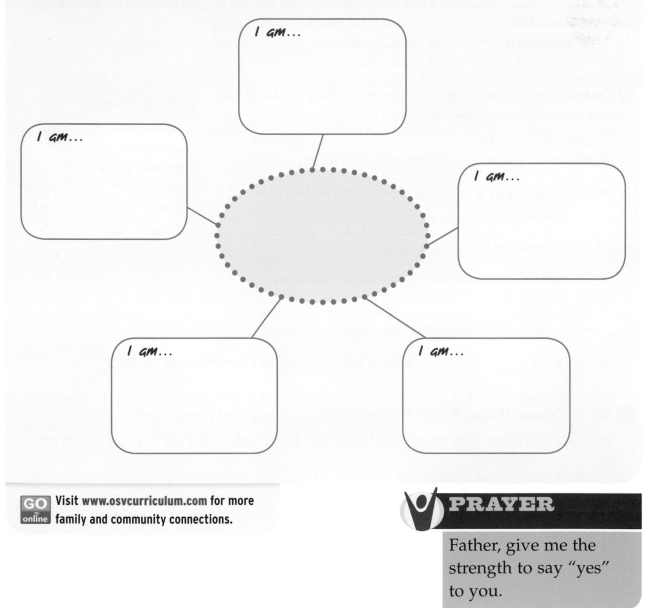

GO online Visit www.osvcurriculum.com for more family and community connections.

PRAYER

Father, give me the strength to say "yes" to you.

PEOPLE OF FAITH

St. Maria Zhao-Guo (mother)
St. Rosa Zhao (daughter)
St. Mary Zhao (daughter)

Jesus calls us to be true to him and true to ourselves. This is what it means to be "authentic." When our authenticity is tested, we look to Jesus as our example of how to face those tests.

Maria Zhao-Guo and her daughters Rosa and Mary found themselves facing such a test in China in the summer of 1900. Even though they were persecuted, their faith in God stayed strong. They gave their lives rather than give up their faith and deny what they believed in so strongly.

For centuries, China's culture and civilization thrived, but it was isolated from the Western world. That all changed by the mid-1800s, when China was invaded and controlled by some of the most powerful nations of Europe. The invaders plundered the nation's natural resources and mistreated its people. However, not all the Westerners who came to China were there to get rich and harm people. Jesuit missionaries and others introduced Christianity to China. The Zhao family was one of the families who believed their message and became Christian converts in the late nineteenth century.

Many Chinese people resented the culture of the Western nations that had invaded their homeland and been cruel to their people. In 1900, this resentment exploded into the Boxer Rebellion. The Boxers wanted to drive the foreigners out of China and return to the old ways of life. Because Christianity was introduced by Westerners, the missionaries and converts to Christianity were targeted by the Boxers.

Maria Zhao and her daughters, Rosa and Mary, were being chased by a band of Boxers, so they tried to hide by jumping into a well. The Boxers dragged them from the well and tried to force them to deny their faith. Rosa's defiant answer was, "We have already made up our minds that we would rather die than deny our faith." Then she turned to her mother and sister, telling them to pray to Jesus for strength to give up their lives for the faith.

Even when a relative tried to help them, Rosa told him, "Uncle, don't waste your time trying to save us. Because we want to keep our faith, we are happy to die for it."

The Boxers took them to the Zhao family cemetery, where they were executed. The Zhaos, along with more than fifty other Chinese martyrs, were beatified by Pope Pius XII in 1955. Pope Saint John Paul II canonized them on the centennial of their martyrdom in 2000.

▲ **The Great Wall of China stretches over 4,000 miles. It was built to protect China from warring neighbors.**

GLOBAL DATA

China

- China is the most populous nation in the world, with over 1.3 billion people, and is the second largest in land area.

- China has a civilization dating back approximately 5,000 years.

- China has been under communist rule since 1949, with no official religion, but restrictions on missionary activity have been eased in recent years and its Christian population is growing.

- China recognizes Catholicism as one of five sanctioned religions.

- China has approximately 12 million Catholics, according to the Vatican.

6 HOLY SPIRIT
Comforter and Guide

PRAYER Lord, help me find you.

*Sometimes I struggle.
I feel like no one really understands me.
How can I get through those times?*

Stan stumbled through the turnstile. His legs felt like lead. The crowd pushed him forward toward the iron chains that snaked up and down, forming long lines. He could hear bits of conversations, excited voices all around him. But the words zoomed past his ears.

Stan remembered the night his parents had told him they'd bought a new house. "Just seven miles away," his mom had said. Stan grunted. Yeah, it was only seven miles, but it felt like seven hundred.

Stan had started the fall semester thinking that it wouldn't take long to have a new group of friends. But here it was, near the end of October, and he hadn't found a group to call his own. He had hoped that he'd be able to hang with some people on the class trip to the amusement park.

Stan could feel the pulse of the crowd. Everyone was having a great time. Stan, however, felt like he was watching it all in slow motion. If Tony and Matt were here, Stan thought, we'd be pushing each other and laughing, scheming ways to cut the line. We'd have mapped out which rides to go on first, and how we would ride the Dragon Master with our hands up in the air during the entire ride.

But Tony and Matt weren't there. Instead, there were hundreds of kids all together, all having fun. He was in the crowd, but he was alone.

Suddenly, Stan's cell phone rang. "Hey, Stan," said a familiar voice on the other end. "Are you at the park?" It was Tony. "I was out sick today, and I thought I'd call you and see if I could hear you screaming on the Dragon Master! Want to cheer me up, man?"

"Sure!" Stan laughed. "I'll go down one time with my cell held up in the air!" He talked with Tony as he got in line. When he told the other kids in his car what he was going to do, they all gave some extra loud screams for Tony. They invited Stan to join them for the next ride. The fun was back—thanks to his old friend.

ACTIVITY

LET'S BEGIN Why did Stan feel isolated, even when he was in the middle of a crowd? How did Stan connect with others? Have you known someone in Stan's situation?

▶ **When are some times you have felt alone? What happened?**

_____

_____

_____

_____

_____

A PROMISE KEPT

Focus Why did God send the Holy Spirit to us?

It's hard when you can't be with a close friend anymore. He or she might have moved away, or you might be going to a new school. You miss your friend, and things you do are different because that person isn't there. You might feel lonely, wondering why people don't understand you and what's important to you.

Jesus knew his friends would miss him when he was no longer with them. His followers were going to feel lost without him. His death would shake them up. His Resurrection would certainly confuse them. His return to the Father in heaven would definitely challenge them. How could they continue the work they had done with Jesus after he was no longer with them?

Always with Them Jesus promised his followers he wouldn't stop communicating with them. In fact, he promised them that he would always be with them through an Advocate, the Holy Spirit. An advocate is someone who speaks on your behalf.

SCRIPTURE So Jesus said to his disciples at the Last Supper, "If you love me, you will keep my commandments. And I will ask the Father, and he will give you another Advocate, to be with you forever. This is the Spirit of truth, whom the world cannot receive, because it neither sees him nor knows him. You know him, because he abides with you, and he will be in you."

—*John 14:15–17*

? How could the Holy Spirit help the Apostles?

? How can he help you?

SCRIPTURE

GO TO THE SOURCE
In **Luke 22:14–20**, we see Jesus and the Apostles sharing a loaf of bread and a cup of wine, which Jesus transformed into his Body given for them and his Blood, which is the new covenant. This simple act forms the basis of our Eucharist. For more on the Last Supper, read **Matthew 26:26–29**, **Mark 14:22–25**, and **John 13:1–17**.

The Soul of the Church The Church *is* the Body of Christ in the world. We are the hands and feet of Christ, bringing the truth, joy, and love of the Good News to all people. Our own bodies are more than just a collection of flesh and bones. In the same way that your body is given life by your soul, the Body of Christ comes alive through its soul, the Holy Spirit.

The Holy Spirit keeps the Church going, giving it life and energy. He makes the wonderful diversity of people, places, and cultures in the Church one. He brings them all into harmony by their belief in Jesus. The Holy Spirit is the source of the many gifts and talents the members bring to the Church.

ACTIVITY

SHARE YOUR FAITH Think about situations in your life when you wished you had someone who could speak for you and look out for your best interests. Discuss ways in which the Holy Spirit could fill that role for you.

THE HOLY SPIRIT, COMFORTER

 Focus How does the Holy Spirit help us in ways that no one else can?

SCRIPTURE

Jesus teaches, ". . . how much more will the heavenly Father give the Holy Spirit to those who ask him!" **Luke 11:13**

CHECK THIS OUT!

Sometimes, silence is golden. St. Ignatius of Loyola (d. 1556) promoted a special form of spiritual retreat held in silence. People on Ignatian retreats are guided by a spiritual director to read and contemplate passages from Scripture. For one hour each day, they meet with this director to talk about how the Spirit moves them. The remainder of their time is spent in total silence.

Ignatian retreat houses offer three- and seven-day silent retreats. Practitioners are also encouraged to make one thirty-day silent retreat in their lifetime. Do you think that one-day silent retreat would appeal to you? Why or why not? Why do you think some people relish so much silence in their retreat?

SCRIPTURE After his Last Supper, Jesus took Peter and two other disciples with him into a secluded area of the garden of Gethsemane. He asked his three friends to sit up and wait. He probably wanted them to be there for him, to support him.

He told them, "I am deeply grieved, even to death." Then, he moved farther into the garden where they could not see him. He addressed his heavenly Father in prayer, asking that the cross be taken from him, if possible. Jesus prayed, "My Father, if it is possible, let this cup pass from me; yet not what I want but what you want."

Meanwhile, as Jesus prepared himself for the cross, his friends fell asleep. Twice he returned to find them sleeping and unaware of his pain. How must Jesus have felt?

—*Matthew 26:38–40*

Have you ever had to do something you knew would be difficult—but you also knew that it was important that you do it?

St. Ignatius of Loyola ▶

We May Seem Alone Often, the support and strength of friends helps us through difficult times. There are times, however, when we must face something all on our own. We might be surrounded by our friends, and they might even offer their help and support. But in the end, whatever it is we must face, we need to do it on our own.

Imagine an Olympic gymnast, about to begin her balance beam routine. She knows that her family and friends are there, sending good thoughts her way. She hears the whistles and cheers of fans she has never met. She feels the support of her coach and teammates. At the same time, she will be alone when she mounts that balance beam and does her routine. No one else can do it for her.

As you have probably discovered already, none of us can avoid pain and difficulties in life. We will have challenges in our lives that we must face on our own. But we will have the help and special comfort of the Holy Spirit as we face these trials and confront these challenges.

The saints often prayed to God for help, and the prayers they prayed still help people pray effectively today. The saints poured out their hearts for help from above. We, too, are sure that the Holy Spirit will personally help us. But that divine help does not mean we are invulnerable.

When do you turn to God?

How do you let God know you need him?

ACTIVITY

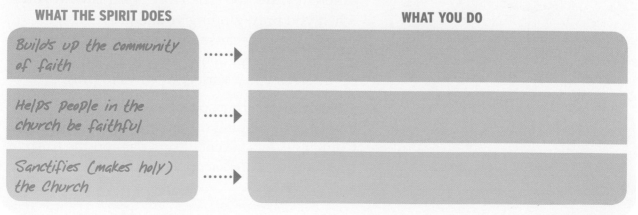

CONNECT YOUR FAITH The left-hand column details three important ways that the work of the Holy Spirit benefits the Church. In the right-hand column, list things that you do in the Church that benefit your brothers and sisters in faith.

WHAT THE SPIRIT DOES	WHAT YOU DO
Builds up the community of faith	
Helps people in the church be faithful	
Sanctifies (makes holy) the Church	

THE HOLY SPIRIT, GUIDE

Focus How does the Holy Spirit help the Church?

A garden grows because someone takes the time and effort to water and weed it. Without weeding, the plants will be choked by unhealthy growth. Without water, the plants in the garden will wither and die.

Similarly, when we raise our minds and hearts to God—which is what **prayer** is—we cultivate our spiritual garden. Requesting bad things from God will produce in us a spiritual garden full of weeds. Neglecting the time and effort for prayer will produce a withered spiritual garden.

Guidance We need someone to guide us through life's questions and help us live for God. That guide is the Holy Spirit. Often, the Holy Spirit works through our parents, parish, and the Christian community.

The Holy Spirit also acts through the living Tradition of the Church to teach and form us as disciples. This living Tradition is our religious heritage. It has been passed down to us from the time of the apostles. The Church leadership guards the Tradition. This living Tradition enriches our personal prayer and the prayer life of the Christian community, so that we raise our minds and hearts to God in healthy, holy, and effective ways.

A Guide to Prayer Just like you talk to your friends in different ways depending upon what you have to share, you can talk to God in different ways, too. The Holy Spirit is with you when you pray, guiding you in prayer as you grow in faith. Because you have different needs and different experiences during life, the Holy Spirit gives you a variety of ways to pray.

The Holy Spirit also teaches you to pray. He does this by helping different generations of Church leaders and believers pass on the truth of Jesus through our sacraments, Creeds, teachings, and devotions.

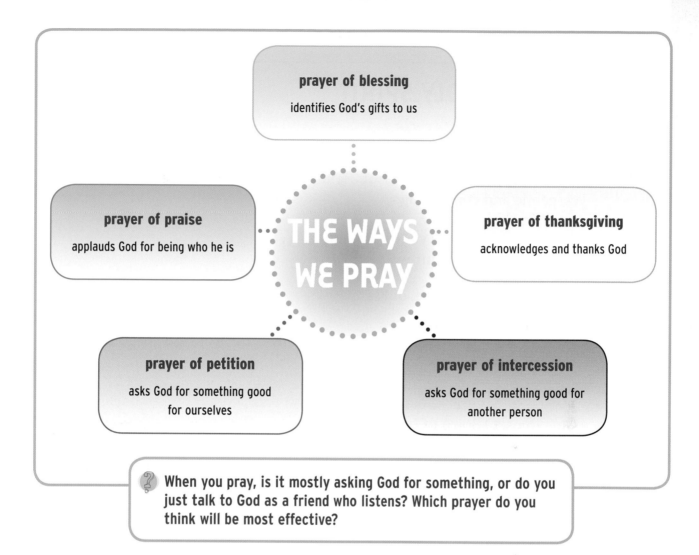

prayer of blessing
identifies God's gifts to us

prayer of praise
applauds God for being who he is

THE WAYS WE PRAY

prayer of thanksgiving
acknowledges and thanks God

prayer of petition
asks God for something good for ourselves

prayer of intercession
asks God for something good for another person

When you pray, is it mostly asking God for something, or do you just talk to God as a friend who listens? Which prayer do you think will be most effective?

ACTIVITY

LIVE YOUR FAITH Some symbols that help us understand the Holy Spirit are flames of fire, holy oil, a dove, and laying on of hands. Choose one that speaks to you of strength, comfort, and guidance. On a separate sheet of paper, draw that symbol. Put it in a place you see frequently.

IN SUMMARY

CATHOLICS BELIEVE

The Holy Spirit is our Advocate, guiding and comforting us, strengthening us to know and live by the truth.

▶ The Holy Spirit, who originally strengthened the first disciples to spread Jesus' message and understand his truth, keeps the Church going, giving it life and energy and uniting us as one Body of Christ.

▶ We all experience difficulties and challenges, some that we must face alone. However, we are never truly alone because the Holy Spirit is with us, comforting, strengthening, and supporting us.

▶ The Holy Spirit guides the Church in her living Tradition and her prayer. The Holy Spirit helps us pray at different times, in different ways, and in different circumstances.

CELEBRATE

PRAYER TO THE HOLY SPIRIT

Leader: Let us pray,

O, Holy Spirit,
God of fire, fierce and powerful,
yet, gentle and comforting,
come to us this day.
Open our ears to hear your wisdom.
Open our hearts to your way.

Reader 1: A reading from the Book of Psalms
Read Psalm 139:1–14.

The word of the Lord.

All: Thanks be to God.

Reader 2: Come to us, O Spirit of truth,
teach us what we need to know,
and remind us of all that Jesus did for us.

Reader 3: Come to us, O Spirit of love,
Walk with us each and every day,
and guide us in all we say and do.

Reader 4: Come to us, O Spirit of compassion,
Be with us when we are lonely and afraid,
when we are confused and don't know how to choose.

All: Come to us, O Spirit of wisdom,
help us to know that you are always near,
help us to know that you will always guide us,
help us to know that you are always for us.

♪ "Confitemini Domino/Come and Fill"

Jacques Berthier, © Taizé, GIA Publications, Inc. Exclusive North American Agent.

80

REVIEW

A **Work with Words** Circle the letter of the choice that best completes the sentence.

1. The Holy Spirit is called an advocate because _____.
   a. he speaks on our behalf   **c.** he is the Word
   b. we can't see him   **d.** he brings healing

2. _____ is the liturgical feast that celebrates the descent of the Holy Spirit upon the Apostles.
   a. Easter   **c.** Pentecost
   b. Christmas   **d.** Mass

3. Prayer involves _____.
   a. thoughts about God   **c.** guidance by the Holy Spirit
   b. raising our hearts and minds to God   **d.** a, b, and c

4. After the Last Supper, Jesus prayed in _____.
   a. Jerusalem   **c.** Gethsemane
   b. the Temple   **d.** Galilee

B **Check Understanding** Complete each sentence with the correct term from the word bank at right.

5. Jesus promised the disciples he would continue to communicate with them after his death through the _____.

6. The Church is the _____ in the world.

7. The Holy Spirit brings _____ to the Church.

8. A prayer of petition asks God for something good for _____.

9. A prayer of _____ asks God for something for another person.

10. _____ passes on to us the authentic teaching of the Church.

> **Word Bank**
> ourselves
> others
> act of faith
> creation
> harmony
> life and energy
> intercession
> Body of Christ
> Holy Spirit
> Tradition

C **Make Connections: Synthesize** Write a one-paragraph response to the questions below.

How are we tied to God? What do you consider the source of your strongest connection to God? Explain.

OUR CATHOLIC FAITH

WHAT NOW?

★ Remember the Holy Spirit when you feel isolated or alone.

★ Take time to pray to the Holy Spirit when you need comfort during a time of difficulty.

★ Ask the Holy Spirit for guidance in making choices.

ACTIVITY

LIVE YOUR FAITH Think of at least five of your favorite movies. Write the title of one in which the main character changes considerably during the movie.

_____

▶ Write a short review of the movie you chose. State the conflict in the story. Show how the character begins to grow emotionally or finds courage to make healthy changes. Give examples of events that may have been the guidance of the Holy Spirit.

_____

_____

_____

_____

_____

_____

 **GO online** Visit www.osvcurriculum.com for more family and community connections.

PRAYER

Come, Holy Spirit, and fill my heart with goodness.

Saint Rafqa (Rebecca)

Many of our saints and other pious men and women have been called by God to serve. Throughout her long life, Saint Rafqa was a guide and source of comfort to those less fortunate, as well as the other members of her religious order.

Born in Lebanon as Boutrossieh Ar-Rayes, she was the daughter and only child of Mourad Saber Shabaq al-Rayes and Rafqa Gemayel. Her mother died when Rafqa was six and she and her stepmother never got along. Working as a maid from age eleven to fifteen, she announced at age fourteen that she felt a call to religious life. Seven years later, she became a nun in the Marian Order of the Immaculate Conception at Bikfaya. She took the religious name Anissa (Agnes) and made her final vows in 1856.

In 1860, she went to Deir-el-Qamar in southern Lebanon. During that year, the Druse sect, goaded by the Turks, killed nearly 8,000 people. They destroyed hundreds of villages, churches, and schools. Rafqa ministered to the suffering people and saved a child's life by hiding him in her skirt as he was being chased by some soldiers.

Following dreams in which Saint Anthony the Great appeared to her, Anissa joined the Lebanese Order of Saint Anthony of the Maronites (Baladiya Order) in 1871. A novice at age thirty-nine, she took the new religious name of Rafqa (Rebecca).

On the feast of the Holy Rosary in 1885, Rafqa prayed that she might share Christ's sufferings. She did suffer, but she never gave up serving God. She became blind and crippled. She spent much of her remaining thirty years in prayer, but always insisted on working in the convent as well as she could with her disabilities, usually spinning wool and knitting. Despite frail health she lived more than eighty years.

Late in life, her close friend and supporter, Mother Superior Ursula Doumit, ordered her to dictate her autobiography, and Rafqa complied. Near the time of her death, Rafqa asked that her sight be restored for a single hour so she could again see the face of Mother Ursula. The hour of sight was granted. Miracles of healing were later recorded at the site of her grave. She was beatified in 1985 by Pope Saint John Paul II and canonized sixteen years later.

▲ The cloister and church of the Maronite Monastery of Deir el Nourieh in Lebanon.

GLOBAL DATA

Lebanon

- Lebanon is located on the eastern shore of the Mediterranean Sea.

- Lebanon is roughly the size of Connecticut.

- Lebanon has a population that is 60 percent Muslim and 39 percent Christian, mostly Catholics.

- Lebanon is recovering from a long civil war between the Muslims and Christians.

Faith in Action!

CATHOLIC SOCIAL TEACHING

DISCOVER | Catholic Social Teaching: Life and Dignity of the Human Person

IN THIS UNIT, you learned that God is a "Trinity," a Community of three Persons whose very Being is Love; and about the importance of loving human relationships. You also learned that the Holy Spirit gives us the courage to love, even when it's hard to do.

Each one of us, every person on earth, is created in the image and likeness of God and is equally precious in the eyes of God. That's the basis of our dignity as human persons. Because God is Love and loves all persons, we too must love everyone, even those who are difficult to love. It almost seems natural to tease certain kids, to make fun of strange-looking adults, to hang out only with people like ourselves. Everybody does it, right? There are some wonderful movies about kids who are "different," whether it's size or disability. These show us the beauty and dignity of kids we don't usually respect. And what about your own experiences of being disrespected? Most kids have been teased, picked on, or talked about at some point. You know how it feels.

One of the most basic aspects of respect is a person's reputation. We all want others to think highly of us. Sometimes the meanest thing we can do to others is tell half-truths about them. Sometimes we do it to look good in the eyes of others. Sometimes we do it because we want to get even with someone or maybe because we're hurting too. No matter what the reason, the Church is clear that this is sinful. Sometimes we hear other kids teasing or telling lies about someone. That's when we are called to stand up for the person being talked about. The Holy Spirit is there to give us the courage to challenge other kids who are doing this. This is where dignity is on the line every day and God is calling us to love every day.

Why is it often easier to disrespect people than to stand up for them?

WE DON'T ALWAYS GET TO see the results of our serving others. Let's look at how young people can make a difference.

"YOUTHSERVE"
JUNIOR HIGH YOUTH IN SERVICE

Whitney and Michael were eighth graders when they joined YouthServe at St. Mary's Parish in Bellevue, Nebraska. YouthServe had been a two-day experience, but the junior high kids complained that they could do more service in the community if the adults would let them. With that, Debra Kaufman, site coordinator for YouthServe and Young Neighbors in Action, both programs of the Center of Ministry Development, went into action. She lobbied for a four-day experience, and Whitney and Michael proved her right.

YouthServe begins on a Sunday, for liturgy, presentations on Catholic social teaching, and service assignments. Monday through Wednesday, from 9 A.M. to 3 P.M., the youth work at sites doing jobs that the staffs don't have time for. Some youth went to inner-city parishes and crisis pregnancy centers; others went to a food bank and a senior center. Whitney and another girl went to a domestic violence shelter, where they scrubbed floors and walls, cleaned toys, and organized donated clothing. Although it bothered them that the women who came there for counseling never talked with them, the girls didn't stop their singing and laughing as they worked. By Tuesday night, when the whole group discussed their experiences, the two girls reported that they felt they had failed—none of the women were paying any attention to them. Other than a cleaner facility, they saw no results

from their presence. Apparently some of the women at the shelter sensed this and wrote them a letter. When Debra shared the letter with the girls, they began to cry as they read how the women so appreciated their joyful presence. "Sometimes in doing service," Debra commented, "you don't see the impact it has right away. You just have to let go and let God take care of it."

This experience changed Whitney and Michael. Debra recalled the skit on prejudice that they had presented during their YouthServe week. "It must have really touched their hearts, for I've seen them stand up for other kids. In a room full of older boys, Michael was the only one who stood up for this nerdy kid the others were teasing. It was amazing!"

? Who are some of the people in your parish or community that you could serve?

▼ In YouthServe, seventh- and eighth-graders spent four days making a difference in the lives of others.

SERVE Your Community

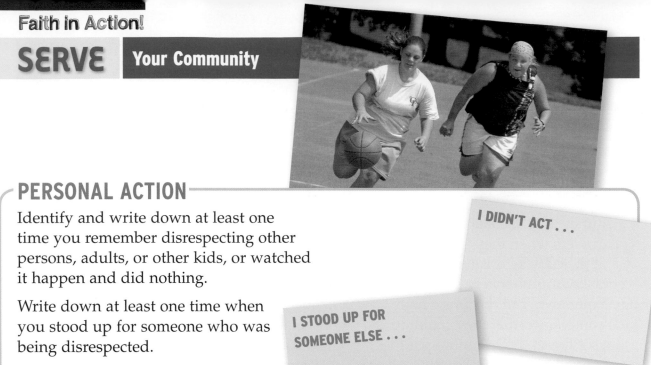

PERSONAL ACTION

Identify and write down at least one time you remember disrespecting other persons, adults, or other kids, or watched it happen and did nothing.

Write down at least one time when you stood up for someone who was being disrespected.

Who are the kids in your class, school, or family who get teased or picked on the most? Choose one of them and decide how you are going to stand up for them the next time it happens.

> **I DIDN'T ACT . . .**

> **I STOOD UP FOR SOMEONE ELSE . . .**

> **I WILL STAND UP FOR SOMEONE BY . . .**

GROUP ACTION

As a class, discuss some of the groups of people who are the least respected in your community and how this disrespect is shown. Choose one group and create a plan for addressing this disrespect.

As a group project, consider creating posters or rap songs expressing your concerns and decide where and how to share them.

Also consider putting together teams of speakers to make presentations in other classes in your school, at a parent-teacher association meeting, or to different parish groups.

Project Planning Sheet

Other specific tasks

_____

_____

Your specific task(s)

_____

_____

_____

Calendar for completing this project

_____

_____

_____

REFLECT On Your Experience

When you think about those times when you disrespected other persons, what were some of the reasons you did it? How did you feel about yourself afterward?

When you think about those times when you stood up for other people who were being disrespected, why did you do it? How did you feel about yourself afterward?

Was it easier to remember times when you disrespected others or times when you stood up for others? Why do you think that is?

What did you learn about disrespect in your community in doing your group project?

What did you learn about yourself in doing the group project?

What did you learn about God and about your faith in doing the project?

List one thing that might be different about you after doing this project. How will your life be different because of these actions?

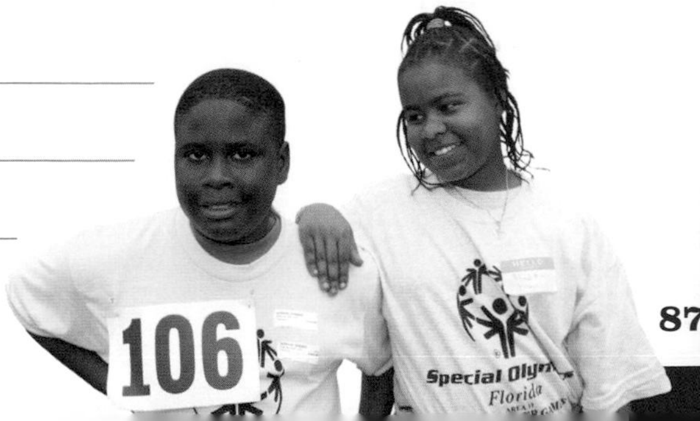

REVIEW

A **Work with Words** Match the words on the left with the correct definitions or descriptions on the right.

_____ **1.** Blessed Trinity

_____ **2.** grace

_____ **3.** Holy Spirit

_____ **4.** Incarnation

_____ **5.** Annunciation

_____ **6.** miracle

_____ **7.** prayer

_____ **8.** Pentecost

A. sign or wonder unachievable by human power that happens through the power of God

B. the Son of God becoming man

C. the third Person of the Trinity

D. raising our hearts and minds to God

E. the outpouring of the Holy Spirit upon the Apostles fifty days after Easter

F. Father, Son, and Holy Spirit

G. the free, undeserved gift of God's life

H. Gabriel telling Mary that she would be the Mother of God

B **Check Understanding** Indicate whether the following statements are true or false. If a statement is false, rewrite it to make it true.

_____ **9.** When God the Father sends his Son to us, he also sends his Spirit.

_____

_____ **10.** Jesus Christ is a guide to the Church.

_____

_____ **11.** In the sacrament of the Eucharist, we become members of God's Church.

_____

_____ **12.** Jesus promised the disciples that he would continue to communicate with them after his death through the Holy Scriptures.

_____

_____ **13.** A prayer of petition is asking God for something good for ourselves.

_____

_____ **14.** A prayer of intercession asks God for something for another person.

_____

_____ **15.** The New Testament alone passes on to us the authentic teaching of the Church.

_____

_____ **16.** In the opening part of the Gospel of John, John calls Jesus "the light of the world."

_____

_____ **17.** The name Jesus literally means "God saves."

_____

_____ **18.** Mary is our spiritual mother because she shows us the way to Jesus.

_____

C **Make Connections** Write a short answer to these questions.

19. Interpret. As a young girl, Mary made a decision to follow God. In what ways is Mary an example for your life as a young person today?

_____

_____

_____

_____

20. Compare. The Church is the Body of Christ. What part of the body are you? Use a part of the human body (hand, foot, eye, etc.) to describe your role in the Body of Christ.

_____

_____

_____

_____

CHAPTER 7 INCARNATION

PRAYER God, help me become my best self.

Sometimes I want to be superhuman!
Other times I think I am too hard on myself.
How do I reach my full potential?

Calvin was exhausted. Swim team practice every weekday and twice on Saturdays! It was starting to get to him. Waiting for his mom to pick him up from practice, he couldn't take his eyes off the basket of candy bars sitting unguarded on the snack bar. "I'm starving!" he thought. "The candy is right there and I'm going to fold if I don't get something to eat. I don't have money today, but I could pay for it tomorrow. No one would blame me; after all, I'm only human! I need to take care of myself—I've got to get something to eat!"

But he walked away from it and went back to the locker room to make sure he hadn't left anything behind. As he opened his locker door, Pete called out, "I'm going to catch up with you in the backstroke soon! I'm less than a half a second behind! You'd better not miss a practice, or I'll be getting first place at the next meet!"

Just hearing this made Calvin more exhausted. He tried to ignore Pete, but it was no use. He buried his head in his jacket like a pillow, "I used to be the fastest, without trying! Now I'm swimming as hard as I can, and I'm losing my edge," he thought. "How can Pete be that close to beating me? He was never all that! Have I already hit the wall? Is this as good as I'll ever get? Maybe I don't have what it takes and I'm just kidding myself. Why get my hopes up? I'm only human! Maybe I'll never be an Olympic swimmer!"

But how could he know for sure—especially if he gave up trying now?

When his mom pulled up, he flopped into the car with a thud. "Tough practice?" she asked. "I'm just wondering," Calvin mumbled, "what if I keep working hard, but I don't keep improving?"

His mom smiled. "You're only human! Just do your best—that's all anyone can ask of you."

ACTIVITY

LET'S BEGIN What do you think of the advice Calvin's mom gave to him? How would you answer the question Calvin asked his mom? When have you been in a situation like Calvin's? What did you do?

▶ **How do you know what your "full potential" is? When have you tried to be "super-human"—tried so hard to do something almost impossible that everything else becomes unbalanced and every setback is emotionally crushing? Do you think that this is what God asks of you?**

_____

_____

_____

_____

TRUE GOD, TRUE MAN

Focus How is Jesus like all of us?

Athletes aren't the only ones to wonder what their full potential is. At some time or another, everyone wants to excel—reach their full potential—in something. People wonder how good they *could* be. People often say it's human nature to want to be the best at something. Is that what it means to be "fully human"? But if you fail, it is okay to just remind yourself, "After all, I'm only human!"

Jesus is "true man and true God," fully human but also fully divine. He is God. And he is also a human being, a man who walked on the planet earth, like all of us. He reached his full potential as both man and God. So what does that mean for us as his followers?

Sometimes it's hard for us to imagine that Jesus actually lived a human life. Can you picture Jesus as a small child learning to put on his sandals? On sunny days, he might have wanted to go outside and play instead of finishing his chores. Maybe he got tired from too much studying. Can you imagine his parents feeling confused because they didn't always understand him and they didn't know how to tell him about it?

Yet, these kinds of things probably happened. How do we know? They are the kinds of things that happen with all human beings—and in all families. We all face new challenges, feel tired, and become confused! After all, we're human!

What are some examples from Jesus' life that show he was fully human? How can these examples help you reach your full potential?

Jesus Became One of Us Jesus is true man, like us. But he is not "only human." He is also true God. Jesus has two natures:

1. He has a divine nature. Jesus is the second Person of the Blessed Trinity.

2. He has a human nature. He was born of a human mother and had to be fed, burped, kept warm, and cuddled like all other human babies.

The Son of God chose to be a man like us in order to show us how to live a full life.

Jesus not only brings us closer to the Father, but he also makes it possible for us to become more like him and the Father. God's Son became human to share his divinity with us. Because of that, we can become united with God the Father. When Jesus the Son of God became the Son of man, we also became God's sons and daughters.

That doesn't mean we should set standards so high that our lives become impossibly stressful and demanding as we try to "prove" ourselves and how good we are. It means we are expected to do our best. When that is not enough, we need to accept our disappointments with humility and learn from our own mistakes.

▲ *Christ Among the Doctors*, by Jusepe de Ribera (1591–1652)

ACTIVITY

SHARE YOUR FAITH In your own words, describe the kind of things you think Jesus expects teenagers to do in order to live a full life. Describe what things you think Jesus doesn't expect teenagers to try to do.

What Jesus expects

_____

_____

What Jesus doesn't expect

_____

_____

JESUS IS THE WAY TO GOD

Focus How does Jesus show us the way?

Before they were called "Christians," the disciples who followed Jesus were called followers of "The Way." Jesus showed them the way to God. He also showed them a new way to live, a way based on truth and love.

How does "The Way" help you trust in God?

How did the disciples of Jesus learn about God? Basically in two ways: Jesus talked about God, letting them know that God is Father, and Jesus showed them God the Father through his life, the life of the Son. Jesus used words to describe what the Father was like, and Jesus used actions to demonstrate what he was like. Jesus' words and actions still show us the way today.

✝ SCRIPTURE

GO TO THE SOURCE
Jesus used words to describe the Father. Read **Luke 11:9–13** and find out why Jesus spoke about giving a hungry child a scorpion or a snake, instead of an egg or some fish.

Some people may have imagined God as someone to be afraid of. Jesus was able to give us a better picture of God—a picture of a loving, gentle, and affectionate Father—a God who takes care of us and gives us what we need. But he is far more—he is eternal Father and source of all life. Jesus told us, "For everyone who asks receives, and everyone who searches finds . . ." (*Luke 11:10*)

► *The Sermon on the Mount*, by Fra Angelico (c. 1387–1455)

Titles for Jesus The Church has given Jesus some titles to describe who he is and what he does. You're probably familiar with Savior, Lord, Christ, and Lamb of God. Here are two titles you might not know: Mediator and Substantial Image.

A *mediator* brings together those who might normally be separated or apart. Because of his uniqueness as true God and true man, Jesus serves as a mediator between God the Father and his people. As our link to God the Father, Jesus is called Mediator because he brings us closer to the Father by his words and his actions.

✝ **SCRIPTURE** As we read in one of Saint Paul's letters,

"For there is one God; there is also one mediator between God and humankind, Christ Jesus, himself human, who gave himself a ransom for all"

—1 Timothy 2:5–6

When Jesus became man, he remained God. So when we look at Jesus, a human being, we get to see God in living color, as if we were watching a video about him. He is sometimes called the Substantial Image of the Father. An image is a visible likeness. *Substantial* implies belonging to its nature. When we say Jesus is the Substantial Image of the Father, we mean that what we see in Jesus reflects the nature of who God is. In the Son of God, you can see what God the Father is like.

❓ **How does knowing Jesus better help you understand what the Trinity is all about?**

✓ CHECK THIS OUT!

Here are some ways Jesus used actions to demonstrate God's love for us.

▶ healing many people who were sick or injured
Read Matthew 8:14–17, Jesus visiting Peter's mother-in-law.

▶ spending time and eating with people who were unpopular
Read Luke 5:30–32, Jesus answering to the Pharisees and scribes.

▶ feeding people who were hungry
Read Mark 6:30–44, the Feeding of the 5,000.

ACTIVITY

CONNECT YOUR FAITH Write three words or phrases to describe Jesus. Tell why you think they are an accurate description of what Jesus is like. Name three people you know who can be described in a similar way.

JESUS	OTHERS

THE WAY TO LIVE

Focus What did Jesus want to show us?

Jesus gave his followers many examples of how they could become more like him. When you follow his example, you are acting like he did. The more you do so, the more you can discover your full potential and live the best life possible.

Being All You Can Be It's not easy to figure out what your full potential is! Whether you are on a swim team, learning chess, practicing the piano, or trying to develop your talent as a painter, it can be frustrating at times. We might start out by asking ourselves, "How good can I become?" But after awhile, we might simply ask, "How good do I have to be?"

Most parents, teachers, and coaches are quick to tell us, "Don't be a quitter!" Even so, sometimes it's easier to quit than to try to push ourselves to become excellent.

LIKE JESUS

Following Jesus means doing the kinds of things he did. Things like this:

▶ taking time to pray *See Mark 6:45–46.*

▶ having a good relationship with his parents *See Luke 2:51–52.*

▶ relying on his good friends *See Luke 8:1–3.*

▶ expressing deep feelings *See John 11:32–37.*

▶ talking about things with those who disagree *See Mark 12:13–17.*

▶ listening to others and sometimes changing his mind *See Matthew 15:21–28.*

▶ taking care of others in need *See Matthew 9:27–31.*

▶ forgiving his enemies *See Luke 23:33–34.*

▶ saying no to temptation *See Matthew 4:1–11.*

▶ going to Church *See Luke 2:41–52.*

▶ standing up for others *See Matthew 21:12–13.*

In what ways do you already act like Jesus?

Jesus didn't come to show us the way to play perfect chess or piano, swim, paint, or get straight A's. Jesus is more concerned with what importance we give God in our lives, how we treat our families and friends, how we pray, how we care for people we don't know, and how we forgive our enemies. Sometimes that is a lot harder than doing laps in the pool or practicing scales on the keyboard.

Reaching your full potential means being the person God created you to be. Of all the good that God wants for you, he most wants you to live in his love, to know his happiness, to become like him. You do all of these things when you follow in Jesus' footsteps, when you become his disciple.

Discipleship is really what reaching your true potential is all about. It isn't easy—just like Calvin's journey to reach his potential as a swimmer isn't easy. But you don't have to reach your potential for discipleship alone. We are all in this together—that's why we have the Church.

ACTIVITY

LIVE YOUR FAITH In a famous address to all the young people of the world, the late Pope Saint John Paul II called on all young people to take on "the noble adventure of discipleship." Why would he call discipleship something "noble" and an "adventure"? List some reasons here. As a group, decide one thing you can do together that is both noble and an adventure.

NOBLE   **ADVENTURE**

WHAT WE CAN DO:

IN SUMMARY

CATHOLICS BELIEVE

Jesus is the Son of God who became one of us to show us the way to live and the way to the Father.

▶ Jesus has two natures. He is fully God and fully man. Jesus is the second Person of the Blessed Trinity.

▶ Jesus showed us the way to his heavenly Father with words and actions. He is our link to the divine, the one person who can mediate between people and God.

▶ Jesus became man to show us how to live. We need to follow his example and become followers of the Way. Doing so will help us reach our full potential.

CELEBRATE

PRAYER OF PETITION

Leader 1: Let us pray,

O loving Father,
your care for us is so awesome.
In the joy and sorrow of our lives,
you sent us your most precious gift, your Son, Jesus,
to be with us always.

Leader 2: In our struggles, in our victories,
in our laughter, and in our sadness,
your Light shows the way.

All: Your Light shows the way.

Leader 1: Take us this day, just as we are, here and now,
we who are happy,
we who are hurting and in need of your guidance,
we who are excited about faith and Jesus,
we who don't know what to believe.

Leader 2: Take us just the same, all of us, just as we are.
Bring forth the gifts you have planted deep within us.

Leader 1: Send us your Spirit to open our eyes to see
all the good that you see in us.

Leader 2: Send us your Spirit to open our ears to hear
the guiding words of your Son, Jesus.

Leader 1: Send us your Spirit to open our minds to know
there is more than the "here and now."

Leader 2: Send us your Spirit to open our hearts to trust
in the plan you have in store for our future.
Open our lives to all you have called us to be.

All: Your Light shows the way.

Leader 1: We ask this in Jesus' name. Amen.

♪ "Take, O Take Me As I Am"
John Bell, © 1995, The Iona Community. GIA Publications, Inc., agent

REVIEW

A Work with Words Circle the letter of the choice that best completes the sentence.

1. _____ is a special prayer form in honor of the blessed virgin Mary.
   a. The Rosary
   b. Hail Mary
   c. Our Father
   d. all of the above

2. Mary's visit to her cousin Elizabeth is known as the _____.
   a. Annunication
   b. Nativity
   c. Visitation
   d. Presentation

3. The Nativity refers to _____.
   a. the birth of Jesus
   b. Elizabeth's visit to Mary
   c. Gabriel's visit to Mary
   d. Jesus at the temple

4. Jesus is called the Substantial Image of the Father because _____.
   a. he brings us closer to God
   b. he communicates with us
   c. he is human and divine
   d. he reflects the Father's love for us

B Check Understanding Complete each sentence with the correct term from the word bank at right.

5. Disciples of Jesus were first called the followers of the _____.

6. The disciples learned more about God through the _____ and _____ of Jesus.

7. Jesus is known as the _____, the link between God and humans.

8. Jesus has two _____.

9. Reaching your full _____ means becoming the person God meant you to be.

10. You become a _____ when you follow in Jesus' footsteps.

Word Bank
- words
- mediator
- the Gospels
- disciple
- way
- the Holy Spirit
- natures
- actions
- inspiration
- potential

C Make Connections: Analyze Write a one-paragraph response to the question.

Jesus is both true God and true man. Which aspect of Jesus is harder for you to identify with? Explain why.

OUR CATHOLIC FAITH

WHAT NOW?

★ Take time to think about your full potential.

★ Remember Jesus when you struggle with the day-to-day frustrations of life.

★ Try to decide which goals are "fully human" and which are "only human."

★ Follow the example of Jesus, especially the way he treated strangers as well as his friends and family.

ACTIVITY

LIVE YOUR FAITH Think about your own life. Reflect on where you are not doing your best. Consider whether you need to try harder in that area.

▶ Make a list of things that you think would be "only human" to try.

▶ Make a list of things that you think would be "fully human" to try.

▶ Pick one "only human" task and commit to improving in that area.

▶ Pick one "fully human" task and at least consider improving in that area.

▶ Ask an adult you trust to look at your goals and give you some advice.

Examine your commitment to "the noble adventure of discipleship." How well are you reaching your true potential for discipleship? Make yourself some notes as to how you might take some positive steps following "The Way."

GO online Visit www.osvcurriculum.com for more family and community connections.

PRAYER

"This is what is needed: . . . a Church which is not afraid to require much, after having given much; which does not fear asking from young people the effort of a noble and authentic adventure, such as that of the following of the Gospel."

Pope Saint John Paul II,
Message for the XXXII World Day of Prayer for Vocations

Saint Joseph

When the Mother of Our Lord first conceived him, she was a very young woman betrothed to Joseph, an elderly carpenter from Nazareth. Many men, if they found out their wife-to-be was pregnant with a child that was not theirs, would have broken off the engagement. Joseph seriously considered doing this, but an angel appeared to him in his sleep and told him the child Mary was bearing was the Son of God. The angel urged Joseph to go ahead with his plans to wed Mary. Joseph obeyed.

Joseph was blessed with compassion for his young wife and when the Son of God became man in the flesh, Joseph was a loving earthly father to Jesus with all his heart. When King Herod received word that the Savior was born, he began to search for the newborn child. The king would have put the child to death if he had found him. Joseph took Mary and his infant son and fled to Egypt until it was safe to return home.

Long before Jesus grew into adulthood and began his ministry, Joseph was already living the Christian life his adopted son would later advocate. He taught Jesus the skills of his trade as a carpenter. He showed his young son the values of living a righteous life, and brought him up in the faith of his ancestors. Every year Joseph and his family would make the pilgrimage for the Feast of the Passover. Joseph was not a rich man and he could not afford a lamb to offer for sacrifice at the altar in the Temple of Jerusalem. But that did not stop him from making the pilgrimage. He offered two doves to the priests and his offering was accepted.

The final reference to Joseph in the Gospels is when Jesus was about twelve years old and he disappeared during a pilgrimage to Jerusalem with his mother and foster father. He was later found in the Temple, arguing Scriptures and their interpretations with the priests there. This was the first sign of the calling of Jesus to restore the true faith in the Lord.

An elderly man at the time of Our Savior's birth, it is assumed that Joseph was dead when Jesus began his public ministry in Judea. None of the accounts of Jesus' final days mention anything about Joseph being present at that time or at the crucifixion. During his long lifetime, Saint Joseph was a shining example of humility, compassion, and devotion. Many years later he was anointed a Patron of the Universal Church.

▲ **Saint Joseph with the Child Jesus**

GLOBAL DATA

Jerusalem

- Jerusalem was the center of faith for the Jewish people for more than 1,000 years before the birth of Our Lord.

- Jerusalem was conquered by the Romans in 63 B.C.

- Jerusalem was the site of the Holy Temple in which Jesus argued Scripture with the priests and overturned the tables of the moneychangers just before his death.

- Jerusalem is today the capital of the nation of Israel and the Holy City of three faiths.

CHAPTER 8 JESUS Model of Wisdom

PRAYER O God, give me your wisdom.

*At times I am so confused!
There are so many different opinions!
How do I know what's right?*

Janelle's face burned. Tears welled up at the corner of her eyes, ready to cascade down her cheeks. She didn't want anyone to see how upset she was, so she hurried out of the classroom into the crowded hall.

It happened in English class. Out of the blue during the group activity, Cynthia said in a voice loud enough for the whole room to hear, "Nice shirt you wore yesterday, Janelle. I used to have one like that, but I gave it to the thrift store. Is that where you got yours?" Janelle was too stunned to think of a good comeback. A hot flush of embarrassment crept up her neck. She wanted to crawl under the floor. She couldn't get out of class fast enough.

She stood in front of her locker, still hurting from Cynthia's comment. Out of the corner of her eye, she noticed a tall kid walking down the hall. Written in black across his hoodie was "Don't get mad. Get even." Janelle thought of ways she could get even. She thought about tripping Cynthia in the lunchroom while she was carrying her food tray. Then the idea to really hurt Cynthia came to her. The week before, Cynthia had confided that she had a massive crush on Javier. "I'll write her little secret in a fake letter from her to Javier and leave it in the bathroom. Tomorrow the whole school will know."

In science lab, Janelle tried to pay attention to the experiment she and her lab partner Tammy were working on. "Your turn." Tammy held out the beaker and thermometer. Janelle noticed a worn leather band around Tammy's wrist with "WWJD" etched into the leather. Janelle took the thermometer and thought, "Yeah. What would Jesus do to Cynthia?"

ACTIVITY

LET'S BEGIN Discuss what could happen in this story. What if Janelle follows her first impulse to hurt Cynthia? How might she feel about herself then? What if Janelle considers what Jesus would advise in this situation?

▶ **Think of a time when there were several ways to respond to a situation. How did you decide what you should do?**

JESUS, THE WISE TEACHER

 Focus What made Jesus different from other teachers?

Lots of young people struggle with finding the voice of wisdom in others and themselves: "What really matters? What choices should I make? How am I supposed to live?"

When Jesus started teaching, the people listening to him probably had similar questions: "Who will help us know God's will? Who can make life better?" Jesus gave the answers to these questions, and more!

A Teacher Like No Other
Once people heard Jesus' words, they realized he was different.

▶ Jesus spoke the truth, even when it was difficult to hear.

▶ He encouraged people to follow the ways of God his Father, even when it wasn't easy.

▶ He spoke across social barriers.

▶ He astounded the crowds with amazing authority given to him by his Father.

Jesus' wisdom challenged the commonly accepted understanding of his time. He did not accept stereotypes. He ignored established practices that judged others by their social or economic status. He spent time with women, children, people who had undesirable jobs, and those who were poor, sick, or in special need. Jesus took the time to get to know those most ignored in society. In all of these ways, he valued the worth and dignity of every person he met.

⊘ Think of someone you know who treats everyone equally, as Jesus did.

⊘ What's this person like? How do people react to him or her?

✝ SCRIPTURE

Rabbi, we know that you are a teacher who has come from God; for no one can do these signs that you do apart from the presence of God. **John 3:2**

▼ *Jerusalem, Jerusalem,* by James Jacques Joseph Tissot (1836–1902)

Ordinary Life, Extraordinary Meaning Jesus knew things were not perfect in the lives of the people. The people needed to turn to God and to work on their relationships with one another. They needed forgiveness.

Those who heard Jesus sensed that he was different. He seemed to be connected to what was important in life and was truly right. He encouraged people to do right, even if it required them to change their way of living.

Jesus wanted his followers to understand the true meaning of forgiveness and the way to live by God the Father's will. He spoke often about God's kingdom of peace and justice. Jesus talked about things that were difficult to describe. So he often taught using parables.

A **parable** is a simple story or an analogy used to describe something larger or more mysterious. Jesus' parables sometimes end with a twist or a surprise, and the people listening didn't always understand the deeper meaning. He talked about things from the everyday lives of his listeners—such as farming, cleaning, cooking, fishing, family relationships—to give a religious or moral lesson, or to emphasize God's great love.

Sometimes Jesus spoke in parables when he was being challenged by a religious leader who wanted to trap him in his words. In the Gospel of Luke a scholar of wanted to test Jesus. He asked, "Who is my neighbor?" to clarify the law, "love your neighbor as yourself." In response, Jesus told the parable of the Good Samaritan. This parable would have surprised Jesus' listeners. The Jewish people and the Samaritans of Jesus' time had religious and ethnic differences. The people would not have expected the Jewish men to ignore one of their own or the Samaritan to help someone considered to be the enemy.

parable

Sermon on the Mount

Beatitudes

CHECK THIS OUT!

You can find more than thirty parables in the Gospels. The parables can be grouped into different themes or categories.

kingdom parables, such as the Pearl of Great Price (*Matthew 13:45–46*)

parables about making choices, such as the Two Sons (*Matthew 21:28–32*)

forgiveness parables, such as the Lost Coin (*Luke 15:8–10*)

parables that upset the order of things, such as the Rich Man and Lazarus (*Luke 16:19–31*)

discipleship parables, such as the Wedding Feast (*Matthew 22:1–14*)

ACTIVITY

SHARE YOUR FAITH Choose a parable with which you are not very familiar. Read and reflect on it. Then use your own words to describe the meaning of the parable.

YOUR PARABLE

ITS MEANING

A UNIQUE MESSAGE

Focus How are Jesus' words surprising and challenging?

✝ SCRIPTURE

GO TO THE SOURCE
Read **Matthew 7:24–29** and think about why the analogy of a house's foundation ended the Sermon on the Mount.

Jesus taught everywhere he went. He preached in homes and synagogues, in boats, on the road as he walked, and on the shores. He gathered with his disciples on hilly areas as the crowds followed him, hoping to hear his message or to receive his healing touch. He offered many words of wisdom throughout his public ministry, and the author of the Gospel according to Matthew collected many of these teachings into what is known as the **Sermon on the Mount**.

Words and Actions Have you ever been told that actions speak louder than words? Or that you need to not only say what's right, but also do what's right? Jesus tells us something similar.

✝ **SCRIPTURE** Jesus said if you listen to his words, and you pattern your actions on his words, you will have a good foundation. It's like building a house on solid rock. The winds will blow, and the rains will fall, but the house will stand. The strong foundation of Jesus' words will hold up your actions that are based on hearing and believing his words.

But if you don't listen to the words of Jesus, it will be like building your house on sand. Your life will have no foundation. The winds and rain will knock it down easily. (See *Matthew 7:24–29*.)

❓ **What can you do to become a person who connects your words and your actions?**

WHERE IT HAPPENED

THE GOSPELS do not tell us exactly where Jesus gathered his disciples and the crowds in Galilee. The geography in the hill country of Galilee contains elevated hills with many associated level places. Some archeologists and people who study the Bible think parts of the Sermon on the Mount took place at Mount Eremos, overlooking the Sea of Galilee. It is often called the Mount of Beatitudes.

Mount Eremos

Sound Bytes from the Mount

You are the salt of the earth.
You are the light of the world.

Where your treasure is, your heart is, too!

Don't judge others harshly, or you will be judged harshly.

Our Father is in heaven; how holy is his name.

When you pray, don't use loud and fancy words.

When you give to the poor, don't brag about it.

When you fast, don't try to look glum and hungry.

Ask and you will receive.
Seek and you will find.
Knock and the door will open.

Love your enemies.

Which of these teachings do you think people most need to hear and act upon today?

Which teachings would be hardest for you to hear and act on?

ACTIVITY

CONNECT YOUR FAITH Name three words or phrases to describe Jesus' wisdom found in the Sermon on the Mount.

WORD 1

WORD 2

WORD 3

DIVINE WORDS FOR WISE LIVING

Focus What do the Beatitudes teach us about our relationships with God and others?

✝ SCRIPTURE

GO TO THE SOURCE

Read either **Matthew's** or **Luke's** version of the Beatitudes to find out how each of these groups of people will be blessed.

Perhaps the most often quoted part of the Sermon on the Mount is the **Beatitudes**, Jesus' teachings on the meaning of and path to true happiness. The word *beatitude* means "happiness or blessedness." In the Beatitudes, Jesus tells how he expects his followers to live in relationship with one another. In the Beatitudes we find the values of the Kingdom of God, and the attitudes and behaviors of Christians living in God's kingdom today. From the Beatitudes we learn about the eternal blessedness, or holiness, to which God calls all of us.

The Beatitudes are recorded in two Gospels: Matthew and Luke. The two versions are similar, but different.

✝ SCRIPTURE

The Words in Matthew 5:3-12

Blessed are:

   the poor in spirit

   those who mourn and the meek

   those who hunger and thirst for righteousness

   the merciful and the pure in heart

   the peacemakers

   those who are persecuted for righteousness

   you when people revile you because of Jesus

The Words in Luke 6:20-26

Blessed are you:

   who are poor

   who are hungry now

   who weep now

   when people hate you, on account of the Son of man

Woe to you:

   who are rich

   who are full now

   who are laughing now

❓ **Why do you think Jesus began his teachings with the word *Blessed*?**

The Message Matthew's version zeroes in on the spiritual and religious virtues of God's kingdom. Luke's version focuses on the social and economic inequality of the time. In both, we find Jesus' teaching that happiness comes from trusting in God no matter what is happening now. We will know true happiness when God's kingdom has come in its fullness. In the meantime, being obsessed with material things or current good fortune will keep us from seeing and living the real values of God's kingdom.

ACTIVITY

LIVE YOUR FAITH Create a modern version of the Beatitudes addressed specifically to people your age.

BEATITUDE

BEATITUDE

BEATITUDE

IN SUMMARY

CATHOLICS BELIEVE

As Catholics we turn to Jesus as our source of wisdom.

▶ Jesus' wisdom came from being the Son of God; he looked at the world and those around him through divine eyes, not society's values.

▶ He taught through his words and actions. In his Sermon on the Mount, he gave advice and specific direction that emphasize just living, honoring God, and making our actions reflect our beliefs.

▶ Jesus' Beatitudes challenge us to live by the values of God's kingdom and to understand that true happiness comes from the hope of eternal life with God.

 **PRAYER**

PRAYER IN THE STYLE OF TAIZÉ

Leader: In the name of the Father, the Son, and the Holy Spirit. Amen.
Let us pray:

(sing or say three times)
God's Chosen People, blest and holy,
what have we done for the poor ones in our midst?

(silence)

Reflection: O Lord, what have we done for those who seek shelter among us?
What have we done for those who are lonely, who long for love
and affection?
What have we done for the "new kids" who want to be welcomed
and accepted?

Chant: *(sing or say three times)*
God's Chosen People, blest and holy,
what have we done for the poor ones here in our midst?

(silence)

Reflection: What have we done for those who are troubled and seek our forgiveness?
What have we done for those who are fragile and need our protection?
What have we done for those who are weary and in need of your peace?

Chant: *(sing or say three times)*
God's Chosen People, blest and holy,
what have we done for the poor ones here in our midst?

(silence)

♪ "What Have We Done for the Poor Ones?"
Lori True, © 2005, GIA Publications, Inc.

REVIEW

Ⓐ Work with Words Circle the letter of the choice that best completes the sentence.

1. The word *beatitude* means _____.
- **a.** wisdom
- **b.** happiness
- **c.** blessedness
- **d.** b and c

2. In the Sermon on the Mount, Jesus said you need _____ to have a strong foundation in life.
- **a.** to listen and follow his words
- **b.** to treat your neighbors fairly
- **c.** to make decisions based upon society's values
- **d.** none of the above

3. A simple story or analogy about everyday life used to describe something larger or more mysterious is a _____.
- **a.** Gospel
- **b.** parable
- **c.** Beatitude
- **d.** Sermon

4. The Beatitudes are found in the Gospels of _____.
- **a.** Matthew and John
- **b.** Luke and Mark
- **c.** Luke and Matthew
- **d.** Mark and John

Ⓑ Check Understanding Complete each sentence with the correct term from the word bank at right.

5. The Beatitudes are the most often quoted part of the _____.

6. Jesus spoke often about God's kingdom of _____ and _____.

7. In the Beatitudes we learn that _____ comes from living the values of his kingdom.

8. God calls each of us to eternal _____.

9. Jesus taught with authority because he was _____.

10. Jesus' parable of the _____ is a good example of how his wisdom crossed social barriers and cultural norms.

Word Bank

- holiness
- Good Samaritan
- truth
- peace
- true happiness
- prodigal son
- Sermon on the Mount
- justice
- blessedness
- the Son of God

Ⓒ Make Connections: Identify Write a one-paragraph response to the question.

What wisdom does Jesus have to offer us and how can following it make a difference in your life?

OUR CATHOLIC FAITH

WHAT NOW?

★ Take the time to learn Jesus' teachings.

★ Use Jesus' values to help you make your choices.

★ Take time to pray for guidance when making decisions.

★ Search out wise people to get to know.

ACTIVITY

LIVE YOUR FAITH Think of one of your teachers, a family member, a coach, or a political figure who is a person of wisdom. Write down why you see wisdom in this person.

▶ List three attitudes or behaviors that reflect the values of Jesus and God's kingdom. Then commit to one thing you can do to put the words into action in your friendships and family relationships.

Attitude/Behavior	Put It Into Action

 Visit **www.osvcurriculum.com** for more family and community connections.

PRAYER

Jesus, help me to do what's right even when it's not popular.

Oscar Romero

He wasn't much of a hero. He didn't like to cause any problems. He was really kind of ordinary. No one thought he'd ever do anything unusual.

In 1977, he became the archbishop of San Salvador. His name was Oscar Romero.

San Salvador (it means "Holy Savior") is in the country of El Salvador (it means "The Savior"). It truly seemed like a city, and a country, in need of our Savior.

There was a lot of violence in El Salvador. Death squads would come in, capture, and kidnap. Often brothers, fathers, sons, and husbands would never be seen again. Those who were poor had no power at all. They couldn't stop the military. Anyone who tried to protect the poor was in danger of being killed.

At first, Archbishop Romero tried to avoid the conflict. He tried to pretend it wasn't as bad as it was. He didn't want to make any waves. He didn't want to upset the other bishops, either.

The death of a close friend who had worked for social justice was the tipping point for Oscar Romero. He had a change of heart. This timid, quiet man became fearless and outspoken. He insisted that the Church must serve those who were poor and must stand against the violence. He brought Jesus' Beatitude living to life. He took "Blessed are the poor" to heart. He placed the values of the kingdom above those of the government, working for justice and the needs of those who could not protect themselves.

He knew his own life was in danger because he was becoming famous for speaking out against the government and supporting people who were poor. He told the people, "I have frequently been threatened with death . . . if they kill me, I shall rise again in the Salvadoran people."

On March 23, 1980, he called upon the soldiers, begging them to refuse to follow orders to kill: "We are your people. The peasants you kill are your own brothers and sisters. When you hear the voice of the man commanding you to kill, remember instead the voice of God. 'You shall not kill!' . . . in the name of God, in the name of our tormented people whose cries rise up to heaven, I beseech you, I beg you, I command you, Stop the repression!"

The very next day, while saying Mass, he was shot and killed.

The people of El Salvador, and all of Latin America, claim him as their saint and martyr.

▲ Oscar Romero, 1917–1980

GLOBAL DATA

El Salvador

- El Salvador is located in Central America on the Pacific coast.

- El Salvador is almost the size of the state of Massachusetts.

- El Salvador has a population of over six million people, more than 57 percent of them Catholic.

- On August 6, the country celebrates the feast day of El Salvador del Mundo (Savior of the World). San Salvador celebrates with carnivals, fairs, soccer games, and a procession.

CHRIST Our Savior

✔ PRAYER Lord, help me to forgive and to be forgiven.

I can't believe I just did that!
If I could only undo what I did, it would fix everything!
What do I do now?

The eighth-graders were going to have to take a vote. Everyone was arguing about the request to let the seventh-graders use the school library lounge.

Javier was against it. "No way! We had to wait until we were in eighth grade! Last year, the eighth-graders kept us out. Now it's our turn! I say we keep it to ourselves. The library lounge should be off limits to everyone except eighth-graders! It should be kept an eighth-grade privilege!"

Monica disagreed. "Yeah? Last year's eighth-graders were awful! That's why you're *still* mad! Don't you think it's time to end this 'war' between the grades? We have a chance to do something positive for our school. Let's share the lounge!"

The vote was close, but the seventh-graders' cause won. They could use the lounge with its recliners, couches, and beanbag chairs. Both grades would share the best spot in the building for relaxing during free period.

Marcus was especially excited—his older brother had been teasing him about everything. Now he teased back: "You got the lounge just one year—but I got it for two!"

But then Marcus decided to disobey the lounge's "no food" rule. He knew he had a bottle of grape juice in his backpack, but he figured that he wouldn't take a drink unless he was alone. That way, no one would see him. While relaxing on the big yellow couch, he leaned over to get some of his books out of his backpack, and took a quick sip of juice. He lost his balance and spilled it all over the favorite couch and rug.

That was it. Not only Marcus but the entire seventh grade class lost their privilege. The library lounge returned to "eighth-graders only." Marcus didn't want to hear what his brother would say now. And he didn't even want to think about what the other seventh-graders would say the next day.

ACTIVITY

LET'S BEGIN Discuss the events of the story. What could Marcus possibly do to "redeem" himself and save the seventh-grade class from losing their lounge rights? What kind of support would he need from others?

▶ **Have you ever done something that hurt or embarrassed a group of people? What was it like? Were you able to patch things up?**

_____

_____

_____

_____

ORIGINAL HOLINESS

Focus How did suffering and sin enter the world?

We've all been there. We think, "What's the big deal?" We deliberately ignore a family rule or a school policy, and the next thing you know, we're in trouble or, even worse, hear the dreaded "I'm disappointed in you." After letting someone down, it's hard to think of a way to make things right, even if we weren't necessarily trying to hurt someone's feelings.

And sometimes, it's even worse. We can be so frustrated or angry that we actually do something hurtful on purpose! We know our actions will hurt someone and affect our friendships. We know it's wrong, a sin, and we still do it anyway. Those results can be pretty bad. We may break the person's trust in us. So what can we do to make it better? Apologize. Promise to do better and not do it again. But what happens when the friendship we've weakened is with God?

A Good Beginning You've probably heard the story of creation many times. But have you ever thought about what it really means? The first humans initially experienced only good, because sin had not yet entered the picture. God made himself known to them, sharing his love. There was no pain or suffering, no arguments or distrust. No concerns about the ozone layer or global warming. The Garden of Eden symbolized true paradise, one in which our first parents lived in holiness and justice. They were happy in a way that we cannot imagine. This is what God created all humans for: to be free, to be his friends, to be close to him.

But that's not how the story ends. Genesis 3 goes on to describe how Adam and Eve took advantage of their freedom and did not turn to God for answers or trust in his word. Instead, they trusted the serpent. He convinced them that if they ate the fruit of the one tree God said not to, they could have the same knowledge as God. So, they disobeyed the one command God had given them, and they ate the fruit. By doing this, the first humans introduced shame, sin, and suffering into the world.

How do you think God might have felt about Adam and Eve's actions?

CHECK THIS OUT!

Have you noticed the Bible never says what kind of fruit Adam and Eve ate? The Bible never mentions an apple! But so often, in art, in stories, and in most people's comments, the fruit painted and described is an apple!

Forever Different So, what happened next? The Book of Genesis tells us that Adam and Eve hid themselves from God, trying to stay away from him because they knew they had sinned. They were afraid. For their disobedience God expelled them from the Garden.

Everything was different now. The pure happiness and holiness had been lost, not just for Adam and Eve, but for all humans after them. Human nature itself had been harmed. Now, all people suffered because of the choice of the first humans. Adam's sin is called **original sin**. All humans inherit the effects of original sin. But what does that really mean? It means many things. Original sin is not something we do; it's something we inherit. Humans can be sad and can suffer because of the sinful actions of others. Humans do not live forever, but die. And all of this is connected with the effects of original sin, including the human tendency to commit personal or **actual sin**, to give in to temptation, and disobey God. In all of these ways, human nature is affected by original sin.

But even though the first humans, and all those who have come after them, disobeyed God, God still loved them. He promised to save them, to bring them back to himself. Throughout history, God sent leaders and prophets to his people, to guide them back to him. Through these people, God promised a Messiah, someone who would bring the people back into the right relationship with God and others, and who would free them from sin.

But why did God allow the physical and moral evil to continue? We do not know the answer to this, but we need to turn to the Son of God whom the Father sent. Jesus Christ died and rose to new life to conquer and defeat evil. In this we must trust.

Words of Faith

original sin

actual sin

Paschal mystery

▲ *Adam and Eve Expelled from Paradise,* **detail from the Annunciation, by Fra Angelico (c. 1387–1455)**

ACTIVITY

SHARE YOUR FAITH Try to think of examples of original sin in the world—times when the human tendency to be sinful, imperfect, or flawed was evident. What examples have you heard about in the news reporting on current events or social issues, or seen in movies or on TV? How would the world be different if those stories were replaced with examples of care, honesty, generosity, and humility?

GOD SO LOVED THE WORLD

Focus Why did Jesus save us?

You might have heard "Jesus is our salvation" and wondered why people need "saving." Well, people need to be restored to God's friendship, like the first humans had with God before original sin. Because God created the first humans holy and just, only he can save us from the effects of original sin and from our sins.

In the second story of Creation in the Book of Genesis, Adam and Eve failed to obey God. They were not faithful. How could things be fixed between them and God? How could the whole human race be redeemed?

For many years, the Jewish people—the people God had chosen to show the whole world his plan of salvation—waited for the Messiah to come and set them free, as their prophets had promised. They were commanded by God to live by the laws of the covenant, but often they strayed. Some of them thought the Messiah was coming to set them free from the Romans, who had captured their land and taken their religious freedom. But God wanted to set his people free from the sin that had captured their hearts and all humankind.

"The New Adam" Because God the Father loved human beings, he sent his Son to them. God the Son freely chose to become human and to offer himself in order to redeem us from the effects of original sin and from our sins. He came into the world as a baby, born from a human mother. Because he did this, no one could ever say that God didn't understand what it was like to be human and be tempted by sin.

Jesus is called "The New Adam." Adam was unfaithful to God, but Jesus remained faithful to God, even when he was tempted.

Jesus the Messiah When Jesus became an adult, many people listened to him tell parables and describe God's love. Jesus came to fulfill the laws of Moses called the Mosaic Law, which included the Ten Commandments, and give them deeper meaning. Jesus fulfilled the Law.

Some of Jesus' followers came to believe that he was the Messiah, the one who would save them. Nathanael, Martha, Peter, and the woman at the well are four examples of people who recognized Jesus in this way.

Jesus the King The Jews before and during Jesus' time used precious oil. When a new king took his place on the throne, a priest anointed him by pouring expensive oil on him as a blessing and sign that God would guide the king. Anointing with oil was a symbol of power and authority. It meant the person being anointed was chosen in a special way. At his baptism, Jesus was anointed by the Holy Spirit to fulfill the Father's will.

✝ **SCRIPTURE**

GO TO THE SOURCE
Look up these readings to see how each person came to recognize who Jesus really was.
Nathanael: **John 1:49**
Martha: **John 11:20–27**
Peter: **Matthew 16:13–20**
Woman at the well: **John 4:25–29**

The Jews were waiting for their Messiah, the one who was to come, the one anointed by God himself, not with earthly oil. The Son of God was the one who came to save and redeem the human race. We call Jesus the Christ, the Messiah, our Savior and Redeemer.

MESSIAH . . . . A Hebrew word that means "anointed," showing he is chosen and empowered. This word was used by Christians to refer to Jesus, "The Much-Awaited Anointed One from God."

CHRIST . . . . . . A Greek word that translates the Hebrew word *Messiah*. It means "The Anointed One."

SAVIOR . . . . . In Hebrew, *Jesus* means "God saves." Jesus is The Savior of the World, the one who saves us from sin and punishment.

REDEEMER . . Jesus is The Redeemer of the World. God accomplished once and for all his plan of salvation by Jesus' redemptive death.

ACTIVITY

CONNECT YOUR FAITH What titles would you give to Jesus? Below, list titles you think of for Jesus and what they mean. Then make a poster or bulletin board with the headline "His Name Is . . ." Cut out graphic symbols to write each name on, such as a crown with the title "King of Kings" written on it, or a scroll with the title "Messiah" on it to show that Jesus was the one who came to fulfill the Old Testament prophecies.

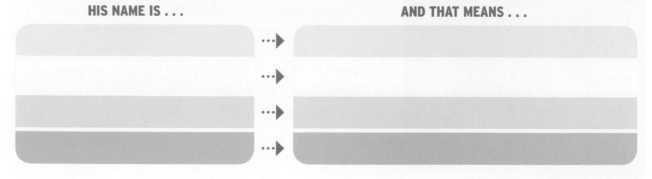

HIS NAME IS . . .   **AND THAT MEANS . . .**

JESUS BRINGS NEW LIFE

Focus What happened when Jesus died?

You might be wondering how Jesus actually brought about our salvation from sin. The ultimate result of sin is suffering and death. So another way to ask the question is, how did Jesus conquer suffering and death?

Jesus willingly offered himself on the cross, which the Church professes in the Nicene Creed every week:

> For our sake he was crucified under Pontius Pilate,
> he suffered death and was buried,
> and rose again on the third day
> in accordance with the Scriptures.

Jesus was free from sin, but he chose to give up his life for the sins of others. He died on the afternoon of what has come to be known as Good Friday. He died for the sins of all people, and we do not hold any one person, or the Jewish people as a whole, responsible for his suffering.

Jesus could not separate his human nature from his divine nature, and the Son of God suffered, died, and was buried. His redemptive death won salvation and eternal life in heaven for all those who had died in God's friendship before him.

His friends saw Jesus die, but nobody saw him rise. They found an empty tomb on Sunday morning. However, Mary Magdalene saw the Risen Christ at the tomb. Later, he appeared to many of his disciples. They talked with him and ate with him, before he ascended (went up) into heaven.

Jesus' redemptive death was something only God-made-man could do. He rose to new life, conquering the power of death. His Resurrection was a victory over death. His death and Resurrection reveal that sin could not keep humans captive forever. Death was not the end, but a passageway to eternal life. This is the salvation that the Son of God won for all who believe in him.

Jesus Continues to Save The **Paschal mystery** is the work Christ accomplished principally by his Passion, death, Resurrection, and Ascension. The Paschal mystery hinges on the great Easter event of our faith: the Resurrection.

How do Jesus' saving activities continue, since he is no longer with us on earth? Jesus' saving actions continue through his Church. Jesus makes his Paschal mystery present in the Eucharist and other sacraments. In so doing, he continues to offer forgiveness, healing, and new life.

▶ Baptism is the first and primary sacrament of forgiveness of sins. It unites us to Christ, so we die and rise with him, and gives us the Holy Spirit.

▶ In the name of God, the Church has the power to forgive the sins committed after Baptism. This happens through bishops and priests, normally, in the Sacrament of Penance, or Reconciliation. We die to sin and rise to renewed life.

▶ The Sacrament of Eucharist cleanses us from venial sins and preserves us from future sins. We share in Jesus' suffering and his rising. The Eucharist does not cleanse us from mortal sins. The proper sacrament for their forgiveness is the Sacrament of Reconciliation.

▶ The Sacrament of Anointing the Sick also forgives personal sins if the person could not participate in the Sacrament of Penance.

ACTIVITY

LIVE YOUR FAITH Think of your own life. Have you ever learned anything "the hard way"? Important lessons can often come from painful experiences. Write a story about a time when a good thing came from a "bad" experience. It can be a true report, or a made-up story.

IN SUMMARY

CATHOLICS BELIEVE

Jesus the Christ is our Savior, Redeemer, and Messiah.

▶ God created humans to live in happiness and harmony with him. By their disobedience, they lost original holiness, introduced sin into the world, and became subject to suffering and death.

▶ God did not abandon his people. He promised them a Messiah who would free them from sin. He sent his own Son to bring that salvation.

▶ Through his Paschal mystery, Jesus conquered death and makes it possible for those who have faith to experience new life through the sacraments.

♪ PRAYER

PRAYER OF PRAISE

Leader 1:   Blessed be God.

All: Blessed be God forever.

Leader 1:   Let us pray,

O Gracious Father,
we praise you, and we thank you for your endless mercy,
your patience and forgiveness,
your endurance and tolerance,
and the gift of your Son, Jesus,
whom you sent to save us
from all that distracts and keeps us far from you.

Leader 2:   In you we find a love greater than any we have ever known.
In you we find hope in the midst of our darkest act.
In you we find faith in knowing we will never be alone.

All: Nothing can keep us from your love.

Leader 3:   Be with us in our daily choices.
Guide our hands for service, not for violence.
Guide our voices for speaking truth, not for gossip.
Guide our eyes for seeing you in all that we meet, not for seeking the bad.
Guide our feet to take the "high road," not for running from responsibility.
Guide our hearts for loving all your people, not for hating or judging.

All: Nothing can keep us from your love.

Leader 4:   Because we are the young who search and seek to grow in faith,
remind us always and often that you are on our side,
that you are for us and never against us,
that you have conquered sin and sadness,
and that through your Son, even in death, your
  love is endless,
because nothing can keep us from your love.

All: Nothing can keep us from your love.

♪ "Nothing Can Keep Us From God's Love"
David Haas, © 1997, GIA Publications, Inc.

REVIEW

A **Work with Words** Circle the letter of the choice that best completes the sentence.

1. Our human nature is affected by _____, which we inherit from Adam and Eve.
   a. Adam's sin
   b. Reconciliation
   c. Original sin
   d. Paschal mystery

2. Jesus came to redeem us—to make it possible for _____.
   a. the Holy Spirit to come
   b. sin to be forgiven
   c. God to become man
   d. man to live a sinless life

3. Jesus is called "The New Adam" because _____.
   a. he was both God and man
   b. he was the son of Adam
   c. he created Adam
   d. he redeemed us from the sin of Adam, the first man

4. The Paschal mystery refers to _____.
   a. Jesus' death
   b. Jesus' Resurrection
   c. original sin
   d. both a and b

B **Check Understanding** Complete each sentence with the correct term.

5. When Adam and Eve chose to trust the serpent rather than God, they introduced _____, _____, and _____ into the world.

6. Adam and Eve _____ after they ate the fruit in the garden.

7. The words *Messiah* and *Christ* both mean "_____ _____."

8. Because of _____ people need salvation.

9. By his death on the cross and Resurrection, Jesus made _____ _____ with God possible.

10. The _____ _____ is made present to us today in the Eucharist and other sacraments.

C **Make Connections: Evaluate** Write a one-paragraph response to the questions.

What is involved in seeking reconciliation with God? What would this reconciliation mean for you?

OUR CATHOLIC FAITH

WHAT NOW?

★ Forgive others when they make a mistake or hurt you—give them a second chance.

★ Ask for forgiveness when you make a mistake or hurt someone.

★ Forgive yourself.

★ Heal your relationship with God, if it's broken—don't forget about the Sacrament of Reconciliation.

★ Pray for the strength to forgive.

ACTIVITY

LIVE YOUR FAITH No matter how far you fall behind in your life with God, God is always there for you. We have a God of second chances. The spirit of second chances is found in the story of Jesus dying between two thieves. One asked for a second chance. Jesus gave it to him. Above Jesus' cross were the letters "INRI" (which stood for the first letters of the Latin inscription "Jesus of Nazareth, the King of the Jews"). The letters can remind you of the Gospel story, and that when you look for a second chance you need to:

IDENTIFY YOUR MISTAKE "I made a mistake . . ."

NO EXCUSES Don't say "But . . ." or "I was only . . ." Either say something like "It was stupid, selfish, insensitive, mean"—or say nothing and move to the next step

RESPONSIBLE ACTIONS MUST FOLLOW "I need to . . ." (fix it, pay the bill, etc.)

IDENTIFY YOUR GOAL "It's really important to me that . . ."

▶ **Outline a real-life response you can make to someone from whom you are seeking a second chance.**

_____

_____

_____

_____

_____

_____

 Visit **www.osvcurriculum.com** for more family and community connections.

⩗ PRAYER

Holy Spirit—forgiveness is so hard! Transform me into a forgiving person and teach me to accept forgiveness, too. Amen.

Saint Madeleine Sophie Barat

"Our Lord who saved the world through the Cross will only work for the good of souls through the Cross."

These were the words of St. Madeleine Sophie Barat, who devoted her long lifetime to Christ our Savior and Redeemer. When called upon to do God's work of educating young women for religious service, Saint Madeleine Sophie rose to the challenge and helped to establish more than one hundred convents and schools.

Born in the wine-producing Burgundy region of France, Sophie was educated by her brother, a priest. Through him she was introduced to Father Varin, who wanted to form an institute for women similar to the Jesuits to teach young girls the virtues of living according to Christ's plan. Sophie and three companions founded the Society of the Sacred Heart of Jesus in 1800 when she was only twenty-one years old. They started their first convent and school at Amiens. Sister Sophie was appointed Superior General, although she was the youngest member of the group. She led it for sixty-three years.

The Society of the Sacred Heart spread throughout France. Convents and schools were founded in many locations throughout the country. A community of Visitation nuns at Grenoble joined the Society, one of whom later became the Saint Rose Philippine Duchesne. She brought the Sacred Heart Society to the United States in 1818, settling near St. Louis, Missouri.

The Society received formal approval from Pope Leo XII in 1826. Four years later, when a revolution ended Bourbon rule in France, the Society's novitiate in Paris closed. Sister Sophie refused to let that stop the work for which Our Lord had chosen her. She went into neighboring Switzerland and founded a novitiate there. From there the Society spread into other European nations and abroad.

By the time of her death in Paris in 1865, the Sacred Heart Society founded and headed by Sister Sophie had opened 105 schools and convents in twelve countries. Among her best-known words of advice were, "Let us attach ourselves to God alone, and turn our eyes and our hopes to Him." So great was her devotion that she was canonized in less than sixty years.

▲ Saint Madeleine Sophie Barat, 1779–1865

GLOBAL DATA

France

- France is the largest nation in Western Europe, about the size of Texas.

- France is the only nation in Europe that borders both the Atlantic Ocean and the Mediterranean Sea.

- France is about 85 percent Catholic.

- Avignon, in southern France, was the Holy See for seven popes from 1309 to 1377.

Faith in Action!

CATHOLIC SOCIAL TEACHING

DISCOVER Catholic Social Teaching:
Rights and Responsibilities of the Human Person

IN THIS UNIT you learned about reaching your own potential and about Jesus' Sermon on the Mount, where he made it clear that it is those we think of as unfortunate who are actually the most blessed.

Rights and Responsibilities

"All men [and women] are created equal and endowed with certain inalienable rights. . . ." This basic principle of the Declaration of Independence is echoed in Church teaching. But the Church goes a step further. Yes, we are all endowed with rights and freedom, but we must also use this freedom constructively, for the common good. Governments, too, must respect the fundamental rights of the human person, promote freedom, and defend the common good. Public authority is part of God's plan for promoting positive values in society and the well-being of all. The Church, too, gets involved in political affairs whenever economic and social issues affect peoples' fundamental human rights.

What are these fundamental human rights? They start with the right to life and the basic necessities of life—food, shelter, clothing, health care, education,

and work. Second, all people have the right to their own dignity and religious and cultural expression. Third, all have a right to participate in decisions that affect their lives. With rights go responsibilities. We all have the responsibility to exercise our own rights and to work with others to gain their rights.

The United Nations (U.N.) was created in 1945 in part to promote human rights worldwide. In addition to the "Universal Declaration of Human Rights" for all persons, the U.N. created a special "Declaration of the Rights of the Child" in 1959. Because children are more vulnerable than adults, we all have a special responsibility to protect and promote their rights.

Why is it important to have an international document like the "Declaration of the Rights of the Child"?

GOD CALLS HIS FOLLOWERS to respect the life and dignity of all human persons. Let's look at how one organization put these beliefs into action.

"THAT'S NOT FAIR"
CHILDREN LOBBYING FOR CHILDREN'S RIGHTS

Seventh-grade students from sixteen schools in the diocese of Kansas City—St. Joseph, Missouri, participate in a program called "That's Not Fair." This program not only teaches them about Catholic social teaching, but also how to put those values into practice. The program culminates with these students making a presentation to state legislators.

In April 2005, over 500 students gathered in a gymnasium to advocate on behalf of the 11,000 Missouri children in foster care. They asked the legislators not to make further cuts in the foster care program. Children who had been in foster care met with students in their classrooms prior to the meeting with legislators, so that students could hear directly about some of the injustices in that system. Also prior to the meeting with legislators, the students made a presentation at the Sunday Masses in their parishes and asked the adults to sign letters in support of their issue. They collected over 5,000 signed letters.

The students, following a prepared script, made a compelling argument to the legislators. The students were successful in helping get a bill passed that would increase funding for certain aspects of the foster care program. Immediately following this presentation, the students celebrated Mass to experience the connection between justice and Eucharist.

After the rally, one of the students remarked, "I never thought at the age of twelve that I would be able to make a difference." John Burnett, a Missouri legislator at the meeting, said, "It's refreshing to see young people apply their faith to social issues."

Is there some policy or law in your state or community that's "not fair"? What could you do about it?

▼ Seventh-grade students helped get a bill passed to increase funding for foster care programs in Missouri.

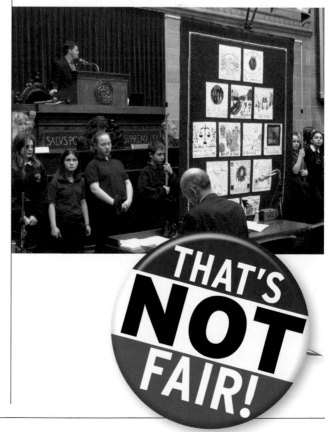

127

SERVE Your Community

STANDING UP FOR OTHERS

As you read about current events, listen to the news, or observe how different people live or are treated in your community or in other parts of the world, who are the people who are treated unfairly? Which of these people do you want to stand up for and help?

Research what you can do to help and decide how you are going to do it. Consider making some kind of slogan or pin you can use or wear to express your concern and invite others to join you in action. See if you can get your family involved.

Your Slogan ▶

PROMOTE THE "RIGHTS OF THE CHILD"

Create a collage or quilt with squares or individual posters for each of the ten principles of the "Rights of the Child."

❶ All children are entitled to have their rights met

❷ to develop their full potential

❸ to have a name and nationality

❹ to have the basic necessities of life and

❺ special care if they are disabled,

❻ to live with their family or someone who cares,

❼ to have education and play,

❽ to be the first helped in disasters,

❾ to be free from all forms of exploitation, and

❿ to be brought up in a spirit of understanding, friendship, and peace.

Create a plan for using the collage, quilt, or individual posters to promote the "Rights of the Child."

Project Planning Sheet

Groups to share the artwork with

Possible actions to ask others to do for promoting these rights

Ways to publicize this project

Specific tasks (list person assigned to complete the task)

Calendar for completing the project

Why do many people in the world still not have their most basic human rights met?

_____

_____

_____

_____

What did you learn about the "Rights of the Child" from doing the project?

_____

_____

_____

_____

What did you learn about yourself in doing both of these projects?

_____

_____

_____

_____

What did you learn about Jesus and about your faith while doing both projects?

_____

_____

_____

_____

List one thing that might be different about you after doing these projects. How will your life be different because of these actions?

_____

_____

_____

_____

REVIEW

A **Work with Words** Solve the puzzle using the clues provided.

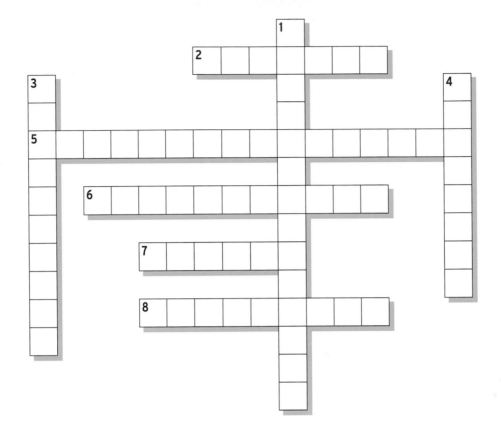

Across

2 A simple story told to teach a larger truth

5 Collection of Jesus' teachings in the Gospels according to Luke and Matthew

6 The sin that affected our human nature which we inherit from Adam and Eve

7 A special prayer form in honor of the Blessed Virgin Mary

8 Word that means happiness or blessedness

Down

1 The mystery of Jesus' Passion, death, Resurrection, and Ascension

3 Elizabeth's visit to her cousin Mary, who was pregnant with Jesus

4 The birth of Jesus

B **Check Understanding** Circle the letter of the best answer to complete the following statements.

9. The disciples of Jesus were first called followers of _____.
   a. The Spirit
   b. The Word
   c. The Way
   d. The Truth

10. Jesus is called the _____ because he reflects the Father's love for us.
   a. Substantial Image of the Father
   b. Lord
   c. Messiah
   d. Savior

130

11. Jesus is _____.

    a. human

    b. divine

    c. human and divine

    d. none of the above

12. The _____ are the most often quoted part of the Sermon on the Mount.

    a. Beatitudes

    b. Psalms

    c. debates

    d. miracles

13. In the Beatitudes we learn that _____ comes from trusting God and living the values of his kingdom.

    a. righteousness

    b. true happiness

    c. salvation

    d. faith

14. Jesus taught with _____ because he was the Son of God.

    a. authority

    b. parables

    c. the Scriptures

    d. humor

15. Jesus is called _____ because he redeemed us from the sin of Adam, the first man.

    a. Messiah

    b. Savior

    c. the New Adam

    d. the Lamb of God

16. Sin came into the world when _____.

    a. Adam and Eve left the garden

    b. Adam and Eve chose to disobey God

    c. Satan tempted Eve

    d. Adam and Eve hid from God

17. Because of original sin, people need _____.

    a. beatitudes

    b. good works

    c. redemption and salvation

    d. the Bible

18. Jesus made eternal life with God possible through _____.

    a. his death

    b. his Resurrection

    c. his parables

    d. both a and b

C **Make Connections** Write a short answer to these questions.

19. Compare and Contrast. How are the truths taught by Jesus in the Beatitudes similar to the values of your friends? How are they different?

20. Interpret. Reaching your full potential means becoming the person God made you to be. What does it mean to you to reach your full potential as a follower of Jesus?

CHAPTER 10 The Community of DISCIPLES

![Prayer icon] **PRAYER** Jesus, lead me.

When should I follow? When should I lead? What are the positives? What are the negatives? Who or what can help me?

"**I give** up!" Hannah cried. She crumpled the spring electives schedule into a ball and lobbed it toward the trash can. "There's no way I can pick a class!" Becca rescued the crumpled schedule from the ground. "Well, with shots like that, you can rule out basketball!" she teased her friend.

"No, this is serious," Hannah protested. "I've just got one class hour left to fill, so I can only take choir *or* speech. Not both. I can't decide which to choose. Everybody says Mr. Thompson's choir is great. It's like a party. He tells jokes, he lets you sing whatever you want, and it's an easy A."

"Sounds like a no-brainer to me," Becca said. "Where's the problem?"

Hannah sighed. "Well, I love singing, and I've taken choir every year. It's easy for me. But I'm kind of interested in speech now. Ms. Sanchez said she thought I'd make a good debater."

"You sure argue enough with me!" Becca giggled.

Hannah ignored her friend's humor. "If I join the debate team, though, it's going to be work, work, work. Ms. Sanchez is a super supportive speech coach, but she's really tough, too. You have to deliver for your grade in her class. I'd be leaving a sure thing behind for something that will be much more difficult."

"I hear the debate team went to state finals this year," Becca said. "Choir didn't do very well in competitions—but they did have a big pizza party."

Hannah smoothed out the crumpled schedule and looked it over one more time. "Hmm," she wondered aloud. "Pizza or pride? Party or work? An easy A, or . . . who knows?"

ACTIVITY

LET'S BEGIN What are the differences in the leadership of Hannah's teachers? What difference will it make to Hannah if she follows one or the other? If you were Hannah's friend, what advice would you give her?

▶ **When have you chosen something difficult over something easy? Why did you make that decision? How did it work out for you?**

_____

_____

▶ **How do you respond when someone expects a lot from you? When have you surprised yourself by living up to someone else's high expectations?**

_____

_____

A SURPRISE INVITATION

Focus What attracted the first disciples to follow Jesus?

We've probably all had a teacher, coach, parent, or grandparent who really pushed us to see things differently, to make a commitment to someone or something that seemed out of our reach. Sometimes the person who challenges us also leads us to see how the impossible can be possible.

In the time of Jesus, just as today, there were people who attracted followers. They were teachers or politicians or religious leaders. John the Baptist was a popular preacher whose message attracted people. He had a group of followers, but he was preparing the way for the Messiah. When Jesus arrived, John pointed to him and told his followers that Jesus was the leader they should be following. John said, "And I myself have seen and have testified that this is the Son of God" (*John 1:34*).

John's followers knew him and knew what to expect from him. They must have had to think about leaving the leader they had trusted to follow someone new.

Tell a Friend Some of John's disciples went to see what Jesus was like. After they saw him and heard him speak, they wanted to get to know him better. Those first disciples told their friends about Jesus and soon the group of followers began to grow. Jesus asked some to follow him.

▲ *Saint John the Baptist*, by Fra Bartolommeo (1472–1517)

SCRIPTURE

GO TO THE SOURCE
Find out more about who Jesus called to follow him and who came to him through the encouragement of a friend.

John 1:43–51
Luke 8:1–3
Mark 1:16–20
Matthew 9:9–17

SCRIPTURE Other people followed because a friend told them to come and see Jesus, like Philip. He went to his friend Nathanael and told him, "'We have found him about whom Moses in the law and also the prophets wrote, Jesus son of Joseph from Nazareth.' Nathanael said to him, 'Can anything good come out of Nazareth?' Philip said to him, 'Come and see.'"

—*John 1:45–46*

❓ When was the last time you tried to convince a friend to try a new activity, join a new group, or go to a new place?

❓ What did you say to try to persuade your friend?

Decisions to Make Each new disciple already had a family and a job. When Jesus invited them, some people asked if they could have a little time to decide. They wanted to go home and take care of things first. But Jesus was looking for people who had been looking for his coming and were ready and waiting to go with him. Some people were ready. Others who were invited did not think following Jesus would be a good idea.

But Jesus was quite an intriguing person. He was a dynamic speaker and an approachable guy with a challenging message. Some of the things he said confused people. Some of the things he did surprised and astounded others. But one thing is for sure: People were talking about Jesus in all the towns and villages in the area.

Wouldn't you want to meet the man who was shaking things up, making things better, giving people something they desperately needed: love, compassion, insight, guidance for living, hope, a new lease on life? And once you met Jesus, would you become a disciple and follow him?

❓ Have you ever had to make a choice that meant changing the way you thought about someone or something, or the way you acted? What was it like?

❓ What are some things about Jesus that surprise or interest you?

ACTIVITY

SHARE YOUR FAITH Imagine you are living in the time of Jesus. Name three reasons why Jesus would choose you to follow him. What would you do if he invited you?

A COMMUNITY OF BELIEVERS

 Focus How did the Apostles and their successors lead other disciples?

LOOKING BACK

You can find the names of the twelve Apostles in Matthew 10:1–4, Mark 3:13–19, and Luke 6:12–16.

▶ **Simon**, who was named "Peter" by Jesus.

▶ **Andrew**—Matthew and Luke say he is Peter's brother.

▶ **James**—Matthew and Mark call him the "son of Zebedee."

▶ **John**—Matthew and Mark say he is the brother of James. Jesus gave James and John the title "Sons of Thunder."

▶ **Philip**—Jesus asked him how they should feed 5,000 people.

▶ **Bartholomew**—Also called Nathanael. Had a hard time believing the Messiah could come from Nazareth.

▶ **Matthew**—Matthew calls himself "the tax collector" in his Gospel. The Gospel of Mark also calls him "Levi."

▶ **Thomas**—The Gospel of John calls Thomas "Didymus," which means "the twin."

▶ **James**—Some called him the "son of Alphaeus" to show he is a different James from John's brother. Sometimes this James is called "James the Lesser."

▶ **Simon**—Matthew and Mark say he is "the Cananean," and Luke called him a "Zealot," to make sure we know he is not Simon Peter.

▶ **Thaddeus**—He is also called "Jude Thaddeus." Be careful not to confuse him with:

▶ **Judas Iscariot**, who was the Apostle who betrayed Jesus.

After they had been with him awhile, Jesus began to send his disciples out ahead of him, two-by-two. They announced the coming of the Kingdom of God and were even able to cure some of the sick people they met as they traveled.

The disciples had some important instructions from Jesus. He told them:

▶ take no money

▶ do not pack a bag or bring extra clothes

▶ do not carry a walking stick

▶ find a home to stay where the people welcome you

▶ leave a town that does not welcome you, and shake the dust of that town from your shoes

Jesus wanted his disciples to trust God the Father to take care of them. He wanted them to "travel light"!

? Have you ever packed too many clothes and other items for a trip? How did the extra baggage help or hinder you?

? Why do you think Jesus might care about how much his disciples carried with them?

? What do you think this message means for us today?

We Receive Guidance We know Jesus had many followers. The Gospels speak of "seventy-two disciples." But Jesus chose twelve men to be his **Apostles** and to share in his work and mission in a special way. They were Jesus' closest followers. The Apostles continued Jesus' ministry after his Ascension to heaven, and since then the Church has been built on the faith and foundation of the Apostles.

To this day, the faith of the Church is built on the faith of the Apostles. The work they began has been continued down through the ages. The teachings they received from Jesus and his Holy Spirit have been handed on through them to us in the Church today.

The night before he died, Jesus said to the Apostles at the Last Supper: "The Advocate, the Holy Spirit, whom the Father will send in my name, will teach you everything, and remind you of all that I have said to you" (*John 14:26*).

? How do you use Church teachings in your life?

? Where do you learn these truths?

Where to Find Church Teachings

How do we know what the Church teaches? How does the Church hand down the teachings of Christ to everyone so that books such as this one can be written? Here is a list of official places where Church teaching is found:

Sacred Scripture	The Old and New Testaments of the Bible
Church Council Documents	Records of all the meetings of the Pope and bishops to explain and make decisions about the Church
The Catechism of the Catholic Church	All the doctrines (official, authentic teachings) of the Church
The Code of Canon Law	All the laws of the Church
Papal Encyclicals	Teachings written by the Pope for all Catholics
Pastoral Letters	Teachings written by bishops for the Catholics in their dioceses

CONNECT YOUR FAITH Jesus wants us to let go of things that might keep us from following him.

Things I Like to Do   *Importance on scale of 1 to 10*

1.

2.

3.

▶ Are any of these so important to you that you forget to pray, to help others, and to live your faith? How can you balance them with following Jesus?

DISCIPLES IN THE CHURCH TODAY

 Focus What does it mean to be a disciple in the Church right here and now?

CATHOLICS TODAY

In 1833, in Paris, France, Blessed Frederic Ozanam and some of his friends were horrified by the poverty they saw around them. They began to look for ways to help people with food, clothes, money, and prayer. They dedicated their work to St. Vincent de Paul, the patron saint of charitable works, who had worked to help the poor in the 1600s. Today there are nearly one million members of the St. Vincent de Paul Society spread out in 130 countries on five continents.

We have the Church to guide us in all parts of our lives and in everything we do. The Church shows us how to live as Jesus lived. His life and his teachings are like a light showing us the way to heaven.

We never have to find our way through life alone. In the Church, we belong to a family of faith, a community of disciples who are following Jesus together. We turn to other Church members for support, guidance, and encouragement. We ask God's forgiveness through the Church. We join with others to help people who are in need—together we can feed the hungry, shelter the homeless, clothe the naked, visit the sick, and try to change laws and policies that keep people from the things they need, like jobs, housing, and food. No one could do as much alone as we can all do together!

A Praying Community The Holy Spirit also teaches us as disciples of Jesus to pray. We pray alone and we pray together in communal prayer and worship. Whether we are praying prayers of blessing, petition, intercession, thanksgiving, or praise, it is the Holy Spirit who inspires us and calls us to pray.

The best way to pray together is to celebrate the Eucharist. When we come together for Mass, we are praying the Church's central and most important prayer. We are worshipping God together and we are receiving the Body and Blood of Christ.

As we grow in our faith, we learn new ways of prayer. Many different **spiritualities** (ways of praying and living as a disciple) have developed over the centuries. In our

two thousand years as a Church, many great saints have guided others in ways of prayer.

There are several "schools" of prayer and Christian spirituality. They are all part of the Church's living tradition of prayer, and although they are very different, they all come from the Holy Spirit.

SCHOOLS OF PRAYER

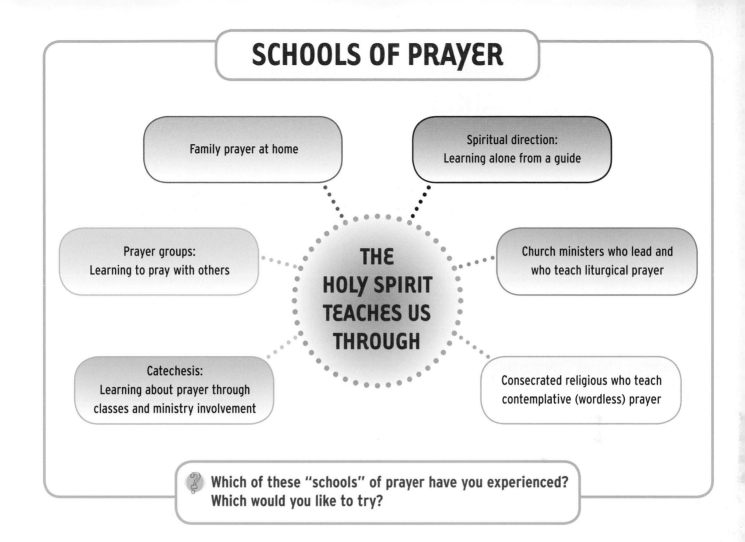

Family prayer at home

Spiritual direction:
Learning alone from a guide

Prayer groups:
Learning to pray with others

THE
HOLY SPIRIT
TEACHES US
THROUGH

Church ministers who lead and
who teach liturgical prayer

Catechesis:
Learning about prayer through
classes and ministry involvement

Consecrated religious who teach
contemplative (wordless) prayer

**Which of these "schools" of prayer have you experienced?
Which would you like to try?**

ACTIVITY

LIVE YOUR FAITH Identify which of the "schools" of prayer you have already experienced. Name someone who taught you to pray in this way.

▶ Look at the "schools" of prayer above. Next to the schools you have not yet experienced, list people you think would be able to teach you how to pray in these ways.

IN SUMMARY

CATHOLICS BELIEVE

We are disciples of Christ together, following Jesus' example by believing, learning, praying, and reaching out to others.

▶ Each follower of Christ receives a personal call from him and must choose whether or not to follow Christ.

▶ Just as Jesus sent the first disciples out two-by-two with nothing extra packed, he asks us to work together to build the Kingdom of God, to "travel light," and follow Church teachings.

▶ The Holy Spirit uses many different spiritualities and "schools" of prayer to teach us how to pray.

CELEBRATE

PRAYER

LITANY OF THE SAINTS

Leader: Let us take time to pray to the saints for their guidance. Begin with the Sign of the Cross.

Saint Thérèse of Lisieux, you relied on God, not possessions, and knew the comforting embrace of God.

All: Saint Thérèse, pray for us.

Leader: Saint Elizabeth Ann Seton, you suffered many losses and felt the comforting embrace of God.

All: Saint Elizabeth Ann, pray for us.

Leader: Saint Francis de Sales, you treated yourself and others with patience and gentleness.

All: Saint Francis, pray for us.

Leader: Saint Thomas of Villanova, you showed freedom to many slaves and care for many orphans.

All: Saint Thomas, pray for us.

Leader: Saint Genevieve, you showed mercy to prisoners and others in need.

All: Saint Genevieve, pray for us.

Leader: Saint Clare, you lived a simple and humble life.

All: Saint Clare, pray for us.

Leader: Saint Francis of Assisi, you sought peace during the crusades.

All: Saint Francis, pray for us.

Leader: Saint Paul Miki, you preached the Word of God and died on the cross.

All: Saint Paul, pray for us.

Leader: In this great community of the saints, we find strength and inspiration to seek and to do God's will.

All: Amen.

♪ "Litany of Saints"
David Haas, © 1988, GIA Publications, Inc.

REVIEW

A **Work with Words** Circle the letter of the choice that best completes the sentence.

1. The _____ continued Jesus' ministry after his Ascension to heaven.
- **a.** Apostles
- **b.** Samaritans
- **c.** Jews
- **d.** Pharisees

2. _____ are the official, authentic teachings of the Church.
- **a.** Papal Encyclicals
- **b.** Catechism
- **c.** Scriptures
- **d.** Doctrines

3. Ways of praying and living as a disciple are called _____.
- **a.** spiritualities
- **b.** church teachings
- **c.** doctrines
- **d.** Papal law

4. _____ prayer is prayer without words.
- **a.** Spiritual
- **b.** Contemplative
- **c.** Personal
- **d.** Proper

B **Check Understanding** Complete each sentence with the correct terms from the word bank at right.

5. _____ prepared for the coming of the Messiah.

6. The laws of the Church are contained in the _____.

7. Jesus called certain disciples to be his _____ and to share in his mission and work.

8. The _____ the Apostles received from Jesus and his Holy Spirit have been handed on through them to the Church today.

9. Jesus promised the Holy Spirit to the Apostles at the _____.

10. The Holy Spirit teaches us as disciples to _____.

Word Bank

Apostles
Old Testament
Code of Canon Law
John the Baptist
Pentecost
Last Supper
pray
sacramental seal
teaching

C **Make Connections: Describing** Write a one-paragraph response to the question.

How is celebrating the Eucharist an important way to pray?

OUR CATHOLIC FAITH

ACTIVITY

LIVE YOUR FAITH Write down the name of someone you personally know who is a true follower of Jesus. Why did you think of this person? List the qualities of a disciple that you see in this person.

Name:

Qualities:

▶ Invite someone to pray with you. Form a small group of students for prayer, or ask members of your family to join you in a time of prayer. Choose a good place to pray and plan enough time. Write a prayer you can use to begin your prayer time.

_____

_____

_____

_____

 GO online Visit www.osvcurriculum.com for more family and community connections.

 **PRAYER**

Jesus, give me the courage to respond, "Here I am, Lord."

PEOPLE OF FAITH

Saint Mother Théodore (Anne-Therese) Guérin

Many people since the time of Jesus' first disciples have studied Jesus' teachings and have committed their lives to teaching, healing, and caring for the needy. Mother Théodore was a woman who committed her life to these ministries. Born in France in the early 1800s as Anne-Thérèse Guérin, she knew she wanted to become a nun from the date of her first Communion at the age of ten. She joined the Sisters of Providence at Ruillé-sur-Loir in 1823, taking the name Sister St. Théodore. She took her final vows in 1831 and taught in Rennes and Soulaines, France. While in Soulaines, she studied medicine with a local physician.

She was sent with five other sisters to the diocese of Vincennes, Indiana, in 1840. She welcomed the opportunity to provide an education to children and to care for the sick and poor. She and the other sisters established the Academy of St. Mary-of-the-Woods the following year at Terre Haute, Indiana. This was the first Catholic women's liberal arts college in the United States. She also established schools at eleven locations in Indiana and one in Illinois. In addition, she founded an orphanage for girls and another one for boys in Vincennes. In all of these ways, she answered Jesus' call to follow him and help to build up his Kingdom.

Mother Théodore followed the example of Jesus in ministering to the less fortunate. Using her knowledge of medicine, she opened pharmacies that gave free medicine to the poor at Vincennes and St. Mary-of-the-Woods. She personally supervised construction of a motherhouse for the Sisters of Providence and several additions to the Academy of St. Mary-of-the-Woods.

During the nearly sixteen years of her ministry in Indiana, Mother Théodore encountered countless hardships, including prejudice against Catholics. But through all those years of growth, struggle, and sorrow, her faith did not waver. She advised the Sisters of Providence, "Have confidence in the Providence that so far has never failed us. The way is not yet clear. Grope along slowly. Do not press matters; be patient, be trustful." She also told the sisters, "With Jesus, what shall we have to fear?"

By the time of her death, she had made a significant contribution to the spread of Catholicism in the Midwestern portion of the United States. Mother Théodore was declared Venerable by Pope Saint John Paul II in 1992 and was beatified by the Holy Father six years later. She was canonized by Pope Benedict XVI in 2006.

▲ Saint Mother Théodore Guérin, 1798–1856

GLOBAL DATA

Indiana

- Indiana was the nineteenth state admitted to the Union in 1816.

- Indiana covers an area of about 36,000 square miles and is home to more than 6 million people.

- Vincennes, the first settlement in the state, was founded by French Catholic fur traders in 1731; the diocese of Vincennes was erected in 1834.

- Indiana has 178 Catholic elementary schools, 25 Catholic high schools, and 11 Catholic colleges or universities.

The Body of CHRIST

PRAYER Lord, help me love your people.

Why do we always do things as a group?
What does being part of a group do for me?
What can I offer a group?
I don't want to lose what makes me unique.

The walls of Ben's parents' garage vibrated as the band finished practicing their best set.

"*YES!!*" Andrea yelled over the echo of her electric guitar. "We're gonna *rock* at the Battle of the Bands!"

Ben shook his head. "I'm not so sure," he said. "Something's missing."

"Yeah," Noah said, "and we all know what it is. If you'd just let me do my drum solo. . . ."

"No!" Shawna pleaded. "That stupid drum solo takes forever, and everybody forgets the rest of us are on stage. What we need is more time for the lead vocals."

"Uh, I can't imagine why the lead singer would say that," Noah replied sarcastically.

"Well, at least I've got rhythm," Shawna said, "unlike you, Mr. Half-a-Beat-Behind."

"Forget it! I don't need this!" Noah put down his drumsticks, grabbed his backpack, and started out the door. He stopped short when Ben grabbed his elbow.

"But we need *you*, Noah," Ben said. "Come on, you guys. We're a band, not just four soloists. We need everybody to make this work. The thing we're missing is harmony."

Andrea looked puzzled. "Harmony? Ben, we're a rock band, not a church choir!"

Ben laughed. "There are all kinds of harmony," he said. "I'm talking about working together. We got into this in the first place because we're *friends* remember?"

ACTIVITY

LET'S BEGIN What's the issue here? What do you think Ben meant when he said a band is more than just four soloists?

▶ **When do you find it hard to be part of a group? What makes you hang in there and keep trying? Think of three groups you are part of. What do you get from each group? What do you give to each group?**

GROUP 1

GROUP 2

GROUP 3

THE CHURCH IS THE BODY OF CHRIST

Focus How are all the different members of the Church united in One Body?

Many amazing things happen when people work together as friends. People gather into groups for many other reasons, but friendship is often the result. It could be that a group forms because there is a job that needs to be done. Sometimes a group forms because of common interests or problems. Some groups become known and visible to others.

Visible and Spiritual Like Jesus, the Church he founded—our Catholic Church—is both human and divine. The Church is both visible and spiritual. This is a great mystery of our faith. For Jesus told us, "For where two or three are gathered in my name, I am there among them" (*Matthew 18:20*).

She brings us in touch with the sacred, but the Church is made up of human beings, with all our imperfections *and* potential.

It is easier to understand the visible part of the Church. You can see how people gather. You can see buildings for worship, for education, and for service. And you can see how the Church is organized into a **hierarchy** with different levels of leadership and membership. However, the visible part of the Church is not enough.

✝ **SCRIPTURE**

GO TO THE SOURCE
Read **Matthew 18:12–20**. Name some times when people gather together in Jesus' name. How do you think Jesus makes his presence known among them?

Visible

The word **church** means a "gathering" or an "assembly." Jesus has gathered all who believe in him into a visible group with leaders and members. In our visible gathering as the Church we are the People of God.

Spiritual

In Christ we become more than just a visible assembly of people. Jesus feeds us his own Body, and we become his Body. As a spiritual group, the Church is called the **Mystical Body of Christ**, for Christ is present among us.

❓ What evidence can you see in your parish that the Church is the visible People of God and the Mystical Body of Christ?

Without the spiritual part, the Church would be like any other club or organization. Our spiritual part is Christ's presence among us through the power of Holy Spirit.

One in Christ Jesus died, but he rose again to new life. Now, through the Holy Spirit, and through his actions in the Eucharist and the other sacraments, Jesus establishes the Church as his own Body. Christ is the head of his Body. The Church lives from him, in him, and for him; Christ lives with and in the Church. Here is how Saint Paul, who was also called "Saul," found out that Jesus considers the Church his Body.

hierarchy
Church
Mystical Body of Christ
Corporal Works of Mercy

✠ **SCRIPTURE** "Meanwhile Saul, still breathing threats and murder against the disciples of the Lord . . . was going along and . . . suddenly a light from heaven flashed around him. He fell to the ground and heard a voice saying to him, 'Saul, Saul, why do you persecute me?' He asked, 'Who are you, Lord?' The reply came, 'I am Jesus, whom you are persecuting.'"

—*Acts 9:1–5*

Paul realized that he was persecuting Jesus himself by persecuting the Church. In letters he wrote to various groups in the early Church, Paul mentions often that we (the Church) are "one in Christ," or that we are "His Body."

❓ **If a nonbeliever visited your parish, how would that person be able to tell that Christ is the head of his Body the Church?**

ACTIVITY

SHARE YOUR FAITH Give some examples of how the Church is both visible and spiritual in your life. Then in small groups make a list of how the Church is visible and spiritual in your school.

THE CHURCH IN MY LIFE	
VISIBLE PART	**SPIRITUAL PART**

ONE BODY, MANY MEMBERS

 Focus Can members of the Church remain separate individuals and still be united as one Body of Christ?

Each person in the Church does not get "lost" as part of the one Body of Christ. The Church is still also a body of many members, each important to the working of the whole Body. Each of us is needed. And each member also needs to remain part of the Church and faithful to its mission. We are ONE Church united in Jesus.

✞ **SCRIPTURE** The Gospel according to John tells us that Jesus explained it this way at the Last Supper.

He said, "Just as the branch cannot bear fruit by itself unless it abides in the vine, neither can you unless you abide in me. I am the vine, you are the branches. Those who abide in me and I in them will bear much fruit, because apart from me you can do nothing."

—*John 15:4–5*

❓ As Jesus' disciples, we are called to bear fruit. How does your parish bear "fruit" as a community of disciples?

All Parts of the Body of Christ Work Together

There is no use being in a band if no one works in harmony with the others. There is no use being part of a group if we do not work together with the other members of the group. When even one member of the Church does not participate with the rest of the Church, the whole Church is affected. And when even one member remains faithful and bears the fruit of good works, the whole Church is also affected.

❓ How do you participate in the Church right now? What can you do to improve the role you play?

❓ How could you make a difference to the whole Church?

BEARING GOOD FRUIT

All over the world today, the Church is bearing good fruit.
The many parts are all connected in Christ.

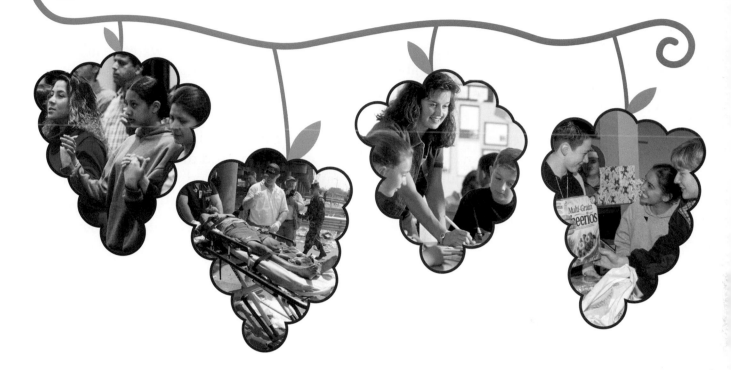

ACTIVITY

CONNECT YOUR FAITH Catholics represent many cultures and countries. Differences in housing, foods, clothing, work, names, and so on can be great. Still, all Catholics are one.

▶ Look at the above pictures. List the types of differences and similarities in the correct sections.

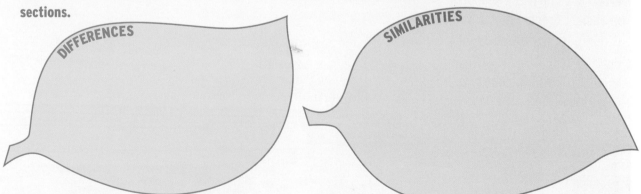

DIFFERENCES

SIMILARITIES

▶ Imagine speaking with one of the people in the pictures about what you have in common. What would you want to tell this person? Write a few ideas on the lines below.

_____

_____

_____

MANY GIFTS FOR THE GOOD OF ALL

Focus How are each person's gifts and talents important to the whole Church?

God gave each person different gifts. If we were all good at the same things, we would probably all be bad at the same things, too. There would be things that would not be done well, or might not get done at all.

Often people use their gifts to compete with each other. Although this can be fun, God did not give us gifts just for competition. As a Church, God wants us to share our gifts to make a positive difference in the world.

Because of this diversity of gifts, the Church is able to help build God's Kingdom in many ways and places. The gifts of every member are needed.

Notice the different gifts people use in your parish. In his letter to the Ephesians, Saint Paul tells us that the gifts God gave were "that some would be apostles, some prophets, some evangelists, some pastors and teachers" (*Ephesians 4:11*). God still gives those gifts in the Church today.

What would your parish or the whole Church be like without all these different people?

WHERE IT HAPPENED

MAYBE IT WAS because there were so many different kinds of people and occupations in Ephesus that Paul wrote to the Church there about different gifts. At the time, Ephesus was a big, important seaport in ancient Greece. That area is now part of western Turkey, and travelers there today can see the ruins of the ancient city, a museum, and a Church shrine to honor Mary.

For Those Who Are in Need Everyone in the Church is linked to everyone else, especially to people who are suffering, poor, and persecuted. In these people we can most closely see Jesus, who suffered and died for us. When we reach out to help others who are in need, we are doing what Jesus did and what he told us to do.

Jesus tells a story about the Last Judgment to teach us that we will be judged by how we help him. In his story, the people are surprised to hear Jesus say that they are going to be rewarded for helping him on earth. They wondered when they had helped him. ". . . just as you did it to one of the least of these who are members of my family, you did it to me" (*Matthew 25:40*).

You might recognize Jesus' words as the **Corporal Works of Mercy**, acts that meet people's physical needs. The complete list adds another work, burying the dead.

Caring for Jesus in Others

▶ I was hungry
  and you gave me food.

▶ I was thirsty
  and you gave me drink.

▶ I was a stranger
  and you welcomed me.

▶ I was naked
  and you clothed me.

▶ I was in prison
  and you visited me.

▶ I was ill
  and you cared for me.

Based on Matthew 25:35–36.

ACTIVITY

LIVE YOUR FAITH Get a copy of your parish bulletin and find all the ways that Church members are using their gifts to help build up the Kingdom of God and to care for those who are in great need.

IN SUMMARY

CATHOLICS BELIEVE

The Church is both visible and spiritual, made up of people with many gifts and talents who together work to continue Jesus' mission in the world.

▶ We call the spiritual part of the Church the Mystical Body of Christ. Jesus is the Head of his Body, the Church.

▶ Each individual member is united with all members as part of Christ's Body; we need one another and Christ to bear fruit in the world.

▶ The Church needs the diverse gifts of all members to help build God's Kingdom.

PRAYER

CELEBRATION OF THE WORD

Leader: Let us pray,

O God, of every good gift,
we praise you and we thank you for this time of prayer,
this time of quiet,
this time to ask ourselves the question,
"What are the gifts you have given me?"

Reader 1: A reading from the letter of Paul to the Corinthians.
Read 1 Corinthians 12:4–11.

The word of the Lord.

All: Thanks be to God.

Reader 2: Open our hearts to receive and understand.
Open our minds to trust in your plan.
Open our hands to take hold of all you give us.
Open our lives to share what you offer.

Reader 3: Let us pray to the God who gives us what we need.

Pray aloud your intercessions, one by one.
After each, respond

All: Lord, hear the prayer of our hearts.

Leader: Help us see how we all fit together,
how each of us offers a different piece,
a different gift to strengthen the whole.
Teach us to know the Holy Spirit is with us,
guiding us and giving us courage and wisdom.
Help us recognize our gifts and use them
    with care.
We ask this through Christ our Lord. Amen.

♪ "Give Your Gifts"
Michael Mahler, © 2001, GIA Publications, Inc.

REVIEW

A **Work with Words** Complete each sentence.

1. The word _____ means a gathering or assembly.

2. As we gather as the Church, we are the _____.

3. As a spiritual group, the Church is called the _____.

4. The Church is organized into a(n) _____ with different levels of leadership and membership.

5. God wants us to use our individual _____ for the good of the Christian community and the world.

B **Check Understanding** Indicate whether the following statements are true or false. Then rewrite false statements to make them true.

_____ **6.** Through the Holy Spirit, Baptism, and the Eucharist, Jesus forms the Church as his Body.

_____

_____ **7.** Jesus taught his disciples that they were the roots and he was the branches.

_____

_____ **8.** Like Jesus, the Church is both human and natural.

_____

_____ **9.** Everyone in the Church is responsible to care for the poor.

_____

_____ **10.** Jesus taught that people would be rewarded at the Assumption for the ways they helped him on earth.

_____

C **Make Connections: Analyze** Write a one-paragraph response to the question below.

What do we need to do so that our efforts "bear fruit" as Jesus instructed?

OUR CATHOLIC FAITH

WHAT NOW?

★ Pray for help to recognize your gifts, and then thank God for them.

★ Think about how you are already sharing your gifts with others. What more can you do to help build God's kingdom?

★ Work on growing some of your God-given talents, and use them to contribute wherever needed.

★ Pay attention to other people in your family, your class, and your parish who are sharing their gifts. Tell them that they are making a difference to the Church.

★ Quietly think about what it means to be part of the Mystical Body of Christ.

ACTIVITY

LIVE YOUR FAITH Explore the hymnbook your parish uses to celebrate liturgies. Make a list of hymns that mention the Body of Christ, our oneness in Christ, our giving of our personal gifts, or our outreach to those in need.

▶ Go through the hymnal and write down your favorite song titles and their main messages.

Favorite Hymn   *Main Messages*

 Visit **www.osvcurriculum.com** for more family and community connections.

PRAYER

Lord, help me to use the gifts you have given me to make your world a better place.

Saint John Bosco

People discover their gifts in many ways. You may identify your gifts by examining the things you like to do and the things you are good at doing. Sometimes other people point out your gifts, or you may try something new and discover that you have a talent for it. Some people use dreams to help them discover their gifts.

John Bosco of Turin, Italy, used his dreams to discover what God was calling him to do. At the age of nine, he began having dreams that would reveal God's plan for him. Eventually, these dreams would lead John Bosco to find his place helping troubled young boys and girls.

In his first significant dream, young John saw himself in a field with a crowd of children. The children started cursing and misbehaving. John jumped into the crowd, shouting and swinging his fists to try to stop the fighting. Suddenly a man appeared in his dream with a face filled with light. The man called John to him and made him leader of the boys.

The man said, "You will have to win these friends of yours not with blows, but with gentleness and kindness." John was skeptical, but the man advised him to be humble and obedient. Then the boys who had been fighting turned into wild animals. John was challenged to grow in humility, faithfulness, and strength. Only then would he see a change in the children. As John changed his ways, the wild animals suddenly turned into gentle lambs.

From that point, John knew that his life's work would be to help troubled young boys—and later girls—to become more Christ-like. He studied for six years to become a priest. In Italy, priests have the title "Don" followed by their last name. Don Bosco ministered to poor and neglected boys and shared Church teachings with them. He would also take them to Mass. Many of the young boys he guided went into the priesthood.

Pope Pius IX took Don Bosco's dreams seriously. He ordered him to "Write down these dreams and everything else you have told me, minutely and in their natural sense."

He used what he saw in the dreams to give the boys moral guidance.

Saint John Bosco founded the Salesian Society. The society opened homes for young boys to be educated and train for the priesthood. By the time of Don Bosco's death in 1888, he had left a lasting legacy of helping those less fortunate.

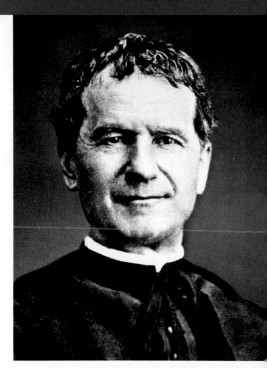

▲ Saint John Bosco, 1815–1888

GLOBAL DATA

Turin

- Turin is the fourth largest city in Italy with just under 1 million people.

- The cathedral houses the Shroud of Turin, believed by some to be the linen winding sheet in which Jesus' body was wrapped when he was removed from the cross.

- Turin was destroyed by Hannibal after he crossed the Alps in 221 B.C.

- Turin was briefly the capital of Italy during unification in 1861.

- Turin was the site of the Twentieth Olympic Winter Games in 2006.

CHAPTER 12 SOURCE of Life

✓ PRAYER — Hear my prayer, Lord.

*God wants me to make a difference in the world!
What does that mean?*

*Is there anything anyone can do
about all the trouble in the world?*

"**H**ey! I'm watching cartoons!" Will glared at his big sister.

Gina clicked the TV remote. "Sorry, but I'm doing an assignment. No time for loony toonies. We have to watch a report about the latest troop movements overseas for civics class."

The two sat staring at the TV screen. "Hmm. This is local news first," muttered Gina. It was a report from the state capital about an execution.

"What do they think they're doing?" asked Will, staring at a group carrying candles and signs. A reporter explained that the group had come to protest the execution and to pray.

"A lot of good that's going to do!" His sister mocked. "A bunch of do-gooders trying to change the world with candles. . . . " She wasn't any more excited about the next story. "And what about them?" asked Gina, as they watched people packing a truck with supplies for people who had just survived another hurricane. "How much good is that little bit of stuff going to do?"

When the war report came on, it showed a group of soldiers at Mass with a chaplain. "Now what's *he* doing there?" exclaimed Will.

Gina and Will were startled when they heard their father behind them. "It looked to me," he said, "like the news showed a lot of folks trying to connect their real faith to real life. I think they *all* believe they're going to do *some* good. I wonder where they'd get an idea like that?"

ACTIVITY

LET'S BEGIN Why do you think Will is skeptical about whether the people in the news stories were doing any good? What reasons would the people in those stories give Gina about their actions if they could?

▶ **Do you think any of the actions being done in these reports can do any good? Why or why not? How do you try to bring your real faith to real life?**

THAT ALL MAY HAVE LIFE

 Focus Why does the Church continue Jesus' saving work?

We have all wondered what difference we can make in the lives of people far away. We may even wonder some days what difference we can make in our family or even in our own lives. Near and far, there seems to be a never-ending tide of problems that need solutions. Where is God in all this?

It's Our Choice We are made in God's image. And God created us to be with him—completely happy and whole. But, he also created us with **free will**, the ability to act freely in making choices. Because humans are free to choose, and because each person is born with original sin, they sometimes choose hurtful, sinful actions. But God can help us learn to use free will to choose what is good. Free will is one of God's greatest gifts to us, but it is very easy to misuse it.

After Jesus died, Paul wrote to the Corinthians about the salvation God offered us through Jesus: "in Christ God was reconciling the world to himself" (*2 Corinthians 5:19*). If we accept Jesus Christ as our Savior, and have faith in him, we will be reconciled, or restored, in our relationship with God. But, it is our free will to choose. And not everyone accepts Jesus as their Lord, not even those who believe in God. Until they do, the world will not be in full communion with God. We who believe have our work cut out for us.

❓ When have you used your free will to decide to do something good?

❓ When has it been hard for you to choose good instead of evil?

Faith and Baptism Jesus is the only one who can save us from our sins. Now that he has returned to be with his Father in glory, he has left on earth his Body, the Church, to continue bringing people hope, new life, and salvation. The Second Vatican Council explained that "all salvation comes from Christ the Head through the Church which is his Body." The Council based this statement on Scripture and Church Tradition. Christ is the one mediator who can bring us to salvation. He is present in the world now in his body, the Church.

We cannot be restored to the right relationship with God without faith. Jesus said, "The one who believes and is baptized will be saved; but the one who does not believe will be condemned" (*Mark 16:16*). We can see that faith is not enough. We need to be baptized into new life in Christ. We receive Baptism in and through the Church, so again we see that the Church is needed for salvation.

But what about those who have never heard of Christ and his Church? Living a good life and following her conscience can still save a person who, through no fault of her own, has not heard of Jesus and the Church. And Jesus is still bringing such a person new life! The same is true for those preparing to become Catholic, but who for some reason are not baptized before they die. And, some people die for the faith even though they are not baptized, and they, too, can be saved.

We might also wonder about children who have died without Baptism. It is best for babies to be baptized, but if they die before they are baptized, we can trust our loving God to have mercy on them and save them. That is what we pray for all unbaptized infants and children.

free will

universal

temporal punishment

**ACTIVITY**

SHARE YOUR FAITH Go back to the words of Gina and Will's dad in the opening story. What do you think their dad means? Share your thoughts with one another.

COMMUNION WITH GOD

 Focus How does the Church help people be close to God?

The Church is the sacrament, or sign, of our salvation. She is also the way of getting to know God, or having communion with him. We are in communion with God when we are members of the Church. Only through the Church do we receive the Eucharist, which unites us with Christ. The Eucharist is also Christ's sacrifice on the cross. The Eucharistic sacrifice is offered to make reparation for people's sins and to gain both material and spiritual gifts from God.

We remember that the one God is the Holy Trinity, three Persons united as one God. We celebrate that through, with, and in Christ, we are united with God.

On our own we could never even imagine being this close to God! It is like a dream that is too good to be true! The Holy Spirit brings about this communion between God and all of us in the Church. Jesus has poured out his Holy Spirit on all the members of the Church. This Spirit builds the Church, brings her to life, and makes her holy.

Missionary Church The Church is **universal**. Jesus did not found his Church to exist in only one time or place. He sent her out to all nations to preach the Gospel to everyone. She is the universal sacrament of salvation.

Bringing salvation would be easy if it were meant for just a select few people. But God wants *everyone* to come to him because he loves all human beings. The Church believes in God's universal plan of goodness, salvation, and redemption, so she has to be a missionary Church.

Salvation is found in the truth. Even before people know about Jesus and his Church, or come to faith in God, they are drawn to seek the truth. They have begun to move toward salvation without even knowing it. They are following the promptings of the Holy Spirit.

God has entrusted the truth about himself to the Church. So while people are *already* searching, she goes out to meet them and bring them the truth.

> **Where do missionaries work in the Church today? What are some things they do to help bring the truth and Good News about Jesus to people?**

The Church's Treasury We have a "treasury" in the Church—not a collection of money, but a spiritual treasury of all the holiness and goodness from Jesus, and from the prayers and good works of Mary and all the saints. There is "an abundant exchange of all good things," among the saints in heaven, the souls in purgatory, and all of us on earth. Jesus gave the Church the authority over this spiritual treasury.

Mary and the other saints can help us overcome the lasting effect of sin. Even though our sins may have been forgiven, we must still be purified before we can enter heaven. This process of purification is called **temporal punishment**. The Church has the power to grant indulgences based on this spiritual treasury. Indulgences, such as particular prayers or actions, allow faithful Christians who have met certain requirements to avoid temporal punishment. We can obtain indulgences for ourselves and also for the souls waiting in purgatory. Indulgences release us from some of the temporal punishment we must pay for our sins. This helps us work toward the salvation and eternal life that God offers all who are willing to respond to his grace.

CATHOLICS TODAY

The Church looks out for the rights of people, the well-being of their bodies, and the ways their material life affects their salvation.

The Church:

▶ speaks out on issues of justice and peace;

▶ helps provide material assistance;

▶ and makes judgments when necessary about the societies and economies of the world.

Everything comes from God and is meant to bring us to God, so that the Church is part of our material and our spiritual lives.

ACTIVITY

CONNECT YOUR FAITH List some ways that you are close to God. Then think of who or what helps you to be close to God. How can you help others realize that God wants to be close to them?

_____

_____

_____

_____

THE CHURCH PRAYS

Focus Why is prayer an important part of the Church's life?

We cannot give ourselves a share in God's life. Salvation is a gift from God, not something we can either cause or earn. God uses the Church to give us the hope of life forever with him.

But we do not have to wait until we are in heaven to be united with God. We can already be in communion with him while on earth. In the Lord's Prayer, Jesus taught us to say: "Your kingdom come. Your will be done, on earth as it is in heaven" (*Matthew 6:10*).

The Lord's Prayer brings us into communion with God the Father and his Son, Jesus. When we pray it, it is a bit like holding up a mirror—the Lord's Prayer shows us who we are as children of God and members of his Church.

There is another side to the Church. It is a quieter side that reflects and prays and silently meets God. The Church must never forget this part of her mission. We are not just a big team or club of people. God tirelessly calls each of us *individually* to meet him and live in his love. He never stops loving individuals and wanting each one to be in communion with him. The history of salvation is not just a story of journeys and battles, of prophets and kings. Salvation history also tells how God has repeatedly called out to individual human beings and how they have answered his call in the quiet of their own hearts.

SCRIPTURE

GO TO THE SOURCE
Read **Matthew 6:9–13**. What do you think the world would be like if all humans truly desired what we ask for in this prayer?

It is not always easy to pray, so people might be tempted to stop or even to skip praying. We can get distracted while we are praying, but God wants us to stay in prayer even when we are distracted. With practice, we can send distractions out of our minds and pay more attention to God.

THE CHURCH'S TRADITION OF PRAYER

There are three major expressions of a life of prayer.

VOCAL PRAYER: prayer that uses words

MEDITATION: prayer that uses the mind, in which we try to understand the "how and why of the Christian life" in order to live closer to Jesus

CONTEMPLATIVE PRAYER: wordless prayer, in which we seek union with God

Sometimes good feelings come to us in prayer, but not always. Sometimes people feel nothing while they pray, unsure if they are really praying. We don't need to have special feelings when we pray. All we need to have is faith. God will speak to us and listen to us if we remain faithful to have a time of prayer.

> When do you like to pray alone? How can you find a certain time of day or a certain place that is best for you?

ACTIVITY

LIVE YOUR FAITH Think about the following questions and discuss your answers with a partner.

▶ When do you pray best?

▶ What are some things that make it hard for you to pray?

▶ When do you like to pray alone?

▶ How can you find a certain time of day or a certain place that is best for you to pray?

IN SUMMARY

CATHOLICS BELIEVE

The Church has a mission to bring all people to believe in God and to be baptized.

▶ Faith and Baptism are necessary for the freedom and new life that come from salvation.

▶ The Church is both a sign and instrument of the communion between God and his people; it is through her actions that people can come to know God and share in his life.

▶ We must have a personal relationship with God nourished by prayer in order to answer our call to bring his love and truth to others.

CELEBRATE

PRAYER FOR PEACE

Leader: God of peace and justice,
you call us this day to be your holy Church,
your holy people here on earth.

All: Lord, make me an instrument of your peace.

Leader: Where there is hatred,
where eyes are lowered, fingers pointed, and tempers rise,
let us be your love, Lord.

All: Lord, make me an instrument of your peace.

Leader: Where there is injury,
where gossip and cutting words damage lives,
let us be your forgiveness, Lord.

All: Lord, make me an instrument of your peace.

Leader: Where there is doubt and we question truth,
when believers lose their way,
let us be your faith, Lord.

All: Lord, make me an instrument of your peace.

Leader: Where there is darkness,
where greed and chaos rule the day,
and fear fills every corner,
let us be your light, Lord.

All: Lord, make me an instrument of your peace.

Leader: When sorrow fills the heart,
when grief is raw, and hope is gone,
let us be your joy, Lord.

All: Lord, make me an instrument of your peace.

Leader: God of mercy and kindness,
let us be your witnesses here on earth.
Let us be your holy Church!

All: Lord, make me an instrument of your peace.

♪ "Make Me an Instrument of Your Peace"
Lori True, © 2005, GIA Publications, Inc.

164

REVIEW

A **Work with Words** Circle the letter of the choice that best completes the sentence.

1. When waiting in the state of purgatory the soul suffers _____ for sin.
   a. final judgment **b.** earthly punishment **c.** eternal punishment **d.** temporal punishment

2. _____ free(s) us from some of the temporal punishment for our sins.
   a. Free will **b.** Indulgences **c.** Reason **d.** Salvation

3. The Church is _____ because she does not exist in only one time or place.
   a. holy **b.** temporal **c.** universal **d.** timeless

4. God created human beings with _____, the ability to make choices.
   a. free will **b.** open will **c.** good will **d.** free choice

5. The Church has a(n) _____ of all the holiness and goodness from Jesus, and from the prayers and good works of Mary and all the saints.
   a. spiritual inheritance **b.** spiritual treasury **c.** limited treasury **d.** universal account

B **Check Understanding** Indicate whether the following statements are true or false. Then rewrite false statements to make them true.

_____ 6. The Church is a sign or sacrament of John.

_____

_____ 7. For the world to be in communion with God, all people must have received communion.

_____

_____ 8. The Lord's Prayer brings us into communion with God the Father and his Son, Jesus.

_____

_____ 9. The Eucharist makes present on our altars Christ's sacrifice on the cross, offered to make reparation for people's sins.

_____

_____ 10. Contemplative prayer is prayer that is spoken communally during the assembly of the faithful.

_____

C **Make Connections: Synthesize** Write a one-paragraph response to the questions.

How does the missionary Church bring people into communion with God? How does the prayerful Church do so?

OUR CATHOLIC FAITH

WHAT NOW?

* Think about your Baptism. How would your life be different if you were not baptized?

* Tell others about Jesus.

* Think of ways you can share in the Church's missionary work.

* Set aside time each day to pray alone.

* Ask your family to pray together once a week.

ACTIVITY

LIVE YOUR FAITH Use newspapers, magazines, and the Internet to find evidence of the Church's influence in the world today. Report on how the Church is working for peace and justice in the world. How is she reaching out to those in need?

The Church reaches out by:

▶ What do you think are two of the most important issues or roles that the Church should focus on in the world today?

_____

_____

_____

_____

GO online Visit www.osvcurriculum.com for more family and community connections.

PRAYER

Holy Spirit, help me pray every day.

Saint Lorenzo Ruiz

Tests in school can prove how strong our study skills are, and tests in our lives can prove how strong our faith is. One important role of the Church is to remind us of Jesus' work and provide us with the tools we need for life's tests.

Sometimes Christians are faced with extreme situations in which our faith is so challenged that our lives may be at stake. This was the case with Saint Lorenzo Ruiz of the Philippines, who was killed as a martyr for his faith. In the early 1600s, he faithfully served the Church in Manila in many ways. When he was younger, he served as an altar boy and later was a helper and clerk-sacristan in his parish church. As an adult, he was a member of the Confraternity of the Rosary. To support his family, he worked as a calligrapher, handwriting documents in neat penmanship.

In 1636, he was accused of a serious crime. While proclaiming his innocence, he fled the Philippines because he was afraid he would not get a fair trial. He traveled by ship with four Philippine and Japanese priests and a layman. They landed on the island of Okinawa, which was under Japanese rule.

The Japanese rulers didn't like the Christians. They felt that their power was threatened by missionaries who had come to the islands for almost 100 years. Lorenzo and his companions were taken by force to Nagasaki, Japan, and brought before the authorities.

They were given the choice of renouncing their faith or being executed. Drawing strength from the Church and its promise of salvation, all six of them refused to give up what they believed in. When told to renounce his faith or die, Lorenzo held firm. He told his captors, "That I will never do, because I am a Christian, and I shall die for God, and for him I would give many thousands of lives if I had them. And so, do with me as you please."

Lorenzo and the others were tortured in an effort to break their spirits, but they still refused to do as their captors ordered. One by one, they were executed. Lorenzo was hung upside-down over a pit for three days until he died. His body was cremated and his ashes thrown into the Pacific Ocean.

In 1981, Pope Saint John Paul II beatified Lorenzo Ruiz along with fourteen other Philippine and Japanese martyrs executed around the same time. All were canonized six years later.

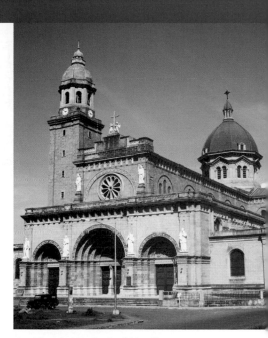

▲ **The Cathedral of Manila**

GLOBAL DATA

The Philippines

- The Philippines is an independent nation in the southern Pacific Ocean consisting of more than 7,000 islands totaling 115,000 square miles.

- The Philippines has a population of nearly 101 million, 81 percent of whom are Roman Catholic.

- The Philippines was first colonized by the Spanish and was under American rule from 1898 to 1946.

- The Philippines was the scene of many key land and sea battles between the Americans and the Japanese during World War II.

DISCOVER

Catholic Social Teaching:
Dignity of Work and the Rights of Workers

IN THIS UNIT you learned about being a disciple of Jesus and participating in the Church's mission of spreading God's love throughout the world.

Rights of the Worker

Part of spreading love is working for justice for those who are treated unfairly. Workers in our own country as well as the rest of the world are often treated unfairly. Because of our oneness in God's family, such unfair treatment is a sin against human solidarity. The equal dignity of all people, no matter what kind of work they do or whether they are able to work at all, demands that we work to eliminate these sinful inequalities. Not to do so would mean we are participating in what the Church calls "social sin"—unjust situations or practices.

Part of what we can do is support the right of workers to form unions to protect their rights. When unions go on strike, we can support them by refusing to cross their picket lines, even when that is inconvenient. When unions call for a boycott, we can join them. Many individuals and some dioceses did so in support of the United Farm Workers and in opposition to apartheid in South Africa. Many young people have participated in boycotts of companies using sweatshop labor or refusing to pay their workers a just wage.

Some people support local workers by buying directly from small farmers in farmers' markets, rather than buying produce in giant supermarket chains. Others choose to eat at locally owned restaurants and shop at neighborhood stores rather than at giant chains, even if they have to pay a little more. Many U.S. communities have challenged giant chain superstores because they put some local stores out of business and pay nonunion-level wages. Where do you shop? There are lots of ways to help. For example, buying "Fair Trade Coffee" supports coffee cooperatives in Latin America and Africa that pay their workers a fair wage.

Which of these ways to help appeals to you the most?

THE RIGHTS OF WORKERS are an important element in maintaining human worth and dignity. Let's look at how one group put this belief into action.

"A PENNY MORE"
SUPPORTING OTHERS

Sr. Rosemary Finnegan, O.P., and Mrs. Ana Forman teach seventh-grade religion at St. Margaret Mary Catholic School in Winter Park, Florida. From 2002 to 2005, their classes were involved in the national boycott of Taco Bell, a favorite "food group" of their junior high. Taco Bell was the largest purchaser of tomatoes grown in Immokalee, Florida. The growers, however, were paying poor wages to the farmworkers who picked the tomatoes. All the workers wanted was "a penny more a pound" and that increase would significantly raise their income. The hope of the boycott was to convince Taco Bell not only of their participation in this unjust situation, but also of the influence they could have to change it.

The faculty educated the children about this situation, stopped serving Taco Bell products on food days at school, and wrote letters home encouraging parents to support the boycott. They also kept parents updated on the progress of the boycott. Finally, after three years, Taco Bell negotiated with the growers to the workers' satisfaction, and the boycott ended. Students discussed the settlement in relation to the dignity and rights of the workers, and wrote letters to the president of Taco Bell, commending his company's actions. When the negotiations were looking very hopeful, Sister Rosemary made a promise to her class. "When an agreement is reached," she said, "we will celebrate the next day by eating tacos!" Of course the students all remembered that part, so the day after the settlement, she brought in twenty-five tacos and they feasted! One of the girls wrote in her letter that that taco tasted even better because she knew it now benefited others!

> **Was the school right to get involved in a labor issue? If you were a student there, would you have joined the boycott? Why or why not?**

▼ Students became aware of the plight of underpaid farmworkers and decided to join a boycott to help change the situation.

SERVE Your Community

PERSONAL SHOPPING DECISIONS

Make a list of all the places you shop or eat. Put an "L" next to those that are locally owned. Put a "C" next to those that are out-of-town chains. For each chain store you list, identify at least one locally owned alternative that is not too inconvenient for you. Make a decision to change one of your shopping habits in order to support workers in your own community. Write this decision down, share it with others you trust, and invite them to join you.

STORE	LOCAL OR CHAIN?	LOCAL ALTERNATIVE

CONSUMER BOYCOTTS

Research with your classmates any consumer boycotts going on in your area. Share your findings, choose one of these boycotts to participate in, and create a plan for doing so.

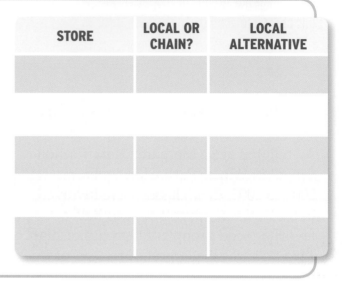

Project Planning Sheet

Others who should be asked to help

_____

_____

Ways to publicize your project

_____

_____

Other specific tasks

_____

_____

Your specific task(s)

_____

_____

Calendar for completing the project

_____

How important is "convenience" for you when you make decisions about where you shop?

_____

_____

_____

How important is "justice" and helping others, even if it's less convenient or costs more?

_____

_____

_____

How did others react to your invitation to join a boycott?

_____

_____

_____

What did you learn about yourself in doing this project?

_____

_____

_____

What did you learn about injustice in the workplace in doing the project?

_____

_____

_____

What did you learn about God and about your faith in doing both of these activities?

_____

_____

_____

List one thing that might be different about you after doing this project.

_____

_____

_____

REVIEW

A **Work with Words** Match the words on the left with the correct definitions or descriptions on the right.

_____ 1. Apostles

_____ 2. doctrine

_____ 3. spiritualities

_____ 4. church

_____ 5. People of God

_____ 6. Mystical Body of Christ

_____ 7. hierarchy

_____ 8. temporal punishment

_____ 9. indulgences

_____ 10. spiritual treasury

A. ways of living as a disciple

B. a word used for the Church, first used to refer to God's Chosen People in the Old Testament

C. the purification of a sinner, here on Earth or in purgatory, due because of forgiven sins or the attachment to sin

D. levels of ordained leadership in the Church

E. official and authentic teachings of the Church

F. the holiness of Jesus and the good words of the saints accounted to the Church

G. group that Jesus especially chose during his lifetime to spread the Good News

H. release from some of the punishment for sin

I. the Church as a spiritual group seen as a spiritual community

J. word meaning a gathering or assembly

B **Check Understanding** Circle the letter of the best answer to complete the following statements.

11. Church laws are contained in the _____.
  a. Bible
  b. Church Council Documents
  c. Code of Canon Law
  d. Old Testament

12. Jesus sent the disciples out two-by-two to announce the coming of the _____.
  a. Kingdom of God
  b. Messiah
  c. Church
  d. Ascension

13. The _____ teaches us as disciples to pray.
  a. Canon Law
  b. Rosary
  c. Roman Missal
  d. Holy Spirit

14. The _____ part of the Church includes Christ's presence among us through the power of the Holy Spirit.

a. spiritual

c. literal

b. invisible

d. allegorical

15. Through the Holy Spirit, Baptism, and the _____, Jesus forms the Church as his Body.

a. Word

c. Eucharist

b. Resurrection

d. Apostles

16. Jesus taught his disciples that he was the _____ and they were the branches.

a. roots

c. fruit

b. vine

d. both a and b

17. Jesus said that faith and _____ are necessary for salvation.

a. judgment

c. hope

b. Baptism

d. marriage

18. _____ is wordless prayer in which we seek communion with God.

a. Intercession

c. Community prayer

b. Vocal prayer

d. Contemplation

· ·

C Make Connections Write a short answer to these questions.

19. Synthesize. Jesus said that we are like branches. He also used other comparisons in the Gospels to describe the Kingdom of God. Now create your own comparison. What is your relationship with Jesus "like"?

_____

_____

_____

_____

20. Evaluate. Imagine that you are standing before Jesus at the Last Judgment. What would you say to him about your readiness for salvation? What would he say to you? Write the dialogue.

_____

_____

_____

_____

173

FREEDOM
and Responsibility

I'm willing to be responsible for my actions, no problem.
How do I know what's really good and right?
What can I do to make better decisions?

It was early morning on a typical spring day. Three neighbors, Kelly, Kyle, and Marietta, were being driven to school by Kelly's mom. Kelly wasn't entirely awake yet. Maybe that's because Marietta hadn't started talking yet. Kyle already had his earphones on, listening to music.

"What're you listening to?" asked Kelly, sleepily.

"New CD I downloaded last night," he said. "For free."

"That's wrong. You're ripping people off. Plus it's illegal," Marietta jumped in—fully awake now.

"Yeah. Right. Everybody does it," Kyle responded casually.

Marietta wouldn't let it go. "That doesn't make it right."

Kelly, whose favorite subject was art, joined in. "Every artist has a right to be paid for his or her work, and a song is *work*—that rapper isn't going to get his share when you download it like that."

"Come on! They make enough money as it is. My clicking and downloading isn't going to hurt a millionaire rap artist."

"But if ten thousand other people are doing what you did, they sure would make a dent in his take. How would you like it if you worked hard for years to make something really good and people took it from you for free?" Marietta argued.

"That's it. We're here!" said Kyle. Putting his player in his backpack, he looked forward to some free time when he could listen to the rest of the song. He thought to himself, *I don't care what they say; my making a copy of this song isn't really hurting someone who's already got enough money.*

ACTIVITY

LET'S BEGIN Do you think Kyle is doing something wrong? Explain. Does Marietta's argument make sense?

▶ **What are some other things that are illegal, but some people think it's okay to do anyway?**

▶ **Have you ever been in a situation when you didn't know what to do, and whatever was happening seemed all right because everyone was doing it? If everyone was doing it, did that make it less wrong? What are some things today that are perfectly legal but still wrong?**

LIVING MEANS THINKING AND DOING

Focus How can you make good choices?

Some people say that life today is more complex than in the past. Your parents, for example, never had to make a decision about downloading music or renting an R-rated DVD. But on the other hand, some of the same kinds of decisions are faced by every generation.

Every day, probably every hour, you are faced with choices that require decisions. Many of these decisions result in actions: what to wear, what to say to someone, where to go, what to do with others. Some decisions seem more important than others, and you might not know how to make the more difficult ones. Just remember, you've been given some important tools to help you.

Your Decisions Sometimes other people make decisions for you because they have authority over you. But all those decisions that you make freely are your own responsibility. Something that you decide to do (or not do) is a decision that belongs to you alone and no one else.

Why is this important? You are not morally responsible for decisions that you have not voluntarily made. Your intentional thoughts, decisions, and actions are yours. So, morally, you are responsible for your freely made decisions, and the actions or non-actions that come from them.

Made to Choose You have the ability to choose to act in a variety of ways. Why? God made humans unique and special from all other creatures.

You have a

▶ **soul**—the spiritual principle that reflects God in you

▶ **intellect**—that which makes it possible for you to think, reason, and judge

▶ **free will**—the power to choose and make decisions on your own without being forced to choose or act in a certain way

This unique combination makes you an image of God. You are created with a great potential to seek what is good and true, and therefore reach happiness with God in heaven.

God gives you another important characteristic to help you make decisions: your conscience. Your conscience is like an inner voice, part of your ability to reason, that helps you know the difference between right and wrong. Conscience is what moves you to know and follow the moral law, to do good and avoid what is evil. You are called by God to develop an informed conscience.

Choices That Lead You from God Listening to your conscience leads you along the right path, the one that keeps you in the right relationship with God and away from sin, any deliberate thought, word, or action that goes against moral law and offends God. Sin is a deliberate choice to disobey God; it's not a mistake or an accident.

There are two types of personal or actual sins, sins for which someone is responsible. **Mortal sin** breaks a person's relationship with God. The effect of mortal sin, without repenting and being forgiven, is total separation from God forever. For a sin to be mortal, three conditions must be met:

1. the matter involved is seriously wrong or believed to be seriously wrong;

2. it must be committed with full knowledge (called *sufficient reflection*); and

3. the person freely chooses or agrees to commit the wrong anyway (full consent of the will to do what is wrong).

The Ten Commandments specify gravely serious matter. But not all sins are gravely damaging or mortal. Less serious sin, called **venial sin**, weakens a person's relationship to God. Venial sins lessen the love of God in your heart and make it more difficult to resist sin. Venial sins arise from not using moderation in less important matters or acting without full knowledge of the situation.

soul

intellect

mortal sin

venial sin

The Vatican has one of the oldest astronomical institutions in the world. But why is the Vatican interested in astronomy (the study of the stars)? At first, in 1582, it was for practical reasons, to correct errors in the calendar and to improve navigation at sea.

Scientists at the Vatican Observatory in Rome, or at the research center at Steward Observatory at the University of Arizona, Tucson, are interested in performing good scientific research. It is part of the Catholic philosophy that God reveals himself through creation. Studying creation in a scientific way is a way to come closer to God. When we listen to the message of creation and to the voice of conscience, we can be certain of the existence of God, the cause and end of everything.

SHARE YOUR FAITH How well (or often) do you listen to your conscience? Why is it sometimes so difficult to follow that inner voice? Discuss this with a partner.

THE SOURCES OF ACTION

Focus What determines whether an action is good?

LOOKING BACK

St. Thomas Aquinas (1225–1274) was a Dominican monk, one of the great philosophers of the Middle Ages. Aquinas argued that whether an act is good or evil depends on the end result of that action. Therefore, human acts are good if they promote the purpose and honor of God. Aquinas also taught that by repeating a good action, people develop a moral habit, which allows them to do good easily. He wrote, "An evil action cannot be justified by reference to a good intention." Today we say, "The end does *not* justify the means." In an extreme example of this moral belief, if asked what to do in a situation where killing one person would save one hundred other lives, a Catholic person's answer is that murder is wrong no matter how many lives it saves. In 1879, Pope Leo XIII recommended that St. Thomas's philosophy be made the basis of instruction in all Roman Catholic schools and the official Catholic philosophy.

There is a way to figure out what is right and wrong. There is a way to develop an *informed* conscience.

But how do you know if what you are doing is morally right? Three things determine the morality of a human action. These three elements are:

▶ the *object*, which characterizes the action in and of itself.

▶ the *intention*, which is the immediate end or purpose the person intends to achieve through the action.

▶ the *circumstances*, which surround the action.

"A *morally good* act requires the goodness of the object, of the end, and of the circumstances together . . . One may not do evil so that good may result from it" (*Catechism of the Catholic Church*, 1755–1756).

Consider this situation:

Your older brother is driving Grandma to the doctor using Dad's car with his permission. The *object* of this action is to drive his grandmother to the doctor.

A bike rider loses control and swerves in front of the car. Your brother makes a split decision and turns the steering wheel, causing the car to jump the curb. There are no pedestrians at the curbside. The *object* of his action and his *intention* are to avoid hitting the bike rider. Your brother's *intention* is not to break the rules of the road or to put pedestrians in danger, but to avoid hitting and hurting the bike rider.

The pertinent *circumstances* are that no pedestrians are at curbside and that your brother drove on the curb long enough to avoid the biker.

In this case, the immediate *object* of the brother's action was to avoid the biker. This, too, was his intention. The *circumstances* permitted him to do this without hurting anyone else. Even though he technically violated the law by going off the road, the immediate *object* of his action was to avoid hitting the biker.

In this episode, the *object*, *intention*, and *circumstances* were good. His was a morally good act.

When making a choice, you have to consider all three elements: what is the action or object itself; why are you doing it, or not doing it; and what are the pressures, environment, or issues surrounding it that might be affecting your judgment.

✝ **SCRIPTURE**
GO TO THE SOURCE
Read **Matthew 6:2–4** to find out more of what Jesus had to say about the intention of good deeds.

CONSIDER THIS

A good intention—such as wanting to help your sister—does not make an object or behavior that is morally wrong—such as lying to your parents—good.

A bad intention—such as the desire to boast—can make an object or behavior that is good—such as donating money or time to a worthy cause—morally bad. As Jesus said, "Beware of practicing your piety before others in order to be seen by them . . ." (Matthew 6:1).

The circumstances of an action can increase or decrease the moral goodness of the action. However, the circumstances cannot change whether an act is morally good or not, only the degree of its goodness or evilness.

Some acts, such as murder, are always wrong no matter the intention or the circumstances because choosing them entails so great an evil they are against the natural moral law.

❓ **Is the brother's action described earlier a morally good act? Why or why not? What about Kyle downloading music for free?**

ACTIVITY

CONNECT YOUR FAITH Write down a moral decision you are currently dealing with, or have dealt with recently: something you are trying to decide is—or was—right or wrong. Use a word or symbol to indicate the situation. Then follow the process we have been talking about in the space below.

WHAT'S THE ACT?

WHAT'S THE INTENTION?

WHAT'S THE CIRCUMSTANCE?

WHAT DOES YOUR CONSCIENCE NOW TELL YOU?

FORMATION FOR DOING RIGHT

Focus How can a well-formed conscience help you?

Athletes know that if a person wants to build up his or her body, he or she has to work at it. He or she has to establish a routine. Along with exercise, he or she must eat the right food.

When you have a moral decision to make, your conscience will move you to make a right (morally good) judgment that follows reason and God's law. Or, it can lead you to make an incorrect (morally bad) judgment that does not follow reason and God's law.

Building and shaping a conscience is similar. If you want to make good decisions through life and do the right things, then forming a conscience is critical. If a conscience has been formed well, it will lead you to what is truthful and just. It will help you make sound, rational judgments and follow what is good.

Conscience Formation Someone who wants to become a more experienced pianist will seek out a teacher who can introduce important skills and guide them to feel the music as they play. The person will spend a lot of time practicing, strengthening her skills, and accepting the fact that her development will be ongoing; if you don't use the skills, you'll lose them.

The same holds true with building up your conscience.

Ways to Form Your Conscience

▶ Scripture: What does the Bible say about it?

▶ Church teaching: What does the Church say about it?

▶ Science: What does science say about it? What are the facts?

▶ Community: What does society say about it? Is it a legal issue as well?

When you are using these resources to inform your conscience and find that there is a conflict between some of these sources, give priority to the wisdom found in Scripture and the teaching of the Church.

CHECK THIS OUT!

You've probably heard that practice makes perfect, but have you ever thought of it in the reverse? What happens when you keep repeating the same negative, sinful behavior over and over? You create in yourself a vice, a habit or tendency to be more sinful. The Church uses the term vices to refer to the seven capital sins that tend to produce other sinful behavior. Traditionally, the Church has identified seven capital sins or vices: pride, covetousness, envy, anger, gluttony, lust, and sloth or laziness. Fortunately the cardinal virtues of prudence, justice, fortitude, and temperance are good habits within us that, when strengthened and practiced, help us counter these vices in our daily lives.

STEPS IN MAKING A MORAL DECISION

1. Think: Take time to consider your options and the possible consequences to yourself, others, and your relationship with God. Take time to hear what your conscience might be saying.

2. Compare: How do your options compare to Jesus' Beatitudes, his new commandment, the Ten Commandments, and Church teachings? If an option contradicts any of these, then it's not really an option anymore.

3. Talk: Find someone who can understand the situation you are in. Tell him or her what you are thinking and why. Ask for advice.

4. Pray: Turn to the Holy Spirit in prayer, asking for guidance to make the right decision.

5. Act: Make your choice and be confident that you have made the right one based upon your conscience.

ACTIVITY

LIVE YOUR FAITH You face situations that require you to make a moral decision almost every day. Choose one of these situations and use the steps below to make a recommendation on how someone could respond.

telling the truth, even if it gets you into trouble

cheating on tests

drinking, using drugs or tobacco

gossiping

obeying parents

maintaining chastity

bullying siblings or others

Decision:

Think:

Compare:

Talk:

Pray:

Act:

IN SUMMARY

CATHOLICS BELIEVE

We are free to choose, responsible for our choices, and guided in our moral decision making.

▶ God made us with a free will, an intellect, and a soul, and our conscience works with these gifts so that we can choose to do good and avoid sin.

▶ Morally good actions require that their object, intention, and circumstance be good; the end does not justify the means.

▶ A well-formed conscience will guide us to do what is right and good, and we can make good decisions if we have the help of Christ's teachings, the Church, the Holy Spirit, prayer, and wise people.

PRAYER

PRAYER OF INTERCESSION

Leader: We live in need of God's guidance in our lives.
Let us take this time to allow God to enter our hearts.
Let us pray.

Side 1: Life can be filled with trouble, Lord.
We get mixed messages and
often we see, hear, and feel the need
to follow things that are not
in line with what you teach us.

Side 2: Violence, abuse, cruelty, war,
selfishness, hatred, racism,
neglect of the poor and elderly,
hunger—
these are all things that you did not make!

All: You are all we need.

Side 1: Help us to always remember
that we are free to choose differently.
Help us to remember that you are all we need.

Side 2: Help us to feel the freedom you give us as something wonderful,
not something to punish us,
or something to deprive us of joy.
Help us to remember that you are all we need.

All: You are all we need.

Side 1: Help us to have the strength,
the understanding,
and the wisdom to know
and to remember
that you are all we need.

Side 2: You alone, O God,
have what we need to be happy.
You alone, O God,
are our delight and joy.

All: We pray in Jesus' name. Amen.

♪ "You Are All I Want"
Lori True, © 2003, GIA Publications, Inc.

REVIEW

A **Work with Words** Complete each sentence with the correct term from the word bank at right.

Word Bank

- soul
- moral law
- conscience
- sin
- free will
- intention
- circumstances
- intellect

1. Your spiritual _____ reflects God in you.

2. Conscience moves you to know and follow the _____, which directs us to do good and avoid evil.

3. _____ is any deliberate thought, word, action, or omission that goes against moral law and offends God.

4. Every human action is composed of three elements—the object, the _____, and the circumstances.

5. The _____ of an action can increase or decrease the moral goodness of the action.

B **Check Understanding** Circle the letter of the choice that best completes the sentence.

6. Your _____ is the spiritual principle that reflects God in you.
   - **a.** intellect
   - **b.** free will
   - **c.** soul
   - **d.** conscience

7. Your _____ is like an inner voice that helps you choose between right and wrong.
   - **a.** intellect
   - **b.** free will
   - **c.** soul
   - **d.** conscience

8. The effect of _____, without repenting and being forgiven, is separation from God forever.
   - **a.** venial sin
   - **b.** mortal sin
   - **c.** free will
   - **d.** moral law

9. _____ lessens the love of God in your heart and makes it more difficult to resist sin.
   - **a.** Venial sin
   - **b.** Mortal sin
   - **c.** Free will
   - **d.** Moral law

10. If a(n) _____ has been formed well, it will lead you to what is truthful and just.
   - **a.** intellect
   - **b.** free will
   - **c.** soul
   - **d.** conscience

C **Make Connections: Evaluate** Write a one-paragraph response to the question.

What types of decisions are people your age currently facing? Write about the process of making a moral decision using the steps think, compare, talk, pray, and act.

OUR CATHOLIC FAITH

WHAT NOW?

★ Make good choices—choices that connect you in your relationship to your loving God, choices that connect you to your family, loved ones, and the communities of which you are a part.

★ Actively inform your conscience. Find out what each of the four resources have to say about some of the moral situations and decisions you are facing.

★ Seek guidance from parents, teachers, and mentors when making big choices.

★ Take time to pray as you make big and little choices in your life.

★ End each day with prayer and an examination of how you helped or hurt others.

★ Read and reflect on Scripture with other believers.

★ Listen for Christ's message for yourself at each Mass you attend.

ACTIVITY

LIVE YOUR FAITH Choose one of the four following moral decisions. See how well you can inform your conscience based on the questions below.

war   capital punishment   euthanasia   stem cell research

WHAT DOES . . . THE BIBLE SAY?	WHAT DOES . . . THE CHURCH TEACH?	WHAT DOES . . . SCIENCE OFFER YOU?	WHAT ARE . . . THE COMMUNITY'S LAWS AND VALUES?

Now choose a tough issue you are dealing with in your life and practice informing your conscience consulting these four resources.

WHAT DOES . . . THE BIBLE SAY?	WHAT DOES . . . THE CHURCH TEACH?	WHAT DOES . . . SCIENCE OFFER YOU?	WHAT ARE . . . THE COMMUNITY'S LAWS AND VALUES?

 GO online Visit www.osvcurriculum.com for more family and community connections.

 **PRAYER**

Lord, lead me to make good choices.

Blessed Aloysius Stepinac

As Catholics, following in Jesus' footsteps, we want to act on what we feel is right in our consciences. That is where the Holy Spirit helps us decide how to do what Jesus would have done. Aloysius Stepinac provides an example of someone who let his conscience guide his actions. He chose to risk his life to save others, even when those others were not Catholics.

Born to a peasant family in Brezani, Croatia, in 1898, Aloysius had an interest in the priesthood. However, World War I put his goals on hold. He was sent to the Italian front, where he received two medals for bravery. By the end of the war, Croatia was no longer independent. It was one of six states incorporated into the nation of Yugoslavia.

Stepinac began studying for the priesthood and was ordained. His honorable deeds led Pope Pius XI to appoint him as the Archbishop of Zagreb. Throughout the 1930s, when German Jews and communists were being persecuted, Archbishop Stepinac hid them from the Nazis. When Croatia briefly became independent from Yugoslavia in 1941, he spoke out against the persecution of the Gypsies and massacre of the Serbs in Glina.

The archbishop's conscience and sense of responsibility compelled him to speak out against injustice and intolerance, even when his own life was at stake. He kept his position as archbishop throughout World War II. He was one of the few leaders in Europe who raised his voice against the Nazi tyranny at a time when it was very difficult and dangerous for him to do so. In 1945, he gave a detailed report on the mass killings of priests and monks that had taken place in Yugoslavia during the war.

Shortly after the end of World War II, during the new pro-communist regime of Marshal Tito, Stepinac was sentenced to sixteen years in prison. He was released after five years on the orders of Tito, who wished to meet him. At their meeting, Stepinac told Tito, "Allow me to tell you that I am for the freedom of the people and accordingly I will raise my voice against you every time you should encroach on this freedom." Tito "encroached" on his people's rights many times, and just as many times Stepinac spoke out against the leader's actions.

Stepinac was named a Cardinal of the Church by Pope Pius XII in 1953. His Holiness called him "the most important priest of the Catholic Church." Pope Saint John Paul II beatified him in 1998.

▲ **The tomb of Aloysius Stepinac is in Zaqreb, Croatia.**

GLOBAL DATA

Croatia

- Croatia is located on the eastern shore of the Adriatic Sea, opposite Italy.

- Croatia has a population of 4.4 million, 88 percent of whom are Roman Catholic.

- Croatia was part of Yugoslavia from 1918 to 1990, and is now an independent republic again.

- Religious instruction is given in Croatian schools under government supervision, with the state paying teachers and supplying textbooks out of public revenues.

14 VALUING Life

INVITE

PRAYER Lord, help me to see others the way you do.

Does every person have the same dignity and value in God's eyes? What does it mean to say we value and respect ALL life?

It was supposed to be a happy time in their lives. At least, that's what David's parents kept telling him. His mom was pregnant, and he was going to be an older brother. But they were nervous—and so was David. Not nervous like every parent is nervous about a new baby, but nervous because there were some serious challenges involved.

After visiting the doctor, they had come home more than a little rattled. Tests showed that his sister might be born with Down Syndrome. The word his parents used to describe her was "special." They never used any kind of words to suggest that his sister might be less a person—only that she would go through life facing challenges. He and his mom and dad already pictured her as a little girl and imagined how he would help her as a big brother.

David got a little angry when he overheard his uncle asking his aunt why his parents would even allow this baby to be born! His uncle couldn't imagine what kind of life the girl would have and whether it was worth it!

David thought his comment was wrong. David had friends at school who were born with limitations that make life challenging. Some had trouble seeing and some were hearing impaired. His best friend, Rob, had been born with only one hand, but he played baseball and soccer and was on the swim team. Some kids had high IQs; others had lower IQs. Some had learning difficulties; others had attention deficits. Tons of kids had something "special" that challenged them.

When he told his parents about what he had overheard and what he was thinking, they said they were so proud of him—he was going to make a wonderful older brother. That's why we're here, they said, to help each other make it through life.

ACTIVITY

LET'S BEGIN Why do other people share the uncle's opinion? As she grows up in this family, how will this girl's special challenges affect the other members, especially her older brother?

▶ **In a week's time, how often do you hear people putting down others? How true is it that seventh and eighth graders are mean to each other? Explain. How often do you laugh at the misfortune of others?**

_____

_____

_____

LOOKING BACK

In an Old Testament lesson, Job tells his neighbors to ask the animals about the truth of creation: God has fashioned all life. But among all creatures, Job reminds them, humans are unique in that our very "life breath" comes from and is upheld by God. Many ancient people, including those in Old Testament times, equated breath with one's "spirit."

✝ SCRIPTURE
GO TO THE SOURCE

Read **Psalm 139:13–16**. What does this song of praise tell you about your relationship to God—past, present, and future? What good can come from praising God for creating you and knowing you?

A SACRED GIFT FROM GOD

Focus Why does human life have value?

If we could choose how we look and what abilities we have, we might change some things. But it's not up to us to choose our challenges. We do not enter this world on our own. Each of us owes his or her life to God. So one life is not more valuable than another. We are all equally valuable because each of us has been given the divine spark of life from God.

Made in the Image of the Divine Sometimes it's possible to tell the manufacturer of one pair of jeans from another. Or, you can always look at the tag. A cartoon shows Adam looking at a "Made by God" tag on his foot with a smile on his face. That's a joke, but there really are ways God has "tagged" us as his creation.

Human beings are so unique and beautifully made because God designed us. For this reason, the author of the psalm praises God, saying,

✝ SCRIPTURE

"For it was you who formed my inward parts;
   you knit me together in my mother's womb.

I praise you, for I am fearfully and wonderfully
   made."

—*Psalm 139:13–14*

Now, we really don't know how the man who wrote that psalm looked or what his limitations were. But he praised God for the way he was made. He believed God had a plan for his life that he was made to fulfill.

Not only are we made by God, but of all the creatures, humans alone have the capacity for "self-awareness"—we know we are individuals, separate from the world around us. We are able to recognize God's presence and freely choose to glorify him in our lives. We are made in the image and likeness of God.

For this reason, each human life has a sacred value from conception to death. This value cannot be taken away or lessened by any condition or situation.

Usefulness What do you do when your favorite pair of shoes is so beat up that they're falling apart? You probably toss them in the trash; they're no longer useful. We tend to throw away or get rid of all sorts of things when they're not useful anymore. Usefulness determines their value to us.

Human beings, however, are different. We are not things. We are not objects to be used or set aside. Value, for us, is not determined by our usefulness at all. Perhaps this is what David's uncle didn't understand about his new niece.

murder

abortion

euthanasia

scandal

Our value comes directly from God, who made us and for whom we exist. We have that value when we are healthy or sick, young or old. Even when dying, our life has worth. When we die, our existence continues. Even beyond life on earth, we are made in God's image. We continue to fulfill our purpose with our Creator.

The fifth commandment instructs us not to kill another person. We who are sacred should not be discarded, judged useless, or killed. Those kinds of decisions are simply not ours to make. **Murder** is the deliberate killing of another person. It is always gravely sinful. It shows the contempt the murderer has for the dignity of human life as well as for the holiness and goodness of God.

Why do you think some people have so little respect for human life?

Sometimes life is so difficult that people don't feel valued or respected; they may be totally overwhelmed, feeling helpless and unsure. Their pain is real, and they may lose sight of the fact that their life is a gift from God. God wants us to stick with this precious gift. Suicide is *never* an option because it goes against God's love and our hope, and it's forbidden by the Fifth Commandment. But asking for help *is* an option.

ACTIVITY

SHARE YOUR FAITH Imagine God has asked you to take notes on the creation of human beings. Make a list of how we are different from the rest of creation.

US . . .	THE REST OF CREATION . . .

HONORING LIFE

Focus What does the Church teach about protecting life at all stages?

In the Sermon on the Mount, Jesus refers to the Fifth Commandment, which bans murder. He then widens the understanding to include anger and vengeance: "But I say to you that if you are angry with a brother or sister you will be liable to judgment . . ." (*Matthew 5:22*). Jesus understands human nature and speaks against destructive emotions that can lead to worse things. Anger, hatred, and vengeance are terrible emotions that tear apart peoples' lives.

Jesus didn't preach one message and live another. His actions and behavior show that he lived a life that valued life. He tells the disciples, "But I say to you, Do not resist an evildoer" (*Matthew 5:39*); if someone strikes them on one cheek, they should offer the other cheek. When Jesus is arrested, he faces his enemies and allows them to lead him to an unjust trial and execution. The Lord of all life upholds and honors every human life to the point of not raising a hand against his oppressors or allowing his disciples to take up the sword against them.

✝ **SCRIPTURE**

GO TO THE SOURCE
Read more of the Sermon on the Mount from **Matthew 5:38–48**. What does Jesus teach about retaliation and loving your enemies?

The Church Follows Her Master

The Church has taken a stand on life issues, advocating for the rights of others. For example, over the centuries the Church has established Church-sponsored hospitals; outreach organizations; and programs for the poor, immigrants, children, victims of domestic abuse, and others in need.

The Church also confronts today's culture. It gets the message out— through preaching, outreach groups, papal encyclicals, bishops' letters, media campaigns, and more—that each human life, from conception to natural death, deserves respect.

Safeguarding Life A human life still in the womb or a life that is no longer as strong as it once was is to be protected from direct harm. Because of this teaching, **abortion**, the deliberate termination of a pregnancy by killing an unborn child, is a grave sin. The Church does not believe that human life begins at some arbitrary point later in a pregnancy. An embryo requires the same efforts of care as any human. Life is bestowed by God at conception. We are called to protect the life of the most vulnerable.

In the same way, our lives cannot be considered less valuable because we are older or sick. For this reason, **euthanasia**—the deliberate action or nonaction that causes the death of someone who is sick, or dying, or has disabilities—is also a grave sin. We owe tender care to those who, at the end of their lives, are most fragile.

It follows from this principle that sometimes we must defend ourselves, or others, from a person or group of people causing harm. It is legitimate and necessary to defend the lives of others, and this is a serious duty for those who have responsibility for the lives of others.

❓ **Who helps you to respect the dignity and sacredness of life?**

"SEAMLESS GARMENT OF LIFE"

"When the soldiers had crucified Jesus, they took his clothes and divided them into four parts, one for each soldier. They also took his tunic; now the tunic was seamless, woven in one piece from the top. So they said to one another, 'Let us not tear it, but cast lots for it to see who will get it.'"

—*John 19:23–24*

The fabric of God's creation is threatened when we tear it, gamble over pieces of it, or claim ownership of any part of it. That's the Catholic belief we have toward human life. No life should be torn, ruined, destroyed.

The late Joseph Cardinal Bernardin, Archbishop of Chicago, described this teaching as a "consistent ethic of life." Catholics should honor, respect, and defend all life. Bernardin taught that Catholics must be consistent, or seamless, in opposing abortion, the death penalty, war, the nuclear arms race, and anything that threatens life. Being seamless in our approach to the sacredness of human life makes the human family, and the Church, stronger.

▲ **Joseph Cardinal Bernardin**

ACTIVITY

CONNECT YOUR FAITH Think about the different organizations or people that protect the right to life of people at different stages of life. In the diagram below, name two ways you can value and honor life at each stage. In the center, name two ways you can value and honor life no matter the age.

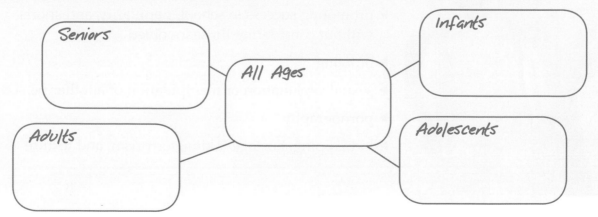

Seniors

Infants

All Ages

Adults

Adolescents

RESPECTING THE HUMAN PERSON

 Focus Why is it important to take care of ourselves and others?

Unkind words are hurtful, they can affect how people think and feel about themselves, and they don't have a positive purpose.

If words can be demeaning and cause damage, think about how much worse it is to allow harmful conditions to continue. Harmful conditions that deny people their rights exist all around us: people living in poverty with no means to change the situation, trapped in unsafe housing, or people who don't have access to an education, health care, or a job.

People need these basic rights met in order to grow and mature. Without them, they are constantly using all of their energy merely to survive. They cannot flourish as God would want.

Raising Ourselves Up A great piece of artwork is meant to be put on display so that everyone can appreciate it and be made better by it. We are God's work of art. The human person is the pinnacle of creation.

We honor the human person, so that all might appreciate and be made better by the creative work of God among us. We avoid all the things that damage the artistry of God at work in the human person, such as overindulgence, extremism, or physical and mental intimidation. For example:

▶ abusing food, alcohol, tobacco, and drugs

▶ sacrificing everything else for the sake of physical perfection

▶ promoting success in school, popularity, and sports without considering those involved

▶ bullying

▶ sexual exploitation or manipulation of another person

▶ pornography

▶ kidnapping, hostage-taking, terrorism, and torture

Care for Others Harsh words are not the only way people harm others. Another way is to encourage others to do sinful things. Jesus warns his disciples against leading others into sin. He says, "If any of you put a stumbling block before one of these little ones who believe in me, it would be better for you if a great millstone were fastened around your neck and you were drowned in the depth of the sea" (*Matthew 18:6*).

Scandal is the name given to the destructive behavior by which we deliberately lead others to sin through our own action or inaction. For example, the sin of scandal is committed when a radio talk show host rallies his listeners to engage in racism.

Those in authority have a greater responsibility to guard against scandal. Teachers and government and business leaders must exercise care for others by not misleading and manipulating them. This special responsibility also includes lawmakers, social institutions, and those who influence public opinion because these are areas of life that can promote or hinder how we perceive and care for one another.

ACTIVITY

LIVE YOUR FAITH Think back over the last couple days and the conversations you've been involved in or overheard. What words were used to respect life? What words were used to disrespect life?

RESPECT:

DISRESPECT:

IN SUMMARY

CATHOLICS BELIEVE

As the People of God, we know that all human life is sacred and a gift from God.

▶ All people possess the human dignity that comes from being made in God's image, and we do not have the right to take that life away from others or ourselves.

▶ We have a responsibility to honor and protect life at all stages, from conception to old age.

▶ We respect the dignity of the human person by respecting the rights of others, taking care of ourselves physically and emotionally, not abusing ourselves or others, and by not leading others into sin.

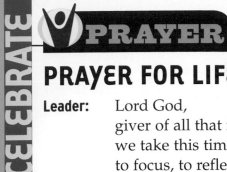

PRAYER FOR LIFE

Leader: Lord God,
giver of all that is good in our lives,
we take this time
to focus, to reflect,
and to consider the awesome gift of life.

Reader 1: You teach us to remember that all life is sacred,
that no one is better or less than the other,
that no one is undeserving of dignity and respect.

Reader 2: Help us to remember,
that it does not matter how talented we are,
how smart we are,
how popular we are,
or how beautiful or good looking we are.

Reader 1: What matters is—that we are—
that we exist,
that you have created us!

Reader 2: Help us to celebrate and show respect and honor
to everyone we meet.

Reader 1: May we be sensitive and compassionate
to those whose life is not as good or comfortable or as fortunate as ours;
to those who we see crying and suffering,
to those who are on the outside, who walk alone in the hallways,
and to all who are cast aside and sometimes invisible to us:
the elderly, the unborn, those imprisoned,
the disabled, the addict, the depressed,
those who are victims of war, abuse,
and those who are simply forgotten.

Reader 2: Help us to help them—
Help us to see them—
Help us always choose for them,
Help us to always choose life!

All: Amen.

♪ "We Choose Life"
David Haas, © 1998, GIA Publications, Inc.

REVIEW

A **Work with Words** Circle the letter of the choice that best completes the sentence.

1. _____ is always gravely sinful because it shows contempt for the dignity of human life as well as for the holiness and goodness of God, the Creator.
   a. Murder   **b.** Suicide   **c.** Venial sin   **d.** Adultery

2. _____ is deliberately ending a pregnancy on purpose by killing an unborn child.
   a. Euthanasia   **b.** Genocide   **c.** Suicide   **d.** Abortion

3. Deliberate action or nonaction that causes the death of someone who is sick, or dying, or suffering because of disabilities is called _____.
   a. euthanasia   **b.** genocide   **c.** suicide   **d.** abortion

4. Behavior or attitudes that lead others to sin are known as _____.
   a. disobedience   **b.** scandal   **c.** free will   **d.** suicide

B **Check Understanding** Complete each sentence with the correct term from the word bank at right.

5. Because humans are made in the image and likeness of God, each human _____ is sacred.

6. According to Job, humans are unique in that our very _____ comes from and is upheld by God.

7. The Fifth Commandment instructs us not to _____ another person.

8. We avoid _____ and extremism because these actions can damage the artistry of God at work in the human person.

9. Jesus warns his disciples that it would be better to drown in the sea than to lead others into _____.

10. Not only are we made by God, but we humans alone, of all creatures, also have the capacity for _____.

Word Bank
- abortion
- overindulgence
- life
- love
- breath
- kill
- sin
- self-awareness
- action
- covet
- scandal

C **Make Connections: Cause and Effect** Write a one-paragraph response to the following questions.

Choose a current issue or situation (local, national, or world wide) in which human life is being valued, respected, or protected. Who are the people involved, and what impact are their actions having on others? How can this be an example of living out the Fifth Commandment?

OUR CATHOLIC FAITH

WHAT NOW?

★ Examine the respect you have for the life that God has given to those around you.

★ Evaluate whether your conscience needs more strengthening.

★ Remind yourself that everyone is a person just like yourself and speak of them as such.

★ Don't use ethnic or racial labels.

★ Imagine yourself in the other person's place.

★ Get involved in groups that push for positive change in society, such as Walk for Life.

ACTIVITY

LIVE YOUR FAITH Think of your life as a garment. What "tears" or "holes" do you need to repair in the way you live your own life? Do your attitudes or actions toward others' lives, as well as all of life, also cause "tears"? Write your observations down on a note card to keep as a reminder to value yourself and others as God does.

My Life: _____

_____

▶ Make a list of movies, television shows, books, or songs that encourage respecting life. As a class, make a list. Discuss the items you have listed in common.

My List	Class List

GO online Visit www.osvcurriculum.com for more family and community connections.

 **PRAYER**

Lord, help me to honor the human dignity of every person I meet.

Venerable Pierre Toussaint

Pierre Toussaint's life stands out as an example of how to show our faith through our works. His generous acts are a shining example of how we, as Catholics, should live our lives in service and in prayer. As a devout layperson, he gave his life to serving the sick, the disabled, and the uneducated.

Pierre was born into slavery on the Berard family plantation in 1766. His family, parents and grandparents, were domestic slaves on the French island colony of Saint-Dominique (now Haiti). The Berard family treated their slaves more kindly than most French colonists, encouraging young Pierre to read and develop his natural musical gifts and talents.

Jean Berard, fearing that a slave revolt was coming soon, moved his family—including Pierre, Pierre's aunt, and sister Rosalie—to New York. They rented a three-story house where Pierre learned how to speak English. Eventually, he became a hairdresser.

In 1789 Jean Berard died. Pierre helped to maintain the house until Mrs. Berard's death ten years later. Meanwhile, he dutifully attended church every morning and began assisting the pastor. Just before Marie Berard died, she drew up papers granting Pierre his freedom.

Once he was free, Pierre married Juliette Noel, who had also worked in the Berard household. He also bought his sister Rosalie's freedom. When Rosalie died soon after giving birth, Pierre and Juliette became the adoptive parents of Rosalie's daughter.

Pierre worked tirelessly with the needy in New York. He raised money to build a new church (St. Peter's), open an orphanage, and start a Catholic school for black children. When yellow fever broke out, he risked infection caring for its victims. His faith kept him strong enough to help others. He often brought homeless African American boys home for a hot meal and helped them find jobs.

Once he was turned away from attending Mass at St. Peter's Cathedral because of his color. Though angered by the insult, he didn't protest. Later he received an apology from the pastor, who hadn't realized that Pierre had helped raise money to build the church. He continued to attend church regularly until he became bedridden.

Shortly before he died, a friend asked him if he wanted anything. He smiled from his sickbed and replied, "Nothing on this earth!" He died in 1853 at age eighty-seven. He was declared Venerable by Pope Saint John Paul II in 1996.

▲ Pierre Toussaint's remains are buried in the crypt below the main altar of St. Patrick's Cathedral in New York.

GLOBAL DATA

■ Haiti is the western one-third of the island of Hispaniola, between the Caribbean Sea and the Atlantic Ocean, sharing the island with the Spanish-speaking Dominican Republic.

■ Haiti was visited by Columbus in 1492 and colonized by the French in 1697, with the help of imported African slaves.

■ Haiti was the first predominantly black nation in the Western Hemisphere to win independence, following a successful revolt against French rule in 1804.

■ Haiti has a population of 9.7 million, about 80 percent of whom are Catholic.

15 BEING Virtuous

PRAYER Lord, I belong to you.

I want to stand up for what my heart tells me is important. And sometimes I want to shut up and go with the flow.

Jen's friends crowded around her as she read the letter from her agent to them. It gave the details he had promised when he called last week. "Jenny O," said Mr. Hara, "this is it! No more department store catalog modeling for you. One of *the* biggest producers in Hollywood saw your portfolio and wants you to test for a part in his next film. What a break! This will get your name out there—it's big, Jen."

Her friends were thrilled for her. They laughed and teased her chanting, "Jenny O! Jenny O!"

"You're ready for the red carpet now," her buddy Mason chuckled as they walked to class. "Have you read the script?"

"No, I should get the first draft from Mr. Hara today," she smiled. "Want to come over and help me read through?"

"Sure, see you later," Mason promised. His opinion would be great to get. Mason was the most talented actor in the school's theater group. Plus he was a great friend who'd given her good advice many times.

Later Mason and Jen settled in to read through the script. Her mom brought them a snack. "Here, 'Movie Theater' popcorn for you two," she laughed.

Jen liked what she read at first. Things changed when they got to scene 12. It called for nudity from her character! She blushed and looked up at Mason, who had stopped reading over her shoulder. "Oh, no," Jen groaned. She had secretly worried about something like this all along. "Now what?"

Mason thought a minute. "It doesn't fit with the way the plot is developing. That scene is just thrown in."

"I don't want to become a sex object; I want to act." As she continued reading, she realized the script also contained way too much cursing.

She talked to Mason and her mom about it and decided to call her agent. She explained her reaction to the script. There was silence on the other end of the line. Then, her agent promised to talk to the director, but he reminded her that a huge break could launch her career. "But not like this," she answered. "That's not the way I want to go."

ACTIVITY

LET'S BEGIN Why do you think Jen felt the way she did? Do you think her stand on nudity and language will make a difference to the producer? What advice would you give Jen?

▶ **When have you been in a situation in which getting something you really wanted also meant giving up something about your moral character?**

STRIVING FOR THE BEST

Focus How do you grow to be the person God wants you to be?

Every day brings us new opportunities and more chances to act on what we think is right. Not all the choices we face are easy, and sometimes the more popular response isn't the one that is best for us or our values. We sure aren't meant to agree to everything that crosses our path. The freedom God gives us is meant to be used for doing good. Living a good life requires practice and self-discipline. The truth is, it's not always easy.

Our Truest and Best Selves God shares his love completely with you. Your response should be just as strong and focused. By responding to God's love, you can discover and strengthen your truest, best self.

Many things contribute to who you are and who you can become, such as your individual talents, gifts, and uniqueness; your body and soul; the way you typically relate to others; and how you learn from life experiences and from others.

These things together can be a powerful force to reach your ultimate goal, to be good and holy, to be loving and welcoming, to become more like God, and to one day be with him forever.

But what does being good and holy look like? Saint Paul tells us that we are to help one another strive for those things that are most worthwhile in life.

✝ SCRIPTURE

GO TO THE SOURCE

Read **Philippians 4:13** and think about the ways God gives you the strength that you need, just as he gave it to Paul.

✝ SCRIPTURE

"Finally, beloved, whatever is true, whatever is honorable, whatever is just, whatever is pure, whatever is pleasing, whatever is commendable, if there is any excellence and if there is anything worthy of praise, think about these things."

—*Philippians 4:8*

❓ If Saint Paul were writing to you and your friends, how do you think he might word his message differently?

Helping Habits Saint Paul's list is pretty challenging! In specific situations, it is sometimes difficult to determine exactly what is true, honorable, just, and so on. All kinds of positive and negative pressures and assumptions can be at play. Some situations require us to really think through how the final outcome will impact everyone.

The virtues help us do this. A **virtue** is a strong habit of doing good that helps us make good moral decisions. Virtues guide our conduct and our emotions.

Faith, hope, and charity (love) are **theological virtues**. They are gifts from God that help us believe in him, trust in his plan for us, and love him as he loves us. We have to respond to God's gift and live out the virtues for them to be strong in our lives.

The theological virtues make the human, or moral, virtues possible. These virtues guide the way we act and feel. They help us live according to our conscience, control our passions, and deal with how we respect others and ourselves in light of our faith.

Moral virtues don't just automatically appear within us. They are cultivated—like a garden. We grow them when we learn about them and are intentional about doing them, even in the face of struggles.

God's grace gives us a boost so that we can cultivate virtue. In this way, the virtues that we are growing get strong inside us.

virtue
theological virtues
cardinal virtues
chastity
modesty
reparation

ACTIVITY

SHARE YOUR FAITH Imagine you are writing a dictionary entry for the term *virtuous*. Write your entry here.

VIRTUOUS (adj.) _____

▶ **Now describe how a virtuous person would act.**

A VIRTUOUS PERSON _____

MORAL VIRTUES

Focus What are the cardinal virtues?

If someone asked you what the word *cardinal* meant, how would you answer? You might say it's a bird, or a special name for a bishop in the Church, or maybe even a tint of the color red.

The Church uses the word *cardinal* to describe the four most important moral virtues: prudence, justice, fortitude, and temperance. They are called the **cardinal virtues**. All the other moral virtues can be grouped under them. The word *cardinal* comes from the term *cardo*, which means "hinge, that which something turns on, its principle point." So other moral virtues—such as patience, piety, gratitude, abstinence, and truth—flow from one of the four cardinal virtues.

We develop the moral virtues by responding to God's help in our lives and through our own efforts. As we learn more about life and how we should respond to different situations and as we practice the virtues in our daily lives, the moral virtues can grow in us.

The Cardinal Virtues

PRUDENCE—wise, careful, and sensible judgments in all circumstances	▶ Helps you to be aware of what's really going on in a situation ▶ Helps you see ahead to the consequences of actions
JUSTICE—giving God and others what is due to them	▶ Helps you act fairly and respect the rights of others ▶ Helps you promote equality in the way you treat others and harmony among groups of people
FORTITUDE—courage to do what is right even if others disagree with or challenge you	▶ Helps you resist temptation and be consistent in your choices and attitudes ▶ Helps you overcome obstacles to doing good
TEMPERANCE—balancing your thoughts, actions, and feelings so that your desires don't rule your life	▶ Helps you enjoy all good things in moderation ▶ Helps you practice self-control

❓ Which of the cardinal virtues do you think would help you the most right now?

❓ Which of the cardinal virtues do you find easiest to live by? Which one is hardest?

Modesty and Chastity God created males and females, and both are made in God's image and likeness. Both share in equal dignity, and both are unique to each other. The gift of human sexuality comes from God, and it is part of his plan for humans to share in his creative abilities. Your sexuality is part of who you are; it's more than whether you are biologically a male or female. It includes the way you think and feel about things, the way you pray, the way you are inclined to act, the interests you have.

The virtue of **chastity** helps you maintain the right balance of body and spirit in human sexuality. Chastity helps you express your sexuality in the right way. It helps you show love in the appropriate ways.

Chastity is not a lack or a denial. Rather, it is through chastity that we include our sexuality in a beautiful and meaningful way with all the other elements of who we are. Everyone who is baptized is called to chastity, even though Catholics have different states in life—married, single, and vowed religious. For women and men religious, this means living a celibate life. Chastity requires discipline. It won't happen overnight. It involves a long process of growth and maturity. Inner peace and wholeness are the fruits of this process.

The virtue of modesty also helps you respect your sexuality. **Modesty** is all about decency. It's about being discreet in the way you dress, the things you say (or choose not to say), and the way you handle curiosity about sexual matters.

CHECK THIS OUT!

As children of God, our connection to the Lord demands that we treat our bodies and the bodies of every other person with great respect. Extreme tattooing and body piercing are forms of disrespect toward one's body. Self-mutilation and disfigurement for the purpose of shocking others would be sinful. When the human body is so intentionally deformed, it shows disrespect for God's creation. Deforming a young body may be regretted later and have a costly price tag to repair.

ACTIVITY

CONNECT YOUR FAITH For each of the cardinal virtues, name a person who you believe exemplifies that virtue and why.

VIRTUE:	PERSON:	WHY:
PRUDENCE		
JUSTICE		
FORTITUDE		
TEMPERANCE		

THE GOOD LIFE

Focus Why should you try to live a life of virtue?

People have dreams for themselves and where they want their lives to go. Some people want to be explorers and travel to distant lands. Some people want to be great teachers, influencing others. Dreams are important. They fuel our lives. They provide the motivation for what we learn and how we grow.

Keys to Excellence In the same way, striving for excellence is fueled by virtues. They are powerful keys that help to open the doorway into a faithful, reasonable life of excellence. In that sense, they help us to follow the Ten Commandments, Jesus' Beatitudes, and his new commandment to love one another as he has loved us.

There are some behaviors that do not build up excellence in our life. The Eighth Commandment has identified some that damage our character and integrity. For example

▶ *lying*, deliberately saying false things by which we intend to deceive others

▶ *slander* or *calumny*, false words or even attitudes that maliciously injure others

▶ *revenge*, words or actions that return injury to another whom we perceive as having harmed ourselves

▶ *not living up to our promises*, behavior that shows that we are not worthy of another's trust

These behaviors are sinful. They hurt the person doing them and others. They are signs that a person is not interested in pursuing what is good and beautiful in life.

These behaviors are opposite the virtue of truth, by which a person shows that he or she is true and honest in words and actions. The virtue of truth helps people avoid being deceitful, hypocritical (saying one thing but doing another), or disguising their true intentions.

A Challenge Pursuing the good life by striving for excellence within ourselves and in our behavior does not necessarily mean that we will have it easy or that life will be comfortable. Just the opposite!

Because society does not always believe as Catholics do, you may end up frustrated that people don't get it. You may be tempted to "sit down and go with the flow." You may have to stand up for things or act in ways that your friends or acquaintances don't understand or agree with. Sometimes this will cost you. You may be laughed at or ignored because of it.

Does this sound like the life of someone you know and have learned about? Jesus faced all of these things, but we know that he was happy in the truest sense of the word. He is our model for living a life of excellence. Living a life of virtues brings true inner peace.

CHECK THIS OUT!

One reason why **poor boxes** are found in Catholic churches is so that the faithful can give to others and help others. Sometimes their gifts are given to make amends anonymously for sins against the truth, that is, lying and slander. It may not always be possible to admit to these sins directly to the one affected, so a donation can be made to the poor to make amends. Such an action of giving is one form of **reparation**—an attempt to directly or indirectly "repair" the damage done by the sin.

ACTIVITY

CONNECT YOUR FAITH Choose two of the four behaviors listed below. Think of a concrete example of that behavior that you or someone you know has encountered. Discuss how you stood up to answer this behavior (or plan to stand up next time you encounter this situation).

| lying | slander | revenge | not living up to promises made |

▶ **Behavior:**

▶ **Concrete example:**

▶ **Standing up:**

▶ **Behavior:**

▶ **Concrete example:**

▶ **Standing up:**

IN SUMMARY

CATHOLICS BELIEVE

We are called to strive for what is right, just, holy, and gracious.

▶ The virtues are strong habits of doing good that help us make good moral decisions and guide our emotions and conduct. The theological virtues make the moral, or human, virtues possible.

▶ The cardinal virtues of prudence, justice, fortitude, and temperance can help us respect ourselves and others and act with integrity.

▶ Learning about and practicing the virtues can help us live truthful, faith-filled lives.

CELEBRATE

ACT OF FAITH, HOPE, AND CHARITY

Leader: God, come to my assistance.

All: Lord, make haste to help me.

Leader: Glory to the Father, and to the Son, and to the Holy Spirit.

All: As it was in the beginning, is now, and will be forever. Amen.

Leader: God,
source of our faith, hope, and love,
give us the strength to stand firm
and be the people you call us to be,
a witness and light for all to see.

All: My God, I believe in you,
I trust in you,
I love you above all things,
with all my heart and mind and strength.
I love you because you are supremely good and worth loving;
and because I love you,
I am sorry with all my heart for offending you.

Lord, have mercy on me, a sinner. Amen.

♪ "Stand Firm"

Cameroon Trad., arr. John Bell, © 1988, Iona Community. GIA Publications, Inc.

REVIEW

A **Work with Words** Circle the letter of the choice that best completes the sentence.

1. A _____ is a strong habit of doing good that helps us make good moral decisions.
   a. virtue   **b.** discipline   **c.** sacrament   **d.** reparation

2. When we attempt to indirectly correct the damage done by sin, we are making amends or
   _____.
   a. forgiveness   **b.** virtue   **c.** reparation   **d.** justice

3. The _____ are the four most important moral virtues.
   a. theological virtues   **b.** divine virtues   **c.** cardinal virtues   **d.** lost virtues

4. The virtue of _____ is being discreet in the way you dress and the things you say.
   a. modesty   **b.** chastity   **c.** prudence   **d.** both a and c

5. The virtue of _____ helps you maintain the right balance of body and spirit in human sexuality.
   a. modesty   **b.** chastity   **c.** fortitude   **d.** prudence

B **Check Understanding** Indicate whether the following statements are true or false. Then rewrite false statements to make them true.

_____ 6. Theological virtues help us live as children of God and gain life everlasting with God.

_____

_____ 7. Prudence, justice, fortitude, and chastity are four of the most important moral virtues.

_____

_____ 8. Temperance is the courage to do what is right even if others disagree with or challenge you.

_____

_____ 9. Your sexuality affects the way you think and feel about things and the way you are inclined to act.

_____

_____ 10. The Tenth Commandment identifies lying, slander, and revenge as sins that damage our character and integrity.

_____

C **Make Connections: Analyze** Write a one-paragraph response to the question.

We should think about things that are true, honorable, just, and pure. Think about some movies, music, and magazines. How do they encourage virtue?

OUR CATHOLIC FAITH

WHAT NOW?

* Identify virtues among your friends.

* Learn more about virtuous living by studying Catholic teachings, Scriptures, and the lives of the saints.

* Learn from family members, leaders, mentors, and friends who exemplify virtuous living.

* Watch how these people handle conflict, promote healthy relationships, communicate with openness, exhibit courage, and so on.

* Make your own spiritual commitment to practice more of these virtues in a disciplined way for a period of time to help develop the "muscles" to make this virtue part of your life.

ACTIVITY

LIVE YOUR FAITH Rate Your Virtue (al) Self

▶ Examine the list of cardinal and common virtues listed below. How well would you rate yourself (on a scale of 1 to 10) in practicing each virtue? Think about things you could do to become more virtuous.

MY VIRTUE GRADE, 1–10

1. GRATITUDE ____	6. FORTITUDE ____
2. PATIENCE ____	7. TRUTH ____
3. PRUDENCE ____	8. TEMPERANCE ____
4. PIETY ____	9. ABSTINENCE ____
5. JUSTICE ____	10. KINDNESS ____

▶ Notes to myself about specific ways to become more virtuous:

_____

_____

_____

GO online Visit www.osvcurriculum.com for more family and community connections.

PRAYER

May your wisdom, Holy Spirit, give me courage to live a life of virtue.

Saint Margaret Ward

Margaret Ward followed her faith and her God so strongly that she gave her life to save the life of a condemned priest. The Bible teaches us to live a good life and be an example for others by what we do throughout our lives. Margaret Ward was one person who showed us what it means to be a faithful Catholic during difficult times. She was one of the Forty Martyrs of England and Wales.

Margaret was born in Congleton, County Cheshire. Her family was part of the English nobility. However, in order to be a practicing Catholic during the time Protestantism was taking root in England, she had to give up many of the privileges that came with nobility.

In 1588, King Philip II of Spain had sent a fleet of warships to England, hoping to conquer the island nation and bring it back to the Catholic Church, but the effort failed. English naval forces loyal to Queen Elizabeth I defeated the Spanish Armada. Because of this conflict, anti-Catholic feeling became fierce in England. Catholics were persecuted to the point of death—there were even six new gallows built in various parts of London.

Father Watson was a priest who spoke out against the persecution. As a result, he was arrested and treated brutally in Bridewell Prison. Even though a fellow clergyman said that Father Watson was bordering on insane, Margaret felt sorry for him. To her, he was a persecuted priest, and she planned to help him escape.

Gaining the favor of the guards, Margaret smuggled a rope into the prison, hiding it in a basket of food. Early the next morning, Father Watson escaped. John Roche, Margaret's servant, also helped. He found Father Watson a boat and exchanged clothes with him. Margaret and her servant were arrested when the authorities traced the rope back to her. In prison, she was strung up by her wrists so that only the tips of her toes touched the ground, causing her to become paralyzed.

Despite being tortured, both Margaret and John refused to tell authorities where Father Watson was hidden. At their trial, they were told that if they asked the queen for forgiveness and joined the Church of England, they would be pardoned. They refused, both saying they had done nothing to apologize for and that it was against their consciences to join a Protestant church. They were drawn, quartered, and hanged on August 30, 1588. Margaret Ward was canonized in 1970 by Pope Saint Paul VI.

▲ **Saint Margaret Ward was imprisoned in York Castle before being executed. The tower is all that remains of the castle.**

GLOBAL DATA

Great Britain

- Great Britain has a history dating back five centuries before Christ and was once part of the Roman Empire.

- Great Britain is an island kingdom of about 93,000 square miles (including Scotland and Wales) off the western coast of Europe.

- Great Britain has not been successfully invaded by a foreign power since the Norman Conquest in 1066.

- Until the mid-1900s, Great Britain controlled the largest empire in recorded history.

- Great Britain has a population of nearly 62 million, many of whom are Roman Catholic, although the Anglican Church is the official state religion.

DISCOVER

Catholic Social Teaching:
Solidarity of the Human Family

IN THIS UNIT you learned about the sacredness of all life and the dignity of every human person, plus the importance of advocating on behalf of others.

Solidarity

This principle of Catholic social teaching makes it clear that it's not just for those around us we should be advocating, but for people throughout the world. It is God's love of all persons that motivates us to care globally. We share in the Church's "missionary mandate" to bring the Gospel to all nations. Jean Donovan of Cleveland, Ohio, heard this missionary mandate as a young businesswoman in the mid-1970s. She left her job and family to go to El Salvador to work with the poor. Realizing that "solidarity" means sharing both spiritual goods and material goods, Jean brought both. She shared her faith and found her own faith deepened by the heroic faith of her people. Her friends in Cleveland sent material goods in response to Jean's appeals.

Each day in the midst of poverty and civil war, Jean grew in her understanding of her mission—to be the sacrificial love of Jesus for others. As the danger increased, her fiancé and family begged her to come

home. But she kept thinking about the children she cared for there. On December 2, 1980, Jean was assassinated along with three other American religious women who worked with the poor in El Salvador.

Although Jean sacrificed her life completely, you are asked to consider other ways of sacrificing in solidarity with others suffering around the world. It starts with your time—taking the time to read about others and learn their realities. It includes sharing your money, not only during Lent through Operation Rice Bowl, but year-round. And it includes your talents—writing letters to political leaders, putting together posters about the needs of the poor, and showing how others can help.

Why would Jean Donovan stay in El Salvador, especially with her fiancé asking her to come home? Explain your answer.

SOLIDARITY MEANS SEEING all human beings as part of one global community. Let's look at how one group practices solidarity.

NICARAGUA CONNECTIONS
SCHOOL SUPPLIES FOR CHILDREN

"Project Clean Your Desks" was created by the Quixote Center near Washington, DC. Since the early 1980s, elementary and secondary schools and parish schools of religion have been collecting school supplies for the children of Nicaragua. At the end of the school year, they donate unused pages from their notebooks, along with pens and pencils, markers and crayons, and other unused paper. Some students buy and donate new supplies as well.

At Notre Dame High School for Girls in Chicago, Illinois, campus minister Christie Billups invites some of her older students to promote the project. They decorate and bring boxes to each classroom. They encourage students to share their resources with others less fortunate by making announcements over the public address system, creating posters, and writing articles for the school bulletin. Each year, five to twelve boxes of supplies have been collected.

Christie's own experience has touched the hearts of many students. As she puts it, "I went to Nicaragua in 1992 and 1995 and learned that many young people were no longer able to go to school at all. I got to know a nineteen-year-old youth who was happy to get the $2 he needed to attend sixth grade. Even $2 a semester was a hardship for his family. It's so different for our students. When some of them drop a pen, sometimes they don't even bother to pick it up because they know they have a spare in their pencil pouch. My students are really moved by this example, and it helps them to remember not to take their own education for granted."

Other elementary schools, like St. Joseph's in Rosemont, Minnesota, have participated in the "Niño a Niño" program, raising $100 to send a Nicaraguan child to school for a whole year, plus wonderful after-school music and art opportunities.

? **What would it be like to be too poor to go to school?**

▼ **Some Nicaraguan children are able to attend school because of the care and concern of American students.**

SERVE   Your Community

PERSONAL/FAMILY SOLIDARITY RESPONSE

Research several groups in other countries that need help and discuss with
the rest of your family how you might be able to act in solidarity with one
or more of the groups. Decide who to help and how. Create some reminder
(e.g., a note or picture on your mirror) to pray for this group every day and
suggest that your family add a prayer for them at dinner.

CLASS SOLIDARITY RESPONSE

Research as a class a variety of groups
or programs in other countries that
could use your help. Missionary groups
like Maryknoll and the Columban
Fathers, aid groups like Catholic Relief
Services, and the USCCB Office on Social
Development and World Peace can be
very helpful in this process. Choose one
group or program and create a plan to
help. Consider sharing your plan with
other classrooms, or other groups in
your parish or local community, and
invite them to help.

Project Planning Sheet

Who else needs to be contacted about this project?

_____

How to publicize the project

_____

_____

Other specific tasks

_____

_____

Your specific task(s)

_____

_____

Calendar for completing the project

_____

_____

REFLECT | On Your Experience

What kinds of sacrifices do you think the Gospel and the needs of God's people are asking of you?

_____

_____

_____

What did you learn through your research into groups in need?

_____

_____

_____

What did you learn about yourself and about your family in doing this project?

_____

_____

_____

What did you learn about what's going on in the world in doing the research on the class project?

_____

_____

_____

What did you learn about yourself in doing this project?

_____

_____

_____

What did you learn about Jesus and about your faith in doing these projects?

_____

_____

_____

List one thing that might be different about you after doing this project. How will your life be different because of these actions?

_____

_____

A Work with Words Use the clues below to complete the crossword puzzle.

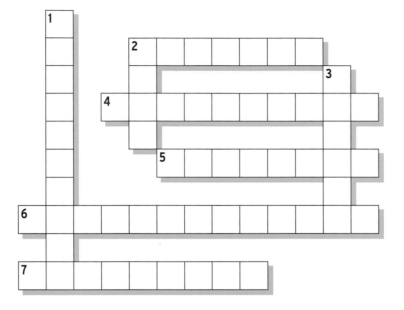

Across

2 Destructive behavior by which we deliberately lead others to sin

4 Deliberate action or nonaction that causes the death of someone who is sick, dying, or suffering

5 Virtue that helps you maintain the right balance of body and spirit in human sexuality

6 The aspect of human action that can increase or decrease its moral goodness

7 The object, the circumstances, and this are the elements included in human action.

Down

1 An attempt to indirectly correct the damage done by sin

2 Your unique combination of intellect, free will, and _____ make you an image of God.

3 A strong habit of doing good that helps you make a good moral decision

B Check Understanding Indicate whether the following statements are true or false. Then rewrite false statements to make them true.

_____ **9.** Your free will is the spiritual principle that reflects God in you.

_____

_____ **10.** The effect of venial sin, without repenting and being forgiven, is total separation from God forever.

_____

_____ **11.** If a conscience has been formed well, it will lead you to what is truthful and just.

_____

_____ **12.** Each human thought is sacred because humans are made in the image and likeness of God.

_____

_____ **13.** The Fifth Commandment instructs us not to kill another person.

_____

_____ **14.** We humans, alone of all creatures, have the capacity for self-awareness.

_____

_____ **15.** The theological virtues are the most important moral virtues.

_____

_____ **16.** The virtue of chastity is being discreet in the way you dress and the things you say.

_____

_____ **17.** Prudence, justice, fortitude, and temperance are four of the most important moral virtues.

_____

_____ **18.** Prudence is the courage to do what is right even if others disagree with or challenge you.

_____

C **Make Connections** Write a short answer to these questions.

19. **Analyze.** Choose a popular television show, movie, or book whose characters struggle with Eighth Commandment issues. What are the issues, how do the characters choose to act, and what is the impact of their actions?

_____

_____

20. **Interpret.** All human life is sacred. What implications does this statement have for your relationships with others—friends, family, neighbors, and strangers?

_____

_____

16 CHRIST with Us

INVITE

PRAYER Open my heart to experience your grace.

Some traditions I never want to stop.
I don't care if they seem silly or other people don't get it.
Somehow . . . a good tradition helps your heart.

"**O**h, come on. I want to see this movie today. Everyone is talking about it. Why can't you come? Your mom can put up decorations without you, can't she?"

Maya's friend Brianna had been begging her to come to the movie today for about five minutes. Maya tried to explain why she wanted to be home today, but Brianna wasn't getting it. No, her mom didn't actually need her help to put up Christmas decorations. But Maya wouldn't miss being there for anything— not even to see the latest movie with her best friend.

It had been a tradition for as long as Maya could remember. Her family set aside one day in December to put up Christmas decorations together. Opening all the boxes of ornaments made over the years was special. Each brought back a different memory. There was the ornament from kindergarten—the lamb made with cotton balls. And the one she and her dad had made together just last year—it looked like a stained-glass window.

This year, her family would start the day as they always did. Each person—Mom, Dad, Maya, and her brother, Manuel—would make a new ornament. Then they would put all the lights and ornaments on the tree. Maya would probably have to give Manuel some advice about which ornaments should go where—and he would probably argue with her. But in the end, they would have a beautiful tree.

Maya's favorite moment was when her dad would take out the nativity scene and set up the manger. Then each person would take turns placing a figure in the scene. With the full scene in place, her dad would read the Christmas story. As he read, Maya could almost see herself there the night Jesus was born. It might seem crazy, but it made Christmas feel so real. Plus, it made her family feel so close. It was a real moment that seemed to touch something more than real.

"No, Brianna. Not today." The movie would have to wait.

ACTIVITY

LET'S BEGIN Why is it important to Maya to be there for her family's Christmas tradition?

▶ **What traditions do you have with family or friends that are special to you? Why do you think traditions are important? What Church traditions are especially meaningful for you?**

_____

_____

_____

_____

IT ALL STARTS WITH JESUS

Focus How is Jesus the source of the sacraments?

The best traditions are always about the people who keep the traditions alive with us. Sometimes a great tradition involves food or special events that come around only once a year.

If you ever made a card or present for your parents when you were a child, someone else probably provided the materials, cleaned up, and helped you wrap.

It is the same way with Christ's presence in his Church and our experience of grace, which is God's help in coming to know and love him. We receive this gift of grace directly from God. There is nothing we can do to earn it.

The Sacraments Although every good work is a work of the Church, the Church celebrates seven "masterworks of God": the seven sacraments. The **sacraments** are effective signs of God's grace given to the Church by Christ.

We, the People of God,

▶ perform the rituals (read, process, sing, anoint)

▶ provide the materials (plant wheat and grapes, sew priestly vestments, order hosts and candles)

▶ participate in the celebration (choir practice, seminary training, lector workshops)

We do these things to praise God and give him thanks, as well as our selves. Yet God took the initiative in sending his Son. We are totally dependent upon God in the celebration of the sacraments.

So where do we begin to understand the sacraments? We start with Jesus Christ. He is the first sacrament. He makes God known to us perfectly because he is God. Jesus said, "Whoever has seen me has seen the Father" (*John 14:9*). Jesus is the perfect mediator between God and humanity, because he is fully God and fully man. So his actions have the power to save—whether it is healing a lame man or carrying his cross. His whole life from his Incarnation to the sending of his Spirit is sacramental: it shows us God, shares God's life with us, and is the source of our salvation and new life.

Through Jesus, we have access to God the Father and God the Holy Spirit; from him, we receive God's help in becoming his children.

The Church Is Sign and Source of God's Life

Our tradition of the sacraments always starts with remembering the works of God the Father, and being thankful, and celebrating Christ's presence. God the Holy Spirit helps us remember all that Christ said and did, and everything he taught about God the Father. In fact, the Holy Spirit, working with the Church, makes Jesus' saving work present in the sacraments. Through the power of the Holy Spirit working in us and in the Church, we not only remember what brings us new life, but that new life is made available to us. The Holy Spirit unites us to the Son of God, drawing us into relationship with the Father as his adopted children.

In this way, the Church herself is a "sacrament of Christ's action at work in her through the mission of the Holy Spirit" (*Catechism of the Catholic Church*, 1118). The Church is a sign of God's love and action in the world.

SCRIPTURE

GO TO THE SOURCE
Read **John 14:1–10**. What does Jesus say about God's works?

ACTIVITY

SHARE YOUR FAITH Place the sacraments in the categories below. Then name one thing you know about each.

Anointing of the Sick	*Baptism*	*Matrimony*
Holy Orders	*Eucharist*	*Reconciliation*
Confirmation		

Sacraments of Initiation	**Sacraments of Healing**	**Sacraments at the Service of Communion**

THE FOUNDATION OF THE SACRAMENTS

Focus How did Jesus institute the sacraments?

At Pentecost, the twelve Apostles became certain that they had to tell the Good News of Jesus. They knew they now had the strength from the Holy Spirit to

▶ carry out Jesus' command to teach and baptize,

▶ remember him in the breaking of the bread,

▶ continue his work of forgiving and healing.

All the sacraments are rooted in the life of Jesus and show us something about him and eternal life. They each draw us into Christ's Paschal mystery, connecting us to his suffering and his rising to new life. Through the work of the Holy Spirit we are made more like Jesus. We share in the divine life so that we can have the hope of life forever with God. Jesus wanted future believers to know him as his first followers did. This is why he told the Apostles to baptize, break bread, forgive, heal, and bless in his name. Jesus did not leave manuals with his Apostles, nor did he dictate the words and symbols to be used in each sacrament. In the Bible, we will find the attitudes and actions of Jesus that are still those of the Church today expressed in the sacraments.

✝ SCRIPTURE

GO TO THE SOURCE

Read:

John 2:1–11	Matthew 8:1–4
Matthew 16:19	Luke 22:4–20
John 21:15–17	Acts 2:1–4
Matthew 28:15–20	

Which passage goes with which action or attitude of Jesus in the chart below?

✝ SCRIPTURE

Read the scripture passages in the "Go to the Source" above. Choose the Scripture that goes with the corresponding action and sacrament of Jesus to complete the chart below.

Actions, Attitudes	Sacrament That Reflects Jesus	Scripture Passage
Jesus told Apostles to make disciples of all nations.	Baptism	
The Holy Spirit filled Jesus' Apostles with his Gifts so they could continue Jesus' work.	Confirmation	
Jesus ate the Passover meal as his Last Supper with his disciples.	Holy Eucharist	
Jesus turned water to wine at a wedding feast.	Holy Matrimony	
Jesus asked Peter to tend his sheep.	Holy Orders	
Jesus gave Peter the keys to the kingdom.	Reconciliation	
Jesus healed a leper.	Anointing of the Sick	

Following Jesus' Command On the day of Pentecost the Apostles baptized nearly three thousand new believers. From Jerusalem they went out to share the message of Jesus.

Everywhere the Apostles and disciples went, the Holy Spirit worked through them to establish the Church in small Christian groupings. They had to fit in houses when they gathered to celebrate the Eucharist in the evening after their day of work. They would gather for a potluck meal followed by *eucharistia*, "giving thanks" with bread and wine in memory of Jesus. They still followed the Law of Moses and worshipped in the synagogues on the Sabbath. They were like the other Jews, but they believed in the Risen Lord.

As people spread the Good News, they settled in other areas like Antioch, where "the disciples were first called 'Christians'" (*Acts 11:26*). The Gentiles—people of non-Jewish cultures—who became believers there wanted to be baptized as well. Eventually Christianity became a separate religion.

The Roman Emperor Constantine issued the Edict of Milan in A.D. 313, which permitted Christians to celebrate their religion. Sunday became a day of rest, and Christians celebrated Eucharist on Sunday mornings. Christians began to shape the Lord's Day; more importantly, the Lord's Day began to shape them. Their daily lives and family traditions began to change to respond to their desire to be a serious part of their Church community.

WHERE IT HAPPENED

AS THE ROMAN EMPIRE grew too large for one ruler to oversee, it was divided into two empires. Byzantium (later named Constantinople) became the center of the eastern empire. Milan became the center of the west. In A.D. 313, Constantine, together with Licinius, the emperor of the east, issued the Edict of Milan that legalized Christianity. When Constantine eventually defeated Licinius in battle over territory, Milan became a stronghold of the new religion.

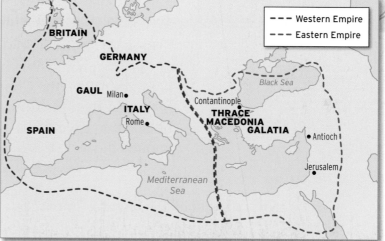

--- Western Empire
--- Eastern Empire

BRITAIN
GERMANY
GAUL Milan•
ITALY
Rome•
SPAIN
Black Sea
Contantinople•
THRACE
MACEDONIA GALATIA
•Antioch
Jerusalem•
Mediterranean Sea

ACTIVITY

CONNECT YOUR FAITH To be a eucharistic person, show gratitude to God and others. Add thanks to your daily prayer. Also express your thankfulness this week in a card, e-mail, or spoken word to persons who have helped you. Write a prayer of thanks or list the people you want to express your thanks to this week.

WHEN THE CHURCH ACTS, CHRIST ACTS

⦿ Focus How is Christ present today when we worship?

God created us to be human, so he knew that we really needed "stuff" to touch and smell and taste and count and hear. The seven sacraments involve symbols and rituals that we can see, touch, hear, taste, and smell. They help us grasp an invisible God who's hard to connect with sometimes.

▶ You taste the Host,

▶ smell the fragrance of incense,

▶ feel the touch of the chrism oil,

▶ hear the words spoken and sung,

▶ and see the light of a candle's flame and the faces of the assembly gathered to pray.

Through our senses, we know the presence of Christ. To receive a sacrament is to meet Christ.

Because Christ is present, he is acting in the celebration of the sacraments. When the Church baptizes, Christ baptizes! When the Church witnesses a marriage, Christ is there! When the Church forgives sins, the power of God's forgiveness is right there! When the Church anoints the sick, it is like Jesus curing the sick of his day.

CHRIST'S PRESENCE IN THE LITURGY

Assembly ▶ Day after day the main place where we meet Christ is in the baptized members of the community.

▶ Next Sunday, look around at the assembled congregation to see the face of Christ.

Priest ▶ The priest gathers our prayers and leads our sacrifice of praise.

▶ Next Sunday, when the priest says, "Let us pray," think of your needs.

Word ▶ When the Gospel is read, it is Christ who speaks to his People.

▶ Next Sunday, let the responsorial psalm and Gospel Acclamation show your belief that Christ is truly present in his Word.

Eucharist ▶ Most importantly Christ is uniquely present under the forms of consecrated bread and wine.

▶ Next Sunday, really mean your "Amen," and then know "you are what you received," as Saint Augustine reminded us.

LOOKING BACK

Jesus was Jewish, and he followed the Jewish traditions of prayer and worship. He celebrated great feasts like Passover. The Apostles were also Jewish; so were many of the first people who came to believe in Jesus.

It's not surprising that the rituals that they would use to remember the presence of the Risen Lord would sound and look like the traditions of their Jewish culture. Here are some connections between the Jewish liturgy and our Christian liturgy:

▶ At the Jewish synagogue service, the Torah is read and reflected upon. As the early Christians gathered, it was only natural to read Scripture. Maybe they even read a letter they just received from Peter or Paul! The structure of proclaiming and responding to the Word of God is now part of the Mass called the Liturgy of the Word.

▶ Some Jewish prayers (*berakoth*) begin with the word "Blessed." Blessing God, calling him Blessed, is a significant part of our prayers, especially in the liturgy. We often say "Blessed be God for ever." During the beginning of the part of the Mass called the Liturgy of the Eucharist, we hear the word "blessed."

▶ As part of their Jewish background, the Apostles and early Christians would have been quite accustomed to celebrating the weekly feast of the Sabbath from sundown Friday to sundown Saturday. Sacred time became part of the Christian faith, too. Christians shifted to celebrating the weekly feast on Sundays—the day of the Resurrection and thus the Lord's Day—by breaking bread, discussing Scriptures, and honoring the Lord.

ACTIVITY

LIVE YOUR FAITH What is your favorite religious tradition? Explain why it appeals to you.

_____

_____

_____

IN SUMMARY

CATHOLICS BELIEVE

We know that Christ continues to be with us and take care of us in the sacraments.

▶ Christ is the first sacrament because he makes God known to us and makes it possible for us to share in God's life. The Church is a sacrament because in it we come to know God and share in his life through the seven sacraments.

▶ Christ instituted the sacraments so that we would always know and experience his welcoming, forgiving, healing, and nourishing power.

▶ Christ is present in the sacraments, through the assembly gathered, the priest presiding, the Scripture proclaiming, and most especially in the Eucharist, his Body and Blood.

CELEBRATE

PRAYER OF LONGING

Leader: Let us begin with the Sign of the Cross.
In faith and in hope we gather here this day,
longing to be active members of your Church, the Body of Christ.
So let us pray,

Reader 1: O God,
we long to hear all your stories, the "good news" of our faith.

Leader: Listen, as Saint Paul tells us there is a place for us in the body of Christ.

A reading from the letter of Paul to the people of Corinth.
Read 1 Corinthians 12:12–27.

The word of the Lord.

All: Thanks be to God.

Reader 2: Father,
we long to be led by your Son, our teacher,
and shepherd.

Reader 3: We long to dine at your table
to share in the feast.
We long to see your Son, present among us.

Leader: We, your newest generation, long to be a part
of the Body of Christ;
to be involved, included, and active members,
who go forth and serve you by serving the poor.
Who share with all people just how much you love us,
how you have saved us, and how much we
love you in return.

We ask this prayer through Christ our Lord,
and brother.

All: Amen.

♪ "Present Among Us"
David Haas, © 2003, GIA Publications, Inc.

224

REVIEW

A Work with Words Complete each sentence with the correct term from the word bank at right.

Word Bank

mediator
counselor
salvation
grace
Baptism
sacraments
Ascension
miracles
Pentecost
the Gospel

1. Through _____ we freely receive God's help in coming to know and love him.

2. _____ are effective signs of God's grace given to the Church by Christ.

3. Jesus is the perfect _____ between God and humanity, because he is fully God and fully man.

4. The Church, a means to _____, is a visible community in the world.

5. On _____ the Holy Spirit descended unto the Apostles and filled them with his Gifts.

B Check Understanding Circle the letter of the choice that best completes the sentence.

6. Jesus' whole life is _____ because it is the source of our salvation and new life.
   a. sacramental   c. holy
   b. tradition   d. mysterious

7. The Church is like a _____ because she is a sign of God's love and action in the world.
   a. Sacramental Spirit   c. Memory of the Church
   b. Power of the Church d. Sacrament of the Church

8. Christ is present in the liturgy in the _____.
   a. word   c. Eucharist
   b. assembly   d. all of the above

9. The seven sacraments use _____ that we can see, touch, hear, taste, and smell.
   a. symbols   c. prayers
   b. rituals   d. a, b, and c

10. Christian liturgy is rooted in the _____ traditions of prayer and worship.
    a. disciples'   c. Gentile
    b. Jewish   d. Church

C Make Connections: Interpret Write a one-paragraph response to the question.

Name the seven "masterworks of God." What role have these celebrations had in your family?

OUR CATHOLIC FAITH

WHAT NOW?

★ Be open to the grace you experience through the sacraments.

★ Recognize grace in your everyday life—in good times and difficult times.

★ Give thanks for the moments of grace God sends you.

★ Keep investing the time and effort in the traditions of your life that "help our heart."

★ Tell those involved how much you appreciate the tradition you share with them.

★ Don't be afraid to start a new tradition that helps you "give thanks" or sustain your spirit. Even if you have to do it alone.

ACTIVITY

LIVE YOUR FAITH Mnemonic devices are ways to remember facts for tests. Here are some mnemonic devices to remember that God's grace is always with you.

▶ Associate God's presence with an object you often see, like a watch, clock, door, or book. When you see this object, remember that God is with you. Perhaps you could say a prayer that uses the object; for example, when glancing at the time, you might say, "God, I give you my time. Help me to use it well."

▶ Place a Bible on your pillow. Before you sleep, read a paragraph. When you make your bed, read another. Think about these passages during the day.

▶ Place a small stone in your pocket. When you feel it, remember that God is your rock. (Remove the stone before laundering!)

▶ Sometimes turn off the radio or CD in the car or your bedroom. Let God speak to you in the silence.

▶ Go five minutes early to Sunday Mass. Thank God for all the blessings of the past week.

▶ When you take a swim, go for a walk, or run, imagine that God is joining you. Use it as your private time with God.

In the space below, create some personal ways for you to remember the presence of God's grace in your daily life.

_____

_____

_____

_____

GO online Visit www.osvcurriculum.com for more family and community connections.

 **PRAYER**

God, help me see your grace in the world around me.

Saint Ludmilla

Receiving the sacraments is one of the greatest gifts of our faith. When we receive them, it is our way of receiving Christ into our hearts and our lives. In the United States today, we receive these sacrments openly. However, there are places in the world where practicing Christian faith means risking family, home, and life. Persecution faced by some in the world today is similar to the persecution Saint Ludmilla and many others like her faced in their time.

In the early Middle Ages in Europe, paganism was widespread. Persecution of Christians was common. It took great courage to keep the faith, but Saint Ludmilla was one of those who remained firm in her beliefs.

Saint Ludmilla was born around A.D. 860 in Bohemia, which is part of the Czech Republic today. In her time it was an independent kingdom, and she was married to Boriwoi, the first Christian Duke of Bohemia. The couple was baptized in 871 by Saint Methodius. They founded the first Christian church in Prague and tried to spread Christianity throughout Bohemia. Pagans who were hostile to Christianity drove them from their throne, but they soon returned. They reigned for another seven years, but then they gave up the throne to their sons.

Their second son, Wratislaw, was married to a woman named Drahomira. She pretended to be a Christian but secretly practiced pagan rituals. One of Wratislaw and Drahomira's twin sons, Wenceslaus, lived for a time with Ludmilla. She taught her grandson Christianity and the importance of experiencing Christ through the sacraments. (Wenceslaus later became a saint himself.) When Wratislaw died in 916, eight-year-old Wenceslaus took his place. Because he was so young, Drahomira set herself up as Regent, to rule until Wenceslaus became an adult.

Jealous of the relationship between Ludmilla and Wenceslaus, Drahomira conspired to have Ludmilla murdered. She hired some noblemen to kill Ludmilla, and they strangled her with her own veil. However, despite her cruel death, Ludmilla's legacy of faith lived on through her grandson. Wenceslaus spread Christianity throughout Bohemia, where it remains a major religion today. He is celebrated in the song "Good King Wenceslaus," and Ludmilla is venerated as one of the Patron Saints of Bohemia.

▲ *The Virgin and Child with Saint Ludmilla and Other Saints*, by Theodoricus of Prague (c. 1359–1381)

GLOBAL DATA

Czech Republic

- The Czech Republic consists of two major regions: Bohemia, which makes up two-thirds of the country, and Moravia, which accounts for the other one-third.

- The Czech Republic has a population of 10.2 million, 38 percent of whom are Catholic.

- The Czech Republic has an ancient history, dating back to the early Middle Ages, and its capital of Prague was an important cultural center of Europe.

- The Czech Republic was part of the Republic of Czechoslovakia from 1918 through 1993 when it split into the Czech Republic and Slovakia. It was under the communist rule of the Soviet Union from 1948 to 1989.

INITIATION in Christ

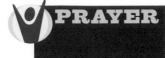

PRAYER God, help me to find my place in your Church.

*I want to be a part of something bigger,
something that makes a difference.
Should I just make my own way?
Or do I join a bigger group and make a bigger contribution?*

"**N**ow, we wait," David's mom had said as she dropped the envelope in the mailbox last spring. They had worked together for days to get his application for McNicholas High School ready. David hoped, really hoped, he would be able to start ninth grade there. His sister and two brothers had gone before him, so it was like a family tradition.

The following weeks of waiting to hear from McNicholas crawled by very slowly. Finally, a letter came. David opened it and read out loud to the family: "We are looking forward to seeing you in the fall." Everyone started talking and laughing at once. "Watch out for Mrs. Kuntz," said his brother. "She's tough." His mom was talking about school uniforms. And his dad was already talking about tryouts for the track team. Later, the family had a little party to celebrate.

In the summer, David enrolled at the school. "One step closer," he thought. He had been really looking forward to this. But doubts started to crowd in. "Will I fit in?" "Can I do the work?" "Will I make new friends there?"

On the first day of school, David felt nervous, but he tried to hide it. At breakfast, it had been hard to eat his cereal. He gave up on it and grabbed his backpack. "Well, here we go," he thought.

At school, the entire student body surged down the hall toward the auditorium. The school year always started with an acceptance ceremony for freshmen. The principal welcomed them, and someone read aloud from Scripture. Other people gave speeches. David looked around. He imagined his brothers and sisters sitting there. Someday, he'd be able to talk about his high school memories the way they did.

He was becoming a part of something more than a school. He felt a part of something bigger—a part of the other kids sitting around him, a part of the values and traditions of McNicholas that were supposed to prepare him for the things life would throw at him. David let out a quiet breath. "Finally, I'm home."

ACTIVITY

LET'S BEGIN Why do you think that David felt that he was finally "home"? Do you think he would have had the same feeling if there wasn't a freshman acceptance ceremony? Explain.

▶ **When in your life have you experienced a real sense of belonging? Did someone do something to make you feel that way, or were there special ceremonies that helped you feel like you belonged?**

▶ **What helps you to feel at "home" with your family? With your friends? With God?**

BAPTISM

Focus What does Baptism do?

Like David, we all want to get to that place where we feel we have made it "home." "Home" for David was the high school he had been longing to go to for years. Spiritually, your faith finds its "home" in the Church. It is that place where your soul can find what it has been longing for.

The Church welcomes new members through the Sacraments of Initiation. These sacraments are about beginnings and belonging. Through them you are initiated into a relationship with Christ and the Church. **Baptism** begins your new life, **Confirmation** strengthens it, and **Eucharist** feeds Christ's life within you so that you can follow him. The Sacraments of Initiation can be received all at once, over a few years, or over a longer period of time. But no matter when they are celebrated, Baptism is always first.

How did Baptism begin the process of bringing you "home"?

✝ SCRIPTURE

GO TO THE SOURCE
Read **Galatians 3:26–28** to find out what else Saint Paul says about Baptism.

IN BAPTISM

A participation in the Paschal mystery—dying to sin and rising to new life—and new identity as belonging to Christ, "As many of you as were baptized into Christ have clothed yourselves with Christ" (*Galatians 3:27*)

Forgiveness of original sin and any personal (actual) sins that may have been committed

A new relationship with Christ as his sister or brother and a new connection to God the Father as his adopted child

The Gift of the Holy Spirit that incorporates the person into the Body of Christ, the Church

A share in the mission of Jesus as priest, prophet, and royalty in God's Kingdom

A special seal or character that blesses the person to worship. This character is permanent and, because of it, the sacrament cannot be repeated

What Happens In the Sacrament of Baptism, the person baptized is immersed in water three times—or has water poured over the head three times—while the priest or deacon says, "I baptize you in the name of the Father, and of the Son, and of the Holy Spirit. Amen" (*The Order of Baptism of Children,* no. 60).

Baptism is God's gift to us; its grace does not require any action on our part. So, Baptism is open to anyone: infant, young child, teen, or adult. In fact, since the earliest times, infants have been baptized in the faith of the Church. In the Baptism of an infant or young child, the parents and godparents agree to bring up the child in the faith.

RCIA In the early years of the Church, there were many adults who chose to become members of the Church. Often they, and their families, would celebrate all three Sacraments of Initiation at one time.

Today nonbaptized men, women, and older children, and those who are baptized from non-Catholic faiths, are initiated in a process lasting several months to two years called the Rite of Christian Initiation of Adults (RCIA). They prepare to receive all three sacraments at the same celebration, usually during the Easter Vigil.

RCIA has several stages:

▶ a time of inquiry in which the person can get to know about the Church and see if they want to learn more

▶ a time for formation and information involving weekly classes. Nonbaptized candidates are called "catechumens (learners)"

▶ the catechumens are now called "the elect" to show that they are preparing for the Easter sacraments of initiation

▶ celebration of the sacraments of initiation

▶ mystagogy, a period of fifty days during which the newly baptized, called "neophytes," reflect on the mysteries of the sacraments, what the celebration meant to them, and how they can live out their faith

CHAPTER
Words *of* Faith

Baptism

Confirmation

Eucharist

transubstantiation

CHECK THIS OUT!

Symbols in Baptism:

▶ **Water** is a sign of cleansing and birth, like the waters God first created.

▶ **Chrism** is a reminder that God has chosen and called each one to be his own.

▶ **The candle and its light** are signs that Christ is the Light of the World and that all who are baptized are called to be the light of Christ to others.

▶ **The white clothing** is a sign of being purified and being clothed in Christ to imitate him and put on his ways.

SHARE YOUR FAITH When do you feel most welcomed by the Church? Explain your answer to a partner.

CATHOLICS TODAY

CONFIRMATION

Focus What happens during Confirmation?

In Baptism persons are "christened," meaning they receive Christ the Anointed One (Greek: *Christos*). In Confirmation there is another very similar anointing, in which we grow in our relationship with the Anointed One and his Spirit. Blessed, scented oil called "chrism" is used in both sacraments.

The Effects of Confirmation:

▶ a deepening and perfection of the life of God in us, which we first received in Baptism

▶ a special outpouring of the Holy Spirit, which increases the Gifts of the Holy Spirit already working in us

▶ a strengthening of our relationship with God as his adopted children and our unity with Christ

▶ a perfection of our connection with the Church

▶ a special strengthening by the Holy Spirit to take part in the mission of the Church, to show others by our words and actions that we are Christians, and to tell others about the Good News of Jesus

At Confirmation, the bishop (or his priest representative) extends his hands over the candidates and prays that the Holy Spirit will come upon them as a Helper and a Guide. Then, taking chrism, he anoints each person on the forehead, which is done by the laying on of the hands, saying, "[Candidate's name], be sealed with the Gift of the Holy Spirit" (*The Order of Confirmation*, no. 27). Like Baptism, Confirmation leaves a spiritual character on the soul. This means that the sacrament can be received only once.

How is the Holy Spirit present in your life now? As a guide? Protector? Comforter? Teacher? What role does the Spirit play in your journey of faith?

An Ongoing Journey The early Church did not practice infant Baptism. Nor was Confirmation separated from Baptism for several hundred years. The term itself wasn't used until the fifth century. In the early Church the bishop laid his hands on the candidates' heads during the Easter Vigil and then anointed them as part of a "total package" of initiation. We know that Confirmation simply *confirms*, publicly shows or seals Baptism, deepening its effects, no matter when it's received.

Being Christ in our world today requires constant conversion. Every week we meet situations that demand more sacrifice, less anger, greater patience, or more stretching in outreach to those in need. No one sacrament on any one day will magically "do the trick," but all sacraments (as well as prayer, service, and other forms of discipleship) give us help along the way.

It's important to understand that the sacraments are not "things" we deserve or earn. Confirmation is not a reward for attending classes and performing hours of service. It's not a graduation ceremony at the end of religious education. It's not a "second Baptism." Confirmation and all the other sacraments are ritual moments that express our ongoing faith. We live the life of Christ 24/7. Whatever we do is a way to live the life of Christ, and that's the really important thing.

ACTIVITY

CONNECT YOUR FAITH How can the Gifts of the Holy Spirit—wisdom, understanding, knowledge, courage, right judgment, reverence, wonder, and awe (also called "fear of the Lord")—help you on your journey of faith? Select the gifts of the Spirit that you would like to grow in, and briefly explain why you think it will help you.

GIFT: _____

GIFT: _____

GIFT: _____

EUCHARIST

Focus What does it mean to eat at the Lord's Table?

Baptism and Confirmation are once-in-a-lifetime sacraments, but we are offered the benefits of the Eucharist over and over again throughout our lives. We need food for the journey, nourishment for the soul through listening to the Scripture and through receiving Holy Communion. This is so important that we are welcomed to take part in daily Mass along with our obligation to attend Sunday Mass.

You've probably heard the saying "You are what you eat." That's why it's important to care about a healthful diet. The food you eat today is becoming you in a true physical way. In Holy Communion, we receive the Body and Blood of Christ and become what we eat—the Body of Christ, the Church.

The Parts of the Mass

▶ We begin with the Introductory Rites, prayers and songs of thanksgiving to God the Father for all of his gifts, especially his Son. This part of the Mass gathers us together and prepares us to hear God's word.

▶ The first main part of the Mass is the *Liturgy of the Word*. This includes readings from the Scripture, usually from both the Old and New Testaments, and always from the Gospels. We also profess the Creed and offer prayers in the Prayer of the Faithful.

▶ The second main part of the Mass is the *Liturgy of the Eucharist*—the recalling of what Jesus said and did at the Last Supper:

THIS IS MY BODY,
WHICH WILL BE GIVEN UP FOR YOU …
THIS IS THE CHALICE OF MY BLOOD …

and the words of the priest and blessing of the Holy Spirit so that the wheat bread and grape wine are consecrated and become the Body and Blood of Christ. For the invitation to the Table of the Lord and reception of Holy Communion, you must be free from serious sin before receiving, so it might be necessary to receive the Sacrament of Penance before Mass.

▶ In the Concluding Rites, we are sent out in peace to announce the Gospel by our words and actions.

The most important aspect of the Mass is Jesus' presence in the Eucharist. During the consecration, in the Liturgy of the Eucharist, through the words and actions of the priest, and by the power of the Holy Spirit, the bread and wine become the Body and Blood of Christ. This change is called **transubstantiation**. Jesus is truly present under the appearances of bread and wine. This is not just a memorial of what Jesus offered to us; Jesus' sacrifice is made present and we are given the gift of his life.

Living Out the Eucharist

The Eucharist has powerful effects in our lives. It:

▶ increases our union with the Lord

▶ forgives venial sins and helps us avoid serious sin

▶ makes our connection with others stronger and supports the unity of all the members of the Church

▶ inspires us to self-sacrifice and commits us to caring for the needs of others

Jesus taught us that all are welcome to his table—especially those who are neglected, the outcasts, and those in need of healing. The table that Jesus creates is a model for our Church. The connection between Eucharist and social justice is real. After we are fed at the Lord's Table, we must go out and feed others with our generosity, talent, service, and resources.

✝ SCRIPTURE

GO TO THE SOURCE
Divide the following Scripture texts among your group. See how Jesus accepted everyone at his table. **Luke 15:1–2; Luke 19:1–10; Luke 22:21–23; Matthew 9:9–13.**

ACTIVITY

LIVE YOUR FAITH What are some ways you "feed" people by sharing your time and gifts and satisfying their hunger for love and attention? What are some ways you could feed people by helping to take care of their physical needs for food, shelter, or clothing?

IN SUMMARY

CATHOLICS BELIEVE

As Christ first welcomed and fed his followers, we are welcomed and belong to the Church through the three Sacraments of Initiation.

▶ In Baptism, the first sacrament, we celebrate new life in Christ through the forgiveness of sins and incorporation into the Church.

▶ In Confirmation, the spiritual life received in Baptism is strengthened and we are sealed with the Gift of the Holy Spirit so that we can live out our journey of faith.

▶ In the Eucharist, the sacrament that we celebrate regularly, we are fed with the Body and Blood of Christ and are brought closer to Christ and one another.

RENEWAL OF BAPTISMAL PROMISES

Leader: On the day of your Baptism, your family and the Church claimed you for Christ. By water and the Holy Spirit you received the gifts of faith and new life. On that day your family and the members of the parish remembered their baptismal promises and professed their faith. Let us now do the same.

Leader: Do you reject Satan?

All: I do.

Leader: And all his works?

All: I do.

Leader: And all his empty promises?

All: I do.

Leader: Do you believe in God, the Father almighty, creator of heaven and earth?

All: I do.

Leader: Do you believe in Jesus Christ, his only Son, our Lord,
who was born of the Virgin Mary,
was crucified, died, and was buried,
rose from the dead,
and is now seated at the right hand of the Father?

All: I do.

Leader: Do you believe in the Holy Spirit,
the holy catholic Church, the communion of saints,
the forgiveness of sins, the resurrection of the body,
and life everlasting?

All: I do.

Leader: This is our faith. This is the faith of the Church.
We are proud to profess it, in Christ Jesus
our Lord.

All: Amen.

Rite of Baptism for Children, 57–59

♪ "I Say 'Yes' Lord" / "Digo 'Sí' Señor"
Donna Peña, © 1989, GIA Publications, Inc.

REVIEW

A **Work with Words** Circle the letter of the choice that best completes the sentence.

1. In _____ a person experiences a rising to new life and new identity as belonging to Christ.
   - **a.** Baptism
   - **b.** Eucharist
   - **c.** Confirmation
   - **d.** Church

2. We receive the Body and Blood of Christ during the Sacrament of _____.
   - **a.** Baptism
   - **b.** Eucharist
   - **c.** Confirmation
   - **d.** Initiation

3. _____ is the changing of bread and wine into the Body and Blood of Christ.
   - **a.** Confirmation
   - **b.** Salvation
   - **c.** Transubstantiation
   - **d.** Transfiguration

4. One of the effects of _____ is that we experience a special outpouring of the Holy Spirit, which increases the Gifts of the Holy Spirit already working in us.
   - **a.** Baptism
   - **b.** Eucharist
   - **c.** Confirmation
   - **d.** Pentecost

B **Check Understanding** Complete each sentence with the correct terms from the word bank at right.

Word Bank

Initiation
venial sins
Invitation
Chrism
mystagogy
Baptism
spiritual character
Last Supper
candle

5. The Church welcomes new members through the Sacraments of _____.

6. In Baptism, the _____ is a reminder that God has chosen and called each one to be his own.

7. The Rite of Christian Initiation of Adults ends with _____, a period of fifty days during which the newly baptized reflect on the mysteries of the sacraments.

8. As in Baptism, the person confirmed receives a _____ on one's soul.

9. During the Liturgy of the Eucharist, we remember what Jesus said and did at the _____.

10. The Eucharist forgives _____ and helps us avoid serious sin.

C **Make Connections: Evaluate** Write a one-paragraph response to the question.

Which part of the celebration of the Eucharist is most meaningful for you? Explain your answer.

OUR CATHOLIC FAITH

WHAT NOW?

★ **Think about the groups you belong to** and let them know your membership is important to you.

★ **Identify the Gifts of the Holy Spirit** working within your family, and acknowledge them.

★ **Brainstorm with your class** some ways to invite and include those who may feel left out.

★ **Participate in the Eucharist** every Sunday.

★ **Be Christ to others.**

ACTIVITY

LIVE YOUR FAITH Here are eight characteristics of Jesus. Choose four that you most understand. Write these in the center circle.

compassionate	loving	helpful	prayerful
just	accepting	strong in faith	welcoming

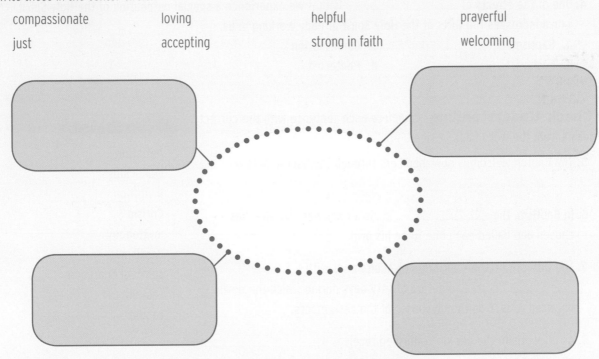

▶ If "you are what you eat," then by receiving Jesus in the Eucharist you can develop these same characteristics. In the outer boxes, write notes to express how you also have or will take on each of these characteristics.

▶ The Sacraments of Initiation serve to help you find a spiritual "home" in the Church. How can you now help others feel "at home" with you?

GO online Visit www.osvcurriculum.com for more family and community connections.

PRAYER

Lord, help me be a part of your Church.

Saint Catherine of Genoa

Saint Catherine of Genoa not only was born into a family that had two popes as members, but she was also blessed with extraordinary visions that guided her life and her writings.

Catherine was born in Genoa in 1447 as the Renaissance was beginning in Italy. At the age of thirteen, Catherine said she wanted to become a nun. However, she was considered too young at the time and was told to wait. Three years later, she was married to Julian Adorno. The marriage was an unhappy one. Julian's vices conflicted with Catherine's devotion to God. As she was seeking guidance in how to deal with them, the answer came to her in a revelation. As she knelt in devotion in a convent in Genoa, she was overcome by a blinding ray of Divine light. She fell into a trance and then lost consciousness. When she regained her senses, she was filled with the Holy Spirit.

She began writing about her feelings and experiences. Her two most famous works are *Dialogues of the Soul and Body* and *Treatise on Purgatory*. She described life as a process of continual purification that would allow the soul to receive Christ pure in heart and mind. "The souls in Purgatory," she wrote, "see all things, not in themselves, nor by themselves, but as they are in God, on whom they are more intent than on their own sufferings. . . . For the least vision they have of God overbalances all woes and all joys that can be conceived. Yet their joy in God does by no means abate their pain. . . . This process of purification to which I see the souls in Purgatory subjected, I feel within myself."

Catherine's life and quest for purity eventually influenced her husband, Julian. Toward the end of his life, he gave up his sinful ways and was sorry for the way he'd lived. After his death in 1497, she devoted herself to the sick at the hospital of Genoa, where she became the director and treasurer. Near the end of her life, a priest named Father Marabotti became her spiritual guide. Father Marabotti began assembling Catherine's memoirs. It is from his writings, more than from her own, that we know so much about her. However, her writings have been examined by the Holy Office in Rome and declared to contain vital Church doctrine. Catherine died in 1510 and she was canonized in 1737.

▲ Genoa was a major port during the Middle Ages.

GLOBAL DATA

Genoa

- Genoa was named after John the Baptist, the city's patron saint.

- Genoa has a population of about 631,000 people and is the largest seaport in Italy.

- Genoa has a history that dates back to the second or third centuries B.C. and is today one of the best preserved ancient cities in Europe.

- Genoa was an important maritime center during the Middle Ages and the Renaissance and was once an independent republic.

- Genoa was the birthplace of Christopher Columbus.

INVITE

 **PRAYER** God, please heal me and help me to forgive.

Life can be so full of hurt and disappointment. How can I begin to heal? Is forgiveness the answer?

Everyone was passing on the mysterious-looking casserole that the lunch line offered, except Dee. She frowned. "I'm *so* wishing I had asked my mom to pack lunch for me." Dee, Steven, and Anthony took their lunch trays to the usual table in the cafeteria.

As soon as they sat down, Anthony started talking. "Dad canceled on me again last night. Said he was called out of town on business. That's always his story. He only thinks about himself." The divorce had happened nearly two years ago, but Anthony was still really angry. He blamed his father for everything that had gone wrong.

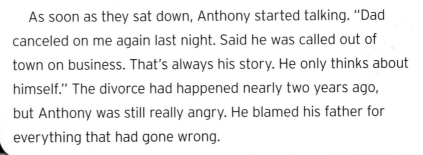

"Why do parents have to make life so hard for us?" asked Dee. "I had a big fight with my dad last night. He said I couldn't go to the party Friday. No parents there, he said. What's that supposed to mean? It's like he doesn't trust me. I really blew up—but I guess I kind of wish I hadn't said some of the things I said to him. I think I really hurt him."

Steven had been staring off blankly for some time now. "Hey you, wake up. Where are you?" Dee threw her napkin at Steven. "Thinking about Lucy," he said quietly. All three fell silent. They all liked Lucy—everybody liked Lucy. She was kind and smart and a good friend. And now she was in the hospital. She had some rare type of cancer, and it was bad. "I can't believe this is happening to her," said Anthony.

All three fell silent again. "I know God could heal Lucy," said Dee. "Yeah, God could have kept my mom and dad together, too," said Anthony. "But he didn't." Steven was thinking again. "Maybe God is doing a different kind of healing. Like what Father Griffin said last week at Mass?"

Father Griffin had talked about emotional and spiritual healing, not just physical healing. And he said that forgiveness—being forgiven and forgiving others—is the key.

"I think I need to have a talk with my dad," Dee said as she tried to swallow the last of her mystery-meat casserole.

"I hear that," Anthony said.

ACTIVITY

LET'S BEGIN When can emotional and spiritual healing be more important than physical healing? Father Griffin said that forgiveness was the key. Do you agree? Explain.

_____

_____

_____

▶ **How have you experienced forgiveness in your life? When have you experienced a kind of healing because you forgave someone?**

A MERCIFUL GOD

Focus Why can we count on God's forgiveness and healing?

At some point or another, each of us realizes that we've done something we regret. Or, that we have been blaming a friend or parent for something that really isn't their fault. We might be confused and worried about someone who is in pain, needing help to get through a really difficult time, or facing an illness. At times like these, we need to give or receive compassion, hope, and possibly forgiveness. And God can give us all of these.

Jesus shows us that God's compassion does not end.

SCRIPTURE

GO TO THE SOURCE
Jesus did not intend for God's compassion to stop with him. Read **Matthew 9:35–38** to find out what Jesus asked of his disciples.

SCRIPTURE ". . . Jesus went about all the cities and villages, teaching in their synagogues, and proclaiming the good news of the kingdom, and curing every disease and every sickness. When he saw the crowds, he had compassion for them, because they were harassed and helpless, like sheep without a shepherd."

—*Matthew 9:35–36*

The Gospels are filled with accounts of Jesus healing those who were sick and forgiving the sins of those who truly believed. Whether emotional, spiritual, or physical healings, these life-changing events had a tremendous impact. Most people believed, changed their lifestyles, and went out to tell others of Jesus and his message.

Always There God is always there to heal us spiritually (when we feel separated from God), emotionally (when we're in psychological pain), and physically (when we are sick or injured). Because Jesus forgave sinners and healed the sick, we know that's just the way God is—forgiving and eager to heal. The Church continues to celebrate Jesus' forgiveness and healing in two Sacraments of Healing: the Sacrament of Reconciliation and the Sacrament of the Anointing of the Sick.

How could your day be different if you remembered God's compassion for you and his desire to heal and forgive?

Holding Ourselves Up to the Light Did you ever put on a "clean" T-shirt only to discover spots in the light? When we hold ourselves up to the light of Christ, we all have "spots": bad attitudes, grudges, prejudices, emotional wounds, bad memories, and sins. With God's help we recognize and admit our need for and desire to change. We are open to conversion.

Conversion can mean many things: a return to God, sorrow for sin, trust in God's mercy, commitment to do better in the future, rooting out bad habits and more. Conversion does not mean unobtainable perfection or no trace of spots. It means making ourselves like Christ. Conversion is ongoing, always possible, always needed.

Conversion and repentance go together. Repentance, also called **contrition**, is being truly sorry for disobeying God and committing to try not to sin again. If contrition comes out of love for God above all things, it is called "perfect"; if someone is sorry for sins because they feel guilty or are afraid of the punishment, it is called "imperfect contrition." Both are promptings of the Holy Spirit in us, moving us to seek forgiveness.

We sometimes stray from the path by venial sin, which weakens our relationship with God. Some people may walk away from God (grave, or mortal, sin). The Sacrament of Reconciliation—also called the Sacrament of Conversion, Confession, or Penance—is the sacrament of forgiveness for sins committed after Baptism. Required for mortal sin and recommended for venial sin, it is a sure way to get back on the path of conversion.

CHAPTER
Words
of Faith

conversion
contrition
Reconciliation
Anointing of the Sick

ACTIVITY

SHARE YOUR FAITH In what ways have you been (or could be) open to conversion? Describe two everyday ways you know to "walk" with Jesus. Describe one or two "conversions" you have been through that improve the way you walk with God. If it helps, try finishing this phrase:

I used to (think/feel/believe/try to) _____ ,

but now I _____

and it has helped my relationship with God because _____ .

RECONCILIATION

Focus What are the rites and effects of this sacrament?

Today the Church celebrates the Sacrament of **Reconciliation** in three ways.

Rite I—Rite for Reconciliation of Individual Penitents (the person seeking forgiveness meets individually with the priest for the entire sacrament)

Rite II—Rite for Reconciliation of Several Penitents with Individual Confession and Absolution (the person seeking forgiveness gathers with others for prayer, Scripture readings, and reflections, but meets with the priest privately for confession and absolution)

Rite III—Rite for Reconciliation of Penitents with General Confession and Absolution, which is not typically celebrated in the United States, and can only be used in "danger of death" or "serious necessity" (*Code of Canon Law*, no. 961).

No matter how the sacrament is celebrated, it always contains four important elements: (1) contrition, which involves an examination of conscience, realization of sin, and true sorrow along with a desire to try to do better in the future; (2) confession; (3) penance, an action or prayer given by the priest as a way to repair the harm caused by sin and to become a stronger disciple of Christ; and, (4) absolution.

Rites I and II have a similar structure that includes

▶ gathering

▶ reading Scripture

▶ expressing contrition

▶ confessing sin individually and privately to a priest who can forgive sins in Christ's name by the authority of the Church. Priests cannot tell anyone what you have told them; this is called the Sacramental Seal of Confession.

▶ receiving a penance and having sins absolved by a priest

▶ praising God

You might be thinking you don't want to tell someone all the things you've done. But, you need to remember that you are actually talking to Christ when you talk to the priest. And, there are so many benefits from receiving the sacrament: reconciliation with God and the Church, freedom from eternal separation from God, a peaceful conscience, spiritual help and guidance, and strength to live as a disciple of Christ.

Let Go Sometimes we hoard a grudge, making it last. It's bitter revenge for our hurt feelings even if the person who hurt us is unaware. The same might be true of prejudices, bad memories, emotional wounds, and psychological scars. We're like Peter who wondered how many times he absolutely *had* to forgive. Or we're like the Unforgiving Servant who was excused a huge debt, but wouldn't let go of a small debt someone owed him. (See *Matthew 18:21–35*.)

Try these ways to let go of bad memories to become freed from emotional pain:

▶ When angry or vengeful thoughts pop into your mind, redirect your thoughts and adrenaline by vigorous activity or short prayers.

▶ Talk with your parents or a mentor, a trusted friend, or your older brother or sister.

▶ Talk to your parents and ask if they think you could talk to a counselor if other things aren't working.

✝ **SCRIPTURE**

GO TO THE SOURCE
Read the Parable of the Unforgiving Servant found in **Matthew 18:21–35**. Do you feel more like Peter, the Unforgiving Servant, or the person who owes? What is your favorite line in the parable? Why?

ACTIVITY

CONNECT YOUR FAITH With a little religious imagination, you can take a two-handed approach to having God help bring you some healing for emotional pain.

▶ **God gave you two hands. When you get to a private place, close your eyes and revisit the situation that gave you some emotional pain. As you revisit that situation, stretch out one hand "toward" that situation and grab onto it. Then take your other hand and stretch it up to heaven, asking God to take it, so that you can move on.**

You are taking a two-handed approach to praying for inner healing.

ANOINTING OF THE SICK

 Focus What are the rituals and effects of this sacrament?

In the District of the Decapolis, people brought a man with a hearing loss and a speech impediment to Jesus. At Bethsaida people brought a man who was blind. When the people of Gennesaret saw Jesus, they scurried about to bring the sick on mats. Wherever Jesus went, people counted on his power to heal. Fortunately, Jesus left his power to heal in his Church.

Healing the sick was so much a part of the life of Jesus that the first thing the seventy-two disciples were told to do was "Cure the sick who are there, and say to them, 'The kingdom of God has come near to you'" (*Luke 10:9*), and they did, just as they'd been told! They had watched what Jesus did and had the simple faith to follow his example.

The early Church continued the practice of curing the sick. The letter of James tells us about praying over sick people and anointing them. We learn that the faith of the community is essential for the healing to take place.

✝ SCRIPTURE "Are any among you suffering? They should pray. Are any cheerful? They should sing songs of praise. Are any among you sick? They should call for the elders of the Church and have them pray over them, anointing them with oil in the name of the Lord. The prayer of faith will save the sick, and the Lord will raise them up; and anyone who has committed sins will be forgiven."

—*James 5:13–15*

The Church does the same today in the **Anointing of the Sick**. Whenever someone falls seriously ill or the illness worsens, or when someone is in danger of death through sickness or old age, they are invited to seek the prayers and anointing of the Church. Only priests can give the sacrament, using oil consecrated by the bishop during Holy Week. The ritual consists of laying on of hands and anointing the forehead and hands while praying the prayers for the grace of the sacrament to strengthen the person to be able to handle the difficulties of serious illness or old age.

Why It's Important What do you think of when you hear words like *courage, health, peace, grace,* and *suffering*? Probably a whole range of things. These words can be used to describe the effects of the Anointing of the Sick. This sacrament has a tremendous impact on those who receive it, and that's why the Church wants to make sure that everyone knows that this sacrament is for anyone who is seriously sick, no matter the age or reason.

As in all the sacraments, the Anointing of the Sick gives a special *grace* to the person who receives it.

In this sacrament, the sick person is united to Christ's *suffering*. That's pretty amazing when you think about it. The Son of God actually suffered, and so God understands our suffering. And, because new life comes from Jesus' suffering, people are connected to his new life in this sacrament.

The sacrament gives *courage* and *peace* to endure suffering or old age, and sometimes *health* is restored. For those who are near death, the sacrament helps prepare them and their sins are forgiven if they are unable to receive the Sacrament of Reconciliation.

ACTIVITY

LIVE YOUR FAITH We sometimes want to help someone who is sick, but don't know how to do it. One way is to simply say, "I will keep you in my prayers, okay?" or "I will say a prayer for you." Name some ways you can reach out to those who are sick.

_____

_____

_____

IN SUMMARY

CATHOLICS BELIEVE

God heals us spiritually, emotionally, and sometimes physically in the Sacraments of Healing.

▶ Jesus' words and actions show us that God is compassionate, always willing to forgive and heal those who are willing to turn to him and believe.

▶ In the Sacrament of Penance and Reconciliation, those who are truly sorry for their sins receive God's forgiveness and are brought back together with him and the Church.

▶ In the Sacrament of the Anointing of the Sick, those who are seriously ill or are suffering from old age receive God's grace to be strong, courageous, and hopeful in their trials.

PRAYER

PSALM OF LAMENT

Leader: Be with us, O God,
As we sit here in quiet,
as we look deep inside at the ways
we have turned away from you.

Side 1: The LORD is my light and my salvation;
whom should I fear?
The LORD is the stronghold of my life:
of whom should I be afraid?

Side 2: One thing I asked of the LORD,
that will I seek after:
to live in the house of the LORD
all the days of my life,
to behold the beauty of the LORD,
and to inquire in his temple.

Side 1: For he will hide me in his shelter
in the day of trouble;
he will conceal me under the cover of his tent;
he will set me high on a rock.

Side 2: Hear, O LORD, when I cry aloud,
Be gracious to me and answer me!
"Come," my heart says, "seek his face!"
Your face, LORD, do I seek.
Do not hide your face from me.

Psalm 27:1, 4, 5, 7

Leader: O God of all goodness,
Your love heals all.
Come now and be with us, as we turn
toward you.
Help us be patient when we stumble and fall,
help us to be forgiving of ourselves and
each other.

All: Amen.

♪ "Turn to the Living God"
Lori True, © 2001, GIA Publications, Inc.

248

REVIEW

A Work with Words Complete each sentence with the correct term from the word bank at right.

Word Bank
Baptism
Reconciliation
Anointing of the Sick
suffering
Contrition
forgiveness
conversion
Eucharist

1. The Sacrament of _____ consists of laying on of hands and putting oil on the forehead and hands while praying for the grace of the sacrament to strengthen the person.

2. _____ is being truly sorry for disobeying God and committing oneself to try not to sin again.

3. The Sacrament of _____ is the sacrament of forgiveness for sins committed after Baptism.

4. In the Sacrament of Anointing of the Sick, the sick person is united to Christ's _____.

5. _____ can mean many things: a return to God, sorrow for sin, trust in God's mercy, commitment to do better in the future, and more.

B Check Understanding Indicate whether the following statements are true or false. Then rewrite false statements to make them true.

_____ 6. Perfect conversion comes out of love for God above all things.

_____

_____ 7. The Sacrament of Reconciliation is required for mortal sin commited after Baptism and recommended for venial sin.

_____

_____ 8. The Sacrament of Reconciliation always includes contrition, confession, anointing, and absolution.

_____

_____ 9. Priests in confession cannot tell anyone what you have told them; this is called the Seal of Confession.

_____

_____ 10. Only priests can give the Sacrament of Reconciliation using the oil consecrated by the bishop during Holy Week.

_____

C Make Connections: Synthesize Write a one-paragraph response to the question.

Write about a time when someone forgave you or a time when you forgave someone. What was the experience of forgiveness like and how did it affect your relationship?

OUR CATHOLIC FAITH

WHAT NOW?

★ When you are in emotional or physical pain, turn to God in prayer.

★ If you are seriously ill, ask for the Anointing of the Sick.

★ Pray for healing. Include your family and friends, but don't forget the world needs healing.

★ If you need to forgive someone, ask God to help you. Ask your teacher or counselor about techniques you can use to help you get rid of the grudge or bad memory.

★ Receive the Sacrament of Reconciliation frequently. Some good times to do so are
   • during Advent and Lent
   • when your conscience bothers you
   • when you have a bad fault that you can't shake
   • when you have seriously gone against God's commandments.

ACTIVITY

LIVE YOUR FAITH Match the beginnings of these scriptural quotes to the correct endings.

1) Forgiving one another . . .

2) I have swept away your transgressions like a cloud . . .

3) You are a God ready to forgive, gracious and merciful . . .

4) The good Lord . . .

A. your sins like mist. (*Isaiah 44:22*)

B. slow to anger and abounding in steadfast love. (*Nehemiah 9:17*)

C. pardon all who set their hearts to seek God. (*2 Chronicles 30:18–19*)

D. as God in Christ has forgiven you. (*Ephesians 4:32*)

▶ Check your answers by looking for the quotes in a Bible.

▶ Choose the Scripture that speaks to you best of forgiveness and explain why on the lines below.

_____

_____

_____

_____

 GO online Visit **www.osvcurriculum.com** for more family and community connections.

 **PRAYER**

Lord, please send the healing we need.

PEOPLE OF FAITH

Blessed Carlos Manuel Cecilio Rodriguez Santiago

The normal course of our lives may inflict many types of pain on us. That pain may be physical, it may be emotional, or it may be spiritual. Most of us experience all three at various times. How we handle our pain often affects how we receive Christ and how we are received by him.

As a child in Puerto Rico, Carlos Manuel Cecilio Rodriguez Santiago began experiencing the first symptoms of what would later become a severe digestive disorder. This illness would cause him much suffering and inconvenience for the rest of his life. However, it never undermined his commitment to Christ and His Church. Nor did the pain he experienced when his parents' house and grocery store burned to the ground. "Charlie," as he was called, simply continued with his life and pursued goals that were both holy and spiritually gratifying.

Determined to receive a higher education, Carlos Manuel attended the University of Puerto Rico. He founded a Liturgy Circle in his hometown of Caguas and used his modest salary as a Spanish/English translator to publish two Christian magazines, *Liturgy* and *Christian Culture*. His principal apostolic work was at Catholic University Center, Rio Piedras, where he evangelized students and teachers. His publications helped university students understand and enjoy liturgical seasons. He was an active member of the Brotherhood of Christian Doctrine, Holy Name Society, and Knights of Columbus and taught catechism to high school students. He also encouraged liturgical renewal among clergy and laity, the use of vernacular language, and devotion to the Paschal Vigil, which takes place near the end of each day. Many of his reforms were adopted by the Church at the Vatican II Council in the 1960s.

Although he never completed his formal higher education, Carlos Manuel was dedicated to the educational process. Many of those who knew him credit him with their growth of a living faith. He lived an exemplary life, dedicating himself to helping others recover or maintain their spirituality. Others testify that Carlos Manuel's zeal for Christ awakened in them their vocation to religious life. He continued to embody and exemplify this spirit throughout his life.

In 1963, he died at the age of 44 after a long and painful illness. So great was his case for beatification that Pope Saint John Paul II beatified him in 2001, only four years after he was declared venerable. He is the first Puerto Rican to achieve that status.

▲ **San Juan Cathedral in Old San Juan, Puerto Rico.**

GLOBAL DATA

Puerto Rico

- Puerto Rico is an island in the Caribbean Sea with an area of 3,500 square miles and a population of four million.

- 85 percent of the residents are Roman Catholic.

- Puerto Rico was claimed for Spain by Christopher Columbus, who landed there in 1493. The name means "rich port" in Spanish, the major language spoken there.

- Puerto Rico became a territory of the United States in 1898 following the Spanish-American War; residents are U.S. citizens.

- Puerto Rico is a popular resort destination with beautiful sandy beaches and a tropical climate; tourism is the island's major industry.

Faith in Action!

CATHOLIC SOCIAL TEACHING

IN THIS UNIT you learned about how the sacraments of Baptism, Confirmation, the Eucharist, and Reconciliation are all ways of belonging to, building, and rebuilding community, the Body of Christ.

Call to Community

By Baptism, you were welcomed and included. Now who needs you to be more welcoming or inclusive to them? Exactly how can you do so? By the Eucharist, you are nourished. Now who needs you to nourish them? Exactly how can you be more nourishing to this person? By Confirmation, you affirmed your call to discipleship. Now what do you need to work on to improve the way you live as a disciple?

Yes, we are the Church, the Body of Christ. With our different gifts, we form one body in Christ made of many parts. Created in the image of God who is a Community of three Persons, we are all called to create community and participate in community.

Today, so many people seem to spend more time at work or in front of the TV or at their computers, while fewer and fewer people seem to care, to participate in events at school or in their parish. And in most elections in this country, the percentage of people who vote is going down rather than up. What's happening? Are people more selfish? Are people giving up? Or are people finding other important things to give their time to?

It's a huge challenge. But for people called, confirmed, and sent forth by God's Spirit of courage and love, we all have a crucial responsibility to say "yes. We truly are Christ's disciples in our world." You are sent to school to help build a community of learners who care about others, especially classmates having a hard time or younger students. At home, you are called to help create a family community. Your parish needs your talents and your ideas. And your country desperately needs you to care about others, to care about your nation's ideals, to care enough that you will speak out when something's wrong. The Church is clear—political authority must be consistent with morality and promote the common good.

Why do you think so many people don't participate in their community?

252

IN ANY COMMUNITY, IT is important for people to make others feel included and valued. Let's look at how one group puts those beliefs into action.

CREATING COMMUNITY

"It's called MSMFN and the kids love it!" That was the comment of Lori Wasner, Director of Religious Education at Christ the King Parish in Richland, Washington. MSMFN stands for "Middle School Mandatory Fun Night," a monthly evening of games organized and conducted by her high school youth group. These dozen youth leaders were community-minded enough to recognize how lost middle school students often feel when they start high school. They decided that these fun nights would help them feel a part of a community that included some high school students. Through this process, the high school youth also discovered that they were building community among themselves. Their sense of mission and willingness to participate in improving the religious education and lives of these younger students also increased greatly.

After ninety minutes of games, there is always a serious note. Each MSMFN has a theme chosen by the youth, and they take turns giving a short faith testimony related to the theme. One youth shared his incredible experience visiting the Nazi concentration camp at Auschwitz. He was overwhelmed by the magnitude of the evil he sensed there. He talked about how so many German people didn't want to know or acknowledge what was happening at the time. That proved to be a powerful testimony to the need for every citizen to take responsibility for what happens in their community and nation and to be willing to participate in changing those things that need changing.

The youth group at Christ the King did just that. They took responsibility to help younger members of their parish family feel more a part of the community.

What can you do to build community at your own school—with your classmates and with younger students?

SERVE   Your Community

BUILDING COMMUNITY

List some things you can do to help build a greater
sense of community in these areas:

> **AT HOME**

> **AT SCHOOL**

> **IN MY NEIGHBORHOOD**

Decide which one you'll do first, second, and third.

_____

_____

PARTICIPATING IN PROMOTING THE COMMON GOOD IN YOUR NATION

Brainstorm with your classmates at least
three different ways you can participate
in challenging political leaders to
improve life for hungry or homeless
families in your local community, state,
or nation. Decide as a class whether
you want the whole class to work on
one of these or create teams to work
on different ones.

Create a plan to accomplish your goal(s).

Project Planning Sheet

Specific tasks

_____

Others who should be contacted about this

_____

Ways to publicize your project

_____

Your specific task(s)

_____

Calendar for completing the project

_____

Did you follow through on the three ways you decided to promote community?

_____

_____

What was the hardest thing about doing the project?

_____

_____

What was the most satisfying thing about completing the project?

_____

_____

What did you learn about yourself while working on this project?

_____

_____

How did your group project go?

_____

_____

What did you learn about working for the common good of low-income families?

_____

_____

What did you learn about yourself in doing the project?

_____

_____

What did you learn about God and about your faith in doing them?

_____

_____

List one thing that might be different about you after doing this project.

_____

_____

REVIEW

A **Work with Words** Use the clues below to complete the crossword puzzle.

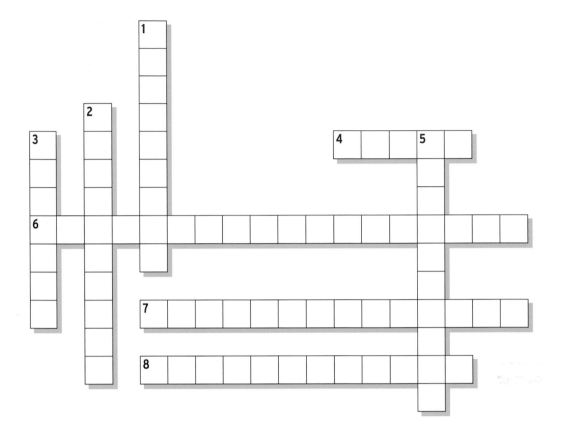

Across

4 God's love and life freely given to help us come to know him as adopted children

6 Happens when the bread and wine become the Body and Blood of Christ

7 Sacrament for forgiveness of sins committed after Baptism

8 One of the Sacraments of Initiation

Down

1 In this sacrament we receive the Body and Blood of Christ

2 Effective signs of God's grace given to the Church by Christ

3 Sacrament through which a person experiences new life and new identity in Christ

5 Being truly sorry for disobeying God and committing to try not to sin again

B **Check Understanding** Circle the letter of the choice that best completes the sentence.

9. Jesus is the perfect _____ between God and man, because he is fully God and fully man.

   a. mediator   **b.** symbol   **c.** division   **d.** conversion

10. The Church, a means to _____ is a visible community in the world.

   a. salvation   **b.** grace   **c.** divinity   **d.** power

11. The Sacrament of Reconciliation reflects Jesus' giving the Church, through _____, the power to forgive sins.

   a. Jesus   **b.** the priest   **c.** John   **d.** Peter

12. All seven sacraments involve _____ and _____ that we can see, touch, hear, taste, and smell.

   a. symbols, rituals   **b.** oil   **c.** attitudes   **d.** signs, words

13. The Church welcomes new members through the Sacraments of _____.

   a. Contrition   **b.** Initiation   **c.** Conviction   **d.** Invitation

14. In Baptism, the _____ is a reminder that God has chosen and called each one to be his own.

   a. water   **b.** candle   **c.** chrism   **d.** prayer

15. Like Baptism, Confirmation imparts a(n) _____ on one's soul.

   a. acceptable character   **b.** invisible sign   **c.** spiritual conversion   **d.** spiritual character

16. _____ can mean many things: a return to God, sorrow for sin, trust in God's mercy, commitment to do better in the future, and more.

   a. Contrition   **b.** Sacraments   **c.** Conversion   **d.** Reconciliation

17. The Sacrament of _____ consists of the priest's laying on of hands and putting oil on the forehead and hands.

   a. Anointing the Sick   **b.** Reconciliation   **c.** Anointing the Dying   **d.** Baptism

18. The Sacrament of Reconciliation always includes contrition, _____, penance, and absolution.

   a. conversion   **b.** confession   **c.** penance   **d.** consideration

· ·

C **Make Connections** Write a short answer to these questions.

19. Interpret. How do you experience God through the customs and practices of the Church? Give a specific example.

_____

_____

20. Analyze. What does it mean to live out the Eucharist? How are you living out the Eucharist in your family, at school, and in the world around you?

_____

_____

257

CALLED by God

✔ PRAYER O God, help me know your will for my life.

What am I supposed to do with my life?
I wish I could do something important.
If we all have gifts, what are mine?

Peter sprinted from the gym as his friends in the carpool, joking, yelled for him to "move it." Basketball practice had gone long, so they kidded him about it as he got into the car. They had done the same to Maria when she made everybody wait, so she wouldn't miss a deadline for the school newspaper. Maya would be next because she had just landed a role in the school play and rehearsals often got out late.

Devon just jumped back into the car behind Peter as he caught his orange Frisbee. He wasn't into clubs or sports, but he didn't mind the wait. He was cool just throwing a Frisbee with anybody hanging around the student drop-off area. Lately he'd taught some tricks to some new kids from Japan, and they had taught him some Japanese.

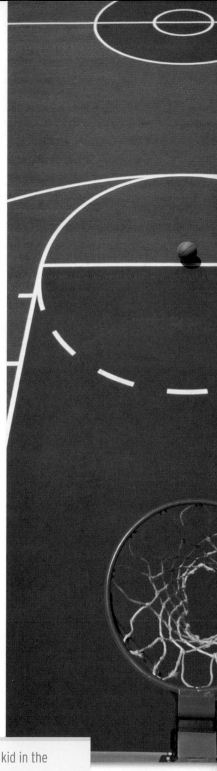

"How did your English test go today?" Peter's mom asked as they hit the road.

"Mom! Coach had a friend at practice today," Peter gasped. "The guy used to play for the Lakers. He said I'm a natural shooting guard! Can you believe that?"

"Wish I could write as well as you can shoot," Maria said. "I want to be a reporter like my aunt, but nobody calls me a natural."

"Yeah, you are more like 'unnatural' girl," Maya grinned. "Who likes to write for fun? The thing is, I think you're born with gifts, but you've still gotta work hard and make the most of your chances. My folks are both teachers, but I want to do my own thing."

"I have no clue what my gifts are," Devon sighed, "but I hope they take me to Tokyo someday. It sounds cool there!"

"That's where my parents met," Maya replied. "They started their careers teaching English in Japan. I bet you'd be really good at that."

"Speaking of which," Peter's mom interrupted, "how'd that test in English go?"

ACTIVITY

LET'S BEGIN Discuss the events of the story. Devon might seem like the least ambitious kid in the carpool, but he has some gifts. What are they, and where might they lead him?

▶ **What gifts or potential gifts seem to come naturally to you? Could any of your gifts be used to make the world a better place?**

_____

_____

_____

_____

_____

THE IMPORTANCE OF FAMILY

Focus What role does the family have in faith?

Each of us has potential gifts and talents. Some of us are artistic, some are athletic, some are thinkers, and some are speakers. We might discover our talents early in life, or we might stumble across them by accident. Our families often point out what our gifts and talents are, and our teachers, coaches, and friends can help us figure them out, too.

When all of us, as God's people, use our talents to work together, we can bring about good in the world. Despite our different talents, we all share the same calling to know and love God. We are first called to this mission in our Baptism, and our parents and guardians play a pivotal role in our responding to that call.

✝ SCRIPTURE

GO TO THE SOURCE
Read **Luke 2:41–52**. Imagine that you were a friend of Jesus when he was growing up. What might you have seen him doing in daily life? What do you think it would be like to have Jesus as a friend or classmate today?

✝ SCRIPTURE A mother found herself praying one day. She and her husband had lost track of their son, who was around twelve years old. Their names were Mary and Joseph, and they finally found their son, Jesus, in the temple, teaching the teachers. They had looked for him for three days, probably worrying and praying all the while. But, even though they were upset, the Bible tells us, they were amazed by him.

The Gospel of Luke also tells us that Mary "treasured all these things in her heart" (*Luke 2:51*). She and Joseph recognized Jesus' great gifts, nurtured him with love, prayed with him, and helped him fulfill God's will.

Prayer begins in our family. Parents and guardians not only put a roof over our heads, clothes on our backs, and food on our plates, but they also provide for our spiritual needs. If you become a parent, it will be your responsibility to help your children grow in faith.

? What different roles do the people in your family have?

Faith Begins at Home Before you were baptized, your parents and godparents were given a big task. They were told:

"You must make it your constant care to bring him (her) up in the practice of the faith."

Constant means all the time, 24/7. This kind of care includes things like teaching you to pray, telling you to "turn the other cheek" instead of getting even, or getting you to Mass on Sunday.

The Christian home is the first place where children learn about God and the Catholic faith. It is here that they should first appreciate what a community of love is. They should experience solid Christian virtues and values. In that sense, a family is a unique dimension of the Church. A Christian home and family is a **domestic Church**—a community of grace and prayer. For example, when such a family gathers around a table for a meal or in the car on the way to school, they can thank God for the gifts they received that day.

No family is perfect. All families face challenges and have growing pains. Sometimes a home seems more like a domestic Church than at other times. The important thing is to keep trying and to ask God for help.

Witnesses to Christ It's not easy for parents to raise their children as Catholics. But lay people are called to be witnesses to Christ at all times and places. A **lay person** is a baptized member of the Church who shares in Jesus' mission and witnesses to him and his message especially in their families, workplaces, and civic communities.

We are witnesses when our words and actions reflect the teachings of Jesus and the Church. At home, in school, on the bus, at work—we can show others what it means to follow Christ. And, we don't do this alone. God gives us the love and strength to make it happen.

Words of Faith

domestic Church

lay person

vocation

discernment

consecrated life

CATHOLICS TODAY

Did you know that there are about twenty-four million Catholic households in the United States today? Some households are small with just parents and children. Others include grandparents or aunts, uncles, or cousins. Sometimes grandparents take on the important role of raising children and creating a faith-filled environment. Other times, guardians do.

ACTIVITY

SHARE YOUR FAITH Think about what you can do to add prayer to your daily routine. Be creative. Keep it simple. Think about how you can do it at different times and in different places—before bed, at breakfast, after a ball game or practice. Try to get ideas from the people in your family on other ways to build your "domestic Church."

Bertha Bowman was born in 1937, in Mississippi. She became a Catholic when she was nine and attended a school staffed by the Franciscan Sisters of Perpetual Adoration. She was so impressed that, at age fifteen, she joined them and was given the name Thea.

Sister Thea's relationship with God was shaped through her family, religious community, prayer, and reading of the Scriptures. After sixteen years of teaching, Sister Thea gave presentations across the country about breaking down racial and cultural barriers—gatherings that combined gospel preaching, prayer, storytelling, and singing.

In 1984, Sister Thea was diagnosed with terminal cancer. During an interview, she stated, ". . . I think one difference between me and some other people is that I'm content to do a little bit. Sometimes people think they have to do big things in order to make a change, but if each one of us would light the candle, we'd have a tremendous light." One of her favorite songs was "This Little Light of Mine." She died in 1990.

A COMMON MISSION

Focus What does it mean to have a vocation?

In Baptism and Confirmation, we are called to be holy in every aspect of our lives—when we're alone, with our family and friends, and as part of our Church. At Baptism, we are anointed with sweet-smelling oil called *chrism* as the priest or deacon tells us that Christ unites us to his people and his Body, and we share in Christ's role as Priest, Prophet, and King.

LAY PEOPLE SHARE IN JESUS' MISSION	
Priest	Like *priests*, we bring the love of Christ to a world in need. We pray for those in need, we offer what we do at school and at home as a gift to God, and we participate in the Mass.
Prophet	Like Jesus and the Apostles, as *prophets* we speak God's powerful truth to people by the way we act and the things we say and do. We show them what it means to follow Christ.
King	When we are like Christ the Servant *king*, we serve those around us and carry the Good News to people in need.

Living It Out You can't apply for a job as a king. It's not as simple as our deciding alone to become an ordained priest, or a religious sister or brother. Those vocations begin with a call from God and require years of prayer and study. A **vocation** is a holy calling, or a call to love and serve God and others.

We all have a vocation as baptized members of the Church. Some have a vocation to priesthood or religious life. Others live out their vocation as married or through single life. God may give married Catholics the gift of children, while sisters and brothers in religious communities dedicate their lives to the faith in many different ministries and lifestyles. Whatever path you follow can be a sacred one when you take Christ's love with you and share it with others.

❓ Who are some people in your school who live up to the roles of priest, prophet, and king? How can you do so?

What About You? Do you get tired of being asked, "What do you want to be when you grow up?" It's normal for the answer to change many times as you grow up. Maybe you wanted to be a star athlete but didn't have the physical skills. Dreams and plans change for many reasons. You might see a movie tomorrow about doctors working to cure diseases and think, "Hey, I want to do that!" Maybe you could. Maybe you will.

Ultimately, you will decide what you do with your talents and time. Weighing your choices and praying for guidance is called **discernment**. Think about what you enjoy doing, and what you are good at. Talk with your parents, family, friends, Church leaders, and those who know you best. Whether you feel called to be a poet or a politician, talk about it with them. They ought to respect and encourage your choices of a vocation. This is more likely if they understand what you are thinking. Pray with them, like Jesus surely did with his parents. Parents can encourage their children to see that they are called to follow Jesus, whatever they do.

> **Who do you turn to for help when you are making a big decision? Why?**

> **Who knows you well enough to help you begin thinking about your vocational path?**

✝ SCRIPTURE
GO TO THE SOURCE
Read **Proverbs 3:5–6**. What does it mean to trust in the Lord with all your heart?

ACTIVITY

CONNECT YOUR FAITH Make a list of the things you enjoy doing and those things you take seriously. How can you use these talents to make a difference in the lives of people around you?

THINGS I ENJOY DOING

THINGS I TAKE SERIOUSLY

LISTENING FOR GOD'S CALL

 Focus What gifts does the Church call on you as a Christian to share?

The words and witness of priests, religious women and men, lay leaders, and good Christian parents can inspire us. There are many needs in our Church, and we're called to listen and respond.

Sometimes we respond with our treasure, as in when disaster strikes a poor country. The collection basket is passed, and we give what we can.

As we grow older, and our gifts develop, we also share our talent and time. We might be altar servers, work at a soup kitchen, or help at Vacation Bible School. We might read at Mass, teach a class, or make an even bigger commitment to participate in parish life.

When a man becomes a parish priest, he will promise to respect and obey his bishop, live a simple lifestyle, and be celibate. *Celibacy* means to not get married and to not have sexual relations. These promises require great sacrifices, but they're made out of love for God and the Church community.

Sacred Vows Other people may choose to serve God by entering **consecrated life**. This includes members of religious orders who are known as brothers or sisters, as well as priests in religious orders. The men and women called to live a consecrated life live in a community and take vows of poverty, chastity, and obedience.

▶ In poverty, a consecrated person owns nothing in his or her own name. His or her few possessions are given to him or her and often shared with others. This helps the person to better understand and to serve poor people.

▶ For men and women in consecrated life, chastity means living a celibate life. It shows that their love for God is the most important thing.

▶ Obedience shows that the common good is more important than our personal needs and helps a person to more fully serve the Church.

Although these vows are required for people in consecrated life, the values they uphold are important for anyone serving the Church. Everyone, whether single or married, should strive to live simply, love God above all things, and care deeply for others. When married, a man and a woman need to treat their relationship as a sacred partnership and mutual vocation. God created both women and men, and through their communion they are meant to grow closer together and nearer to the Lord.

In what ways do you feel called to serve the Church community and all God's people?

CHECK THIS OUT!

"Lord, make me an instrument of your peace. Where there is hatred, let me sow love; where there is injury, pardon; where there is doubt, faith; where there is despair, hope; where there is darkness, light; and where there is sadness, joy . . ." *Peace Prayer*, attributed to *Saint Francis of Assisi*

Saint Francis of Assisi founded an order of religious life known as the Franciscans during the wars and unrest of the crusades in the A.D. 1200s. In which Christian vocation(s) would you find his prayer especially helpful?

ACTIVITY

LIVE YOUR FAITH Brainstorm a list of all the different ministries and vocations that keep your parish running. Share a brief report with your class or ask one person in your parish if he or she will speak to the class about his or her vocation.

1.

2.

3.

4.

5.

IN SUMMARY

CATHOLICS BELIEVE

We share a common call to glorify the Lord by our lives. The Church helps us respond to our unique call.

▶ We are called to relationship. We discern our vocation with the help of family, the Church, and prayer.

▶ We are called to work. The Church asks us to share our time, talent, and treasure.

▶ We are called to faith. Each of us must live our particular vocation, whether married, single, ordained, or consecrated.

 **PRAYER**

PRAYER OF SERVICE

Leader: Throughout all time, through all generations,
people have gathered for prayer.
Today, we too come together,
to offer thanksgiving and to praise God.

Reader 1: O God,
as you once called Isaiah,
and sent him as prophet,
a much needed voice for the people of Israel,
call us, and send us to proclaim hope in our day.

Reader 2: O God,
as you once called Moses,
to deliver your children safely to your holy land,
call us and send us,
to lead and guide your people safely home to you.

Reader 3: O God,
as you once called Jeremiah,
and sent him as servant,
a young boy speaking truth to whomever you chose,
call us and send us,
to make your message of peace fill every silence.

Reader 4: O God,
as you once called Mary,
and sent her as Mother,
a servant who gave her wholehearted yes,
call us and send us,
to bring your light to the shadows of darkness.

Leader: O God,
you call to us too, by our own names.
As you once had a plan for Moses and Mary,
there's a map and a mission for each of us here.
Help us to know your voice when it's calling.
Help us be open and eager to follow.
Help us to trust in your plan for our future.

We ask this through the one who also calls us
to "come and follow,"
Christ our brother.

All: Amen.

♪ "Here I Am"
Tony Alonso, © 2003, GIA Publications, Inc.

REVIEW

A **Work with Words** Complete each sentence with the correct term from the word bank at right.

Word Bank

chrism
lay person
witness
family
domestic School
domestic Church
vocation
priest

1. A _____ is a baptized member of the Church who shares in Jesus' mission and witnesses to him, especially in their families, workplaces, and the civic community.

2. A holy calling, or _____, is a call to serve God and others.

3. _____ is the first place to learn about the good within people and discover Christ's love.

4. A home and family can be a _____—a community of grace and prayer.

5. The sweet-smelling oil used at Baptism is called _____.

B **Check Understanding** Indicate whether the following statements are true or false. Then rewrite false statements to make them true.

_____ 6. Parents and godparents promise to make it their "constant care to bring him (her) up in the practice of the faith" before a child is confirmed.

_____

_____ 7. Men and women called to live a consecrated life take vows of poverty, modesty, and obedience.

_____

_____ 8. Lay people share in Jesus' priesthood by praying and offering what we do as a gift to God.

_____

_____ 9. In Baptism and Confirmation, we are called to be holy in all parts of our lives.

_____

_____ 10. When you use discernment, you pray silently and wait for God's sign.

_____

C **Make Connections: Interpret** Write a one-paragraph response to the question below.

What vocation do you think you will be called to, and how will your gifts from God help you follow that path?

267

OUR CATHOLIC FAITH

WHAT NOW?

* Consider your gifts.
* Talk to someone you admire about his or her vocation.
* Dream about the good you can do.
* Be honest with your parents about what you see in your future.
* Think about obstacles and how you can avoid them.

ACTIVITY

LIVE YOUR FAITH You're called to many things. Take some time to evaluate how you're responding. Then answer the questions below.

▶ How are you responding to the call of faith at this time in your life?

▶ How are you responding to the call of relationships? To whom are you giving your best, being your true self, treating with love? To whom should you be giving more?

▶ How are you responding to the call of work in the grades you are making, the subjects you are studying, the skills you are being invited to develop, your after-school commitments?

 Visit www.osvcurriculum.com for more family and community connections.

PRAYER

Give me the gifts I need, Lord, so I can be the gift others need.

Saint Martin de Porres

Each of us, in our own way, is called by God for a special purpose. Whether we enter the religious life or not, we all have a purpose under God's plan. Our faith in God and in his plan for us helps us respond to our unique calling.

Saint Martin de Porres experienced a very holy calling in his home city of Lima, Peru. Born in 1579, his father was a Spanish nobleman and his mother was a freed black servant from Panama. He wanted to follow the Lord from a very young age. He was only eleven years old when he became a servant in the Dominican priory of Lima. He was promoted to an almoner, someone who solicits donations for charitable purposes. He was good at that job. He helped collect more than two thousand dollars a week from the rich to support the city's poor and sick people.

Martin succeeded brilliantly at everything they gave him to do. When he was put in charge of the Dominicans' infirmary, he showed tender care for the sick. He was also widely known for his spectacular cures, many of which were strongly rooted in faith. He was so good at what he did that his superiors dropped the rule that "no black person may be received to the holy habit or profession of our order." Martin was allowed to take vows as a Dominican brother.

Following his Divine calling, Martin established an orphanage and hospital for the poor children of Lima's slums. His love of all living creatures prompted him to establish a shelter for stray cats and dogs, and he nursed those that were sick back to health. All the while he lived in self-imposed austerity. He never ate meat, fasted continuously, and spent much time in prayer and meditation. He was also known for his great devotion to the Eucharist and was a friend of Saint John de Massias and Saint Rose of Lima. Gifted in his knowledge of the faith and its precepts, he was called upon to solve theological problems for his Order and for bishops of the city.

Martin continued in his Divine calling until his death in 1639. Almost immediately, miracles were attributed to him, including the raising of the dead. At his canonization in 1962, Pope Saint John XXIII in his homily said, "The example of Martin's life is ample evidence that we can strive for holiness and salvation as Christ Jesus has shown us: first, by loving God 'with all your heart, with all your soul, and with all your mind; and second, by loving your neighbor as yourself.'" With these words, Brother Martin de Porres became the first black saint in the Western Hemisphere.

▲ Saint Martin de Porres, 1579–1639

GLOBAL DATA

Peru

- Peru, in pre-Columbian times, was part of the great Incan empire that covered a vast area of western South America.

- Peru was colonized by Spain under Francisco Pizarro in 1533 and supplied Spain with vast quantities of gold, silver, and precious gems.

- Peru won its independence from Spain in the 1820s under Simon Bolívar and Jose de San Martin.

- Peru has an area of nearly 500,000 square miles and a population of almost 30 million.

- Eighty-one percent of Peruvians are Roman Catholic.

ACT with Justice

PRAYER | Jesus, guide me.

Sometimes I feel like I'm the only one who cares about other people. How can I act the way I know I should? What do we owe other people who are in need?

Jessi was eating lunch alone for the third straight day in her new school, but she'd get used to it, she supposed. All around her the lunchroom hummed with noise, but none of it had anything to do with her. Not yet.

Lynn, the biggest gossip in school, hurried to her usual table. "I just heard the gym teachers talking about that new kid," Lynn blurted to the table full of friends. "They must have thought the locker room was empty, but I was having trouble with my lock again. Anyway, they said she moved here to live with her grandma. Get this . . . her parents just got thrown in jail! I guess they were in the newspaper today."

"No wonder she's so quiet!" Julian chimed in. "I just thought she was weird. I should have guessed she had something to hide."

"Hey, I have the paper here in my backpack," Chris said. "Here's the article. Should I go over and say 'Hey, your mom looks great in stripes?' Anybody know her name?"

"I haven't met her yet, and neither have you," Greg said, grabbing the paper. "Man, you guys are acting like you're enjoying the poor girl's pain." Greg stood up and spoke loudly enough for *everyone* around him to hear. "Just try to be as good to *everybody* as you want them to be to you, okay? Is that too much to ask?" Greg started toward Jessi's lonely table.

Everyone was shocked. It wasn't like Greg to hassle people. He was popular because he was a good athlete and a nice guy. Some kids were afraid of him because he was so big, but usually he was pretty quiet. Why had he defended the new kid? Why did he care?

Jessi flinched as she saw Greg coming. Then she winced when she saw the newspaper in Greg's hand. It looked like the big guy was going to throw it at her. Greg flipped the paper over Jessi's head. It landed in the trash can. "Nice shot," Jessi chuckled.

"That's about all it's good for," Greg said as he sat. "Same old stories every day. My name's Greg. What's yours?"

ACTIVITY

LET'S BEGIN Why was Greg's reaction surprising? How did Jessi's reaction to Greg change during their meeting? Why do you think Greg acted as he did?

▶ **Think of a situation in which you wanted to do the right thing but worried what others might think. How did you decide what to do? Are there any behaviors in your school that take away from the dignity of others? What could people do to change those attitudes or actions?**

ALL ARE INVITED

Focus What does Jesus offer us?

SCRIPTURE
GO TO THE SOURCE
Read **Luke 4:14–22** to discover where Jesus announced his mission and how those who heard him responded.

We all have dignity; we all deserve to be treated fairly and to be given the same respect. Jesus told us to "[D]o to others as you would have them do to you" (*Matthew 7:12*). And Jesus' words and actions remind us that we are equal in God's eyes. As his followers, we need to show the world by our actions that all people are equal, deserving of what is their due, worthy of fair treatment. We all also have the responsibility to make sure that groups of people, society, and its organizations promote that dignity and don't undermine it. Sometimes we have to work to change the way things are so that people can get what they deserve and need. This is the **justice** Jesus taught us, giving God and others what is due to them.

On a Mission It was the Father's will that Jesus bring the kingdom of heaven to life right here on earth. "The kingdom of God has come near," Jesus said as he began his ministry. "Repent, and believe in the good news" (*Mark 1:15*).

But what is God's kingdom? It's not a place on the map or a physical location in which a king rules over his subjects or a fairy tale. The **kingdom of God**, sometimes called the kingdom of heaven, is God's rule of love, peace, and justice in our hearts, lives, and the world. Jesus invited everyone to the kingdom. All are welcome. All that's required is that they chose to believe, to have faith, and to make a change in their lives and the way they looked at the world and others.

Jesus came to teach us about the kingdom of God. At the beginning of his ministry, he made it clear that he had fulfilled the words of the prophet Isaiah: that he had come to bring the Good News to the poor, to proclaim liberty to captives, recovery of sight to the blind, and to free the oppressed. (See *Luke 4:14–22*.)

? In what ways did Jesus do the things he said he had come to do?

Making It Real Jesus reached out to people who most leaders in those days would have pushed away— women, children, lepers, and especially those who were poor and in need. He challenged society and those in authority to act justly themselves, to change the attitudes and structures that kept people from having what they needed to live.

An important attitude of the kingdom is that we prefer God to all else. We put God first in our lives, and working for the kingdom seems second nature. Through his parables and other teachings, Jesus tells us that words are not enough to enter the kingdom. Our actions need to show that we believe and are working toward what is just, peaceful, and loving. The kingdom and justice are so closely tied that you can't have one without the other. That's something Jesus showed us.

Words of Faith

justice

kingdom of God

solidarity

CHECK THIS OUT!

One in eight Americans lives in poverty. What can you do about this? Start by visiting **www.osvcurriculum.com** to link to the website of the Catholic Campaign for Human Development (CCHD). You'll discover plenty of information about the causes of poverty and how CCHD helps millions of Americans by supporting economic development and community organizing projects. You also can be part of CCHD's efforts by giving to its collection each year on the Sunday before Thanksgiving.

GO online

ACTIVITY

SHARE YOUR FAITH Think of someone in your community who has made it his or her life's work to help others. How does this person's work help solve poverty, end hunger, or fight injustice? List two things you could do to help this person.

I could help _____ by

1.	2.

We can do a lot to work with God to bring about his kingdom, but we might underestimate the power of praying for it to come. We do this each time we pray the Lord's Prayer: "thy kingdom come, thy will be done on earth as it is in heaven." When you think about it, the Lord's Prayer is what prayer is all about. In this prayer that Jesus gave us, we begin by giving glory to God, our Father. We praise the goodness of God's name. We ask God to build up his kingdom and do his will here on earth. We hope that our world might be as loving, peaceful, and just as we know heaven will be.

But building God's kingdom is hard work! So we also ask for what we need to help make it happen. We need "daily bread"—not just a loaf to eat, but also the love and joy that keep us going. And we ask God not only to forgive our sins, but also to help us forgive those who have hurt us.

The Lord's Prayer is often called the perfect prayer because it really captures the message of the Gospels. Praying to our Father should make our hearts more trusting and humble, and at the same time inspire a desire to be more like God.

NOT YET COMPLETE

Focus How can we work for the kingdom?

If Jesus came to proclaim and witness to God's kingdom, why isn't the world a place of perfect peace, love, and justice? Why does so much injustice still exist? It's because the kingdom is here, but it's not yet complete. Jesus gave us the Church to continue his mission and work. When Christ comes again, then the kingdom will be complete.

The Kingdom Grows The amazing thing about the Kingdom of God is that it's meant to grow and expand. Jesus once told this parable to help his followers understand the kingdom.

✝ SCRIPTURE "The kingdom of heaven is like a mustard seed that someone took and sowed in his field; it is the smallest of all the seeds, but when it has grown it is the greatest of shrubs and becomes a tree, so that the birds of the air come and make nests in its branches."

—*Matthew 13:31–32*

But how does the kingdom grow? By God's presence and work and the ways we work with him to spread the Gospel message. What an amazing idea that, like the first disciples, Jesus sends us on a mission to bring his life and love to others.

? **How do you think the kingdom has grown since Jesus' time?**

? **How can you continue to help the kingdom to grow?**

So What Should We Do? We need to say and do things that reflect God's love, peace, and justice. We can start with our family and friends. How do we respond to their needs? Are we trustworthy? Do we tell them the truth even when it might be difficult? Do we consider how our choices will affect them? When we make the wrong moral decisions, we affect others, perhaps even taking away from their dignity. We can avoid saying hurtful things during tense conversations as a way to resolve conflicts.

There's a lot we can do in our immediate circle, but then we need to take it a step further. We realize that social justice comes about by people working together. Our parishes make choices to do good, to participate in activities that treat people fairly, and to take a stand for what is right regarding local, national, and global issues. The Church has many nonprofit agencies and organizations that look out for others and seek to change what harms others and keeps them from following Jesus. In all of these activities, the Church trusts that the Holy Spirit leads us where we need to be.

What can you do with your family to show that you are working for the kingdom?

ACTIVITY

CONNECT YOUR FAITH Work in small groups to make a collage of signs of the kingdom in your local community. Use photos cut from magazines or newspapers, or create your own drawings. Write captions to describe how the images are signs of God's love, peace, and justice.

✝ **SCRIPTURE**

GO TO THE SOURCE
Read **Luke 18:18–30**. Jesus teaches that we must detach ourselves from our riches if we want to enter the Kingdom of God. Discuss what your riches are, how difficult or easy it is to give them up, and where you might start simplifying your lifestyle.

CHECK THIS OUT!

In the Gospel according to Matthew, Jesus teaches us: "Blessed are the poor in spirit, for theirs is the kingdom of heaven" (*Matthew 5:3*). Poor in spirit doesn't mean we don't have money. A lot of rich people are poor in spirit. It means that we humans cannot make money or riches into a god, but we need to depend on the one true God for strength and guidance. The Tenth Commandment teaches us:

▶ to be glad for others' good fortune and not envious of them

▶ not to be jealous of the things others have

▶ not to be greedy or overly concerned about power or being in charge (See *Exodus 20:17*.)

It's sometimes difficult not to want what others have and seem to enjoy. But we can keep things in perspective. Prayer, goodwill toward others, and trusting in God's care of us help us resist envy.

LIVING FOR THE KINGDOM

🔘 **Focus** What attitudes reflect God's kingdom?

You can't fight City Hall. . . Whoever gets the most toys, wins. . . Bigger is better. . . If you can't beat 'em, join 'em.

We hear messages like these a lot, whether it's in TV commercials or real life. Sometimes the lines blur, and our lives become too much like a video game or a reality TV show.

Often, competing and consuming become more important than cooperating. In the struggle for money, popularity, and power, many good people get chewed up and spit out. Maybe you've heard this message: Nice guys finish last. Is that what happened to Jesus?

We know better than that. Through his death on the cross and his Resurrection, Jesus accomplished the coming of his kingdom. Some people might see a crucifix and think "What a loser!" We know that Jesus won the ultimate battle when he defeated death itself by rising from the dead.

Our Brothers' and Sisters' Keepers Our Church teaches that government and business leaders must respect people's fundamental rights and also the conditions that let them use their rights. Everyone has a right to life and to the necessities of life like food, clothing, shelter, medicine, and education—things we sometimes take for granted. People have the right to vote, speak freely, own property, and run their own businesses. If governments or businesses don't let people have these rights, the Church speaks out. Ultimately, as it says in Acts 5:29, "We must obey God rather than any human authority."

Solidarity is a word our Church uses to describe unity with all of our brothers and sisters throughout the world. In solidarity, we practice the sharing of spiritual and material goods. It encourages us to be generous and to live simply, so that others might be blessed with our generosity. Solidarity is a Christian virtue that motivates us to share our spiritual gifts, even more so than our material ones.

Life is freer and simpler when you make God's love your true goal. Have faith, and don't let anything or anyone distract you from that goal. Believing in God makes it possible for you to put him first in your life, not things or accomplishments. Objects and people, even the ones you love or who love you the most, are no substitute for God.

WHERE IT HAPPENED

THE CHURCH calls for acts of justice around the world. A brave example of this happened in the 1980s, when Pope Saint John Paul II showed his support for a workers' movement in Poland called "Solidarity." He encouraged workers to rise up for their rights. This led to new freedom in Poland and the end of oppressive governments throughout Eastern Europe, including Russia.

ACTIVITY

LIVE YOUR FAITH List three popular slogans, sayings, or ads that do *not* reflect the attitudes of the kingdom. After that, make up one that does.

IN SUMMARY

CATHOLICS BELIEVE

Jesus made justice a priority. It was the heart of his message of the kingdom toward which we all work.

▶ Jesus welcomes all people to God's kingdom of love, peace, and justice. As his followers we have to show others we are called to end hunger, poverty, and injustice.

▶ God's kingdom is present but not yet complete; we prepare for and work toward the kingdom through prayer, sharing Jesus' Good News, just action, and advocacy for those in need.

▶ We need to rely on God, trust in his care, and have the right attitude toward money and things; doing so helps us concentrate on what's important and work for the rights of others.

CELEBRATION OF THE WORD

Leader: Throughout all time and in every generation,
people have gathered to listen to God's word.
We too come to hear God's message
for our time and our place.

Reader 1: A reading from the holy Gospel according to Luke.

Read Luke 5:27–32.

The Gospel of the Lord.

All: Praise to you, Lord Jesus Christ.

Reader 2: O God of compassion,
you call us to set a place at our table;
a place for the poor and homeless among us.
Where water runs clear and blankets give warmth,
and mothers rest safe and secure through the night.

Reader 1: O God of all justice,
you call us to set a place at our table;
a place for the worker, the women and children.
Where wages are fair and justly divided,
where all have a chance to improve their position,
and schoolwork and learning provide a solution,
and all have a dream and invest in a future.

Reader 2: O God of the lonely,
you call us to set a place at our table;
a place for the outcast, the elders and strangers.
Where hands reach to welcome,
where smiles invite friendship,
where medicine and care are well within reach,
where respect and compassion melt hearts
    that can judge.

Leader: O God,
we hear your call and the challenge before us.
Help us to be your people of welcome
    and justice.
In all that we do and in all that we say,
give us the heart of Jesus, your Son,
our way, truth, and life.

All: Amen.

♪ "A Place at the Table"
Lori True, © 2001, GIA Publications, Inc.

R3VI3W

A **Work with Words** Circle the letter of the choice that best completes the sentence.

1. _____ gives God and neighbor what is due to them.
   - **a.** Tolerance
   - **b.** Justice
   - **c.** Patience
   - **d.** Kindness

2. The word *solidarity* is used by the Church to describe _____.
   - **a.** the Kingdom of God
   - **b.** Church traditions
   - **c.** unity with all people around the world
   - **d.** the sacraments of the Church

3. To _____ means to be sorry for our sins and change our ways.
   - **a.** anoint
   - **b.** pray
   - **c.** repent
   - **d.** rehabilitate

4. _____ is God's rule of love, peace, and justice in our hearts, lives, and the world.
   - **a.** The Kingdom of God
   - **b.** Repentance
   - **c.** Holiness
   - **d.** Jesus' mission

B **Check Understanding** Complete each sentence with the correct term from the word bank at right.

5. The Tenth Commandment teaches us not to be _____ of what others have and accomplish.

6. Hunger, poverty, and injustice all come from _____.

7. When Christ comes again, the _____ of God will be complete.

8. In a parable, Jesus tells us that the Kingdom of Heaven is like a _____.

9. Jesus showed us that you cannot have the kingdom without _____.

10. The _____ is often called the perfect prayer because it sums up the message of the Gospels.

Word Bank

- Rosary
- sin
- salvation
- Church
- justice
- Kingdom
- Lord's Prayer
- envious
- mustard seed

C **Make Connections: Synthesize** Write a one-paragraph response to the question below.

How does the Lord's Prayer connect with your life? Rewrite the prayer in your own words, making it personal and specific to your life.

OUR CATHOLIC FAITH

WHAT NOW?

★ Learn about the kingdom that Jesus preached.

★ Reflect on your lifestyle—do you treat others justly?

★ Make a commitment to simplify your life and become less attached to possessions.

★ Get involved in helping people who are poor, homeless, and without access to jobs, medical help, or education.

ACTIVITY

LIVE YOUR FAITH What can you do to make acts of justice part of your life? Try this:

▶ **SEE, JUDGE, AND ACT**

1. Think about a social justice problem.
2. Learn more about it.
3. Find out what Jesus says about it.
4. Do something about it!

SEE First, *get involved* as Christ teaches. When you see a poster advertising for the food drive, you recognize a need and think about what you can do to help.

JUDGE Next, *explore* the problem by performing research online or in magazines and newspapers. You'll learn that one in six children in the United States lives in poverty. Then *reflect* on what Jesus and the Church say. (Matthew 25:35, 40 might inspire you.)

ACT Finally, *do something about it*. Volunteer to help out at the food pantry. Maybe while you're there, you'll hear people talk about struggling to feed their families when their jobs pay so little. You'll see that something needs to be done, and think that maybe you can help.

▶ **Think about a justice issue that concerns you or an event that disturbs you, and follow the steps.**

SEE An event that gets me thinking _____

JUDGE What I've learned from the news _____

What Jesus and the Church say _____

ACT What can I do? _____

GO online Visit **www.osvcurriculum.com** for more family and community connections.

 **PRAYER**

Lord, help me do something to change the world to be more like your kingdom.

Pope Leo XIII

Gioacchino Vincenzo Raffaele Luigi Pecci lived ninety-three years, between 1810 and 1903. He witnessed political and social upheavals that changed the face of Europe and helped define the role of the Church in modern times. His papacy, as Leo XIII, from 1878 until his death, helped the Church survive a stormy period in history.

Following the example of Jesus in his pursuit of justice and peace, Leo helped settle troubles between nations and within nations. He showed his talent for diplomatic skills early in his career. His skills were useful to the popes he served before he became pope himself.

Italy was in turmoil in the middle of the 1800s. Disputes between states that had formerly been independent or under French control were widespread. Ruthless bands of outlaws roamed freely over southern Italy. The papacy itself was surrounded, under political siege in the middle of the Italian peninsula. Officials of the clergy were attacked by secular authorities seeking to limit their power.

Leo skillfully led the Church through this difficult time. Drawing upon his diplomatic experience as a papal legate to Belgium, he helped guide the government of that nation and others down the path of justice and religious tolerance. His friendship with King Leopold I and Queen Louise enabled Belgium to avoid the religious upheavals taking place in neighboring Germany. Catholic schools were established in Belgium and for Belgians living in Rome.

As Germany was in the process of unifying under Bismarck, Leo helped Bismarck win the much-needed support of the nation's Catholics in exchange for ending *Kulturkampf*, the persecution of Catholics there. Exiled bishops were restored to their offices. Leo also helped solve problems the Church faced in the British Isles, Eastern Europe, North and South America, the Far East, and India. He aided in the creation of new religious orders, and he elevated 147 cardinals.

Historians have noted how much the careers of Leo and Pope Saint John Paul II have been alike, although they lived one hundred years apart. In addition to their diplomatic skills, both were linguists and scholars. They both wrote extensively and both beatified and canonized a large number of saints. Both strongly opposed Marxism and the spread of its atheism. By the time of Leo's death, he was already regarded as one of the greatest popes of all time.

▲ **Pope Leo XIII, 1810–1903**

GLOBAL DATA

Italy

- **Italy is a long, boot-shaped peninsula jutting out into the Mediterranean Sea in southern Europe.**

- **The Holy See is centered at Vatican City in Rome.**

- **Italy was the center of the Roman Empire that lasted for six centuries.**

- **Italy was the center for learning and the arts during the Renaissance and was the mercantile hub of the Mediterranean region for nearly two thousand years.**

- **Italy was unified into one nation in the 1870s.**

- **Italy now has 61 million people, 90 percent of whom are Roman Catholic.**

CHAPTER 21 OUR Reason for Hope

✓ PRAYER O God, teach me to watch and pray.

Where do people go when they die?
Will I ever see that person again?
What do I need to do to go to heaven?

"**Lock** the door behind me, Jimmy. I'll be home soon."

"Mom, please call me James. I'm not six. And don't worry so much."

"Sorry, honey," his mom said, giving him a squeeze and looking into his face through sad, swollen eyes. "It's been a long day. I'm so sorry about your birthday. This just isn't fair for you." Her voice caught in her throat.

"Don't sweat it," James said. "It's been rough for everyone, and a party would just feel wrong with everything that's happening. Hug Grandma for me."

James flipped the deadbolt and flopped on the couch. Tonight he felt numb after his uncle's funeral.

Even though he was named after Uncle Jim, they had never been really close. When James was little, his uncle would come to their home every Christmas and would call every year to shout "Happy B-day, Jimbo!" But then he got busy.

Lately, Uncle Jim visited whenever he drove through town on business. Last week, he watched James play baseball. They had plans to go to a game next month. Then, just like that, he was gone. It all seemed unreal.

James wondered if he would see Uncle Jim in heaven. Grandma said Uncle Jim had just started coming back to church. He'd even gone to confession.

Where was Uncle Jim now? What wouldn't he give to hear Uncle Jim's voice again! Even that corny name, "Jimbo . . ."

James flipped through the mail and held up an envelope. He couldn't believe it. It was from Uncle Jim. He opened it cautiously and found a picture of himself pitching last week. On the back was scrawled, "Great game! You're growing up fast. But isn't 'James' a bit *too* formal? Love, Uncle Jim.

P.S. Happy Birthday, Jimbo! Can't wait to see you at the ball game next month!"

ACTIVITY

LET'S BEGIN In this story James wondered if Uncle Jim would go to heaven. How could he be sure? What were some of the feelings James was having about Uncle Jim's death?

▶ **Which of your friends or relatives who have died do you miss the most? What makes you think they're with God? Do you worry about getting to heaven? Does that affect decisions you make?**

JESUS GIVES US HOPE

Focus What does Jesus promise about eternal life?

We always worry about death when someone is seriously ill. But it's also natural to wonder about what will come after. We might think about how things will be different when someone we love is no longer with us. Our concern for a relative or friend who is very sick would send us running to be with that person and help however we could.

✝ **SCRIPTURE**

GO TO THE SOURCE
Read **John 11:1–44** and think about Jesus' love for his friends.

✝ **SCRIPTURE** One day while traveling with his disciples, Jesus heard that his friend Lazarus was ill. Then Lazarus died. When Jesus arrived at their home, Lazarus's sister Martha said "Lord, if you had been here, my brother would not have died. But even now I know that God will give you whatever you ask of him."

Jesus told her:

"I am the resurrection and the life. Those who believe in me, even though they die, will live . . ."

Martha told Jesus that she believed he is the Messiah. Because of her belief, and because Jesus wants people to believe in him and give glory to his Father who sent him, Jesus called Lazarus out of the tomb. Lazarus did not rise under his own power, but under the power of God. Jesus showed that he had power over humanity's greatest fear, death.

—*John 11:1–44*

❓ **What kind of life is Jesus offering us?**

Is There Hope for Us? Lazarus and his sisters were great friends with Jesus. Because of this, Jesus came for Lazarus. Because of Martha's belief, he raised Lazarus. Like so many people back then, they hoped for a messiah. And because of their hope and belief, Jesus gave them even more reason to hope.

Lazarus's return to earthly life is very different from what happened at Jesus' Resurrection. Jesus rose to new life, a glorified life in which he returned to the Father. Jesus' Resurrection gives those who believe hope.

As you know, hope is one of the three theological virtues. The other two are faith and charity (which can also be called "love.") The theological virtues are

▲ *Resurrection of Lazarus,* by Fra Angelico (c. 1387–1455)

gifts from God that help you live your life in ways that strengthen your relationship with the Holy Trinity: God the Father, Son, and the Holy Sprit.

Christian hope puts things into this perspective—that happiness comes from life with God. It helps you put your trust in Jesus' promises and the strength of the Holy Spirit. This hope keeps you motivated and going even during difficult times. It helps you put the right emphasis on the things that really matter, the things that relate to loving God and others.

heaven

hell

particular judgment

purgatory

last judgment

Spiritual Works of Mercy

CHECK THIS OUT!

For hope, look to Paul, who wrote to the Colossians that Jesus is "the beginning, the first-born from the dead" (*Colossians 1:18*). There will be more to come. Because of Jesus' Resurrection to new life, we, too, hope to rise again.

Paul wrote to the Romans that if the Spirit of God is in us, it will give life to our bodies, even though they are dead. (See *Romans 8:11.*) Our Baptism joins us with Christ; we die with him to sin, and we live a full and new life in God.

ACTIVITY

SHARE YOUR FAITH In groups of three, give the reason(s) you have hope in eternal life. Also talk about what makes it hard to have such hope. What do you think it takes to get to heaven?

I HAVE HOPE

IT'S HARD TO HOPE

WHAT IT TAKES

LIFE AFTER DEATH

Focus How will we be judged by God?

No one can be sure what heaven will be like, but our tradition tells us that **heaven** is the state, or experience, of being happy with God forever.

Jesus warns us about judgment at our death in a parable he tells about a rich man who ignored a beggar. They both eventually die; the beggar is carried away by angels, and the rich man winds up in the netherworld, which we know as **hell**. There he suffers in flames.

Jesus also describes a great chasm—a gap that would probably make the Grand Canyon look like a gopher hole—between the rich man and heaven. (See *Luke 16: 19–31*.) Hell is being apart from God forever. God is the source of our life and happiness. Imagine being without life or happiness forever.

If you knew your life would end tomorrow, what would you do?

◀ *Paradise*, by Jacopo Robusti Tintoretto (1518–1594)

How Late Is Too Late?

When we die, we'll be out of time to accept or to reject the love and grace Jesus offers us. We can take it or leave it today, but at the moment we die our destiny for eternity will be based on whether we have accepted God's love. At the moment of death, each person's soul is rewarded with the blessings of heaven, given a time of purification in purgatory, or condemned to eternal separation from God in hell. We call this the **particular judgment**.

God's willingness to accept our repentance, forgive us, and bring us to eternal happiness is available to us as long as we live. Jesus proves this on the cross. One of the criminals crucified with Jesus admits that he has sinned and asks, "Jesus, remember me when you come into your kingdom." Jesus tells him ". . . today you will be with me in Paradise." (See *Luke 23:42–43*.) But think about this: Isn't it much more satisfying to go through life with the inner peace that comes with knowing that you are living as God asks? God's way is not just about happiness later in heaven; living in his love and guidance is the surest way to peace and joy in this lifetime, too.

Why is it such a challenge to live as God asks?

What's Purgatory? We receive God's grace through Baptism and accept God's loving friendship. If we live our lives and have repented for our sins, die in God's grace, and are perfectly purified, we are welcomed into heaven. However, if we have remained in God's friendship but are in need of forgiveness or satisfaction for temporal punishment for sins already forgiven, we will enter a condition called **purgatory**. Purgatory is not a place, but a state of being in which we are purified before we enter heaven. This cleansing needs to happen before we experience the joy of eternal happiness with God.

Purgatory purifies us, but it's very different from the punishment of hell. Our prayers for the dead help provide the grace that the souls in purgatory need to be welcomed into God's heavenly kingdom.

ACTIVITY

CONNECT YOUR FAITH Think about some actions and behaviors that might lead you to disobey or turn away from God. Then list three positive behaviors or actions that can counter these and help you strengthen your relationship with God.

1. _____

2. _____

3. _____

THE SECOND COMING

Focus How can we be with Jesus on the last day?

Someday, at God's word, our world will end. Nobody knows when or why, or what it will look like. We just know that life as we know it will end and creation will be transformed. And as we pray at Mass, Jesus "will come again in glory to judge the living and the dead."

Who Will Inherit the Kingdom? Jesus described pretty simply what will happen when he comes again. At the second coming, the **last judgment** will take place, during which all the living and dead will be judged. Those who have died will appear in their own bodies before Christ. In the Gospel according to Matthew's description of this judgment, the glorified Christ will sit on a throne, putting the righteous people on his right side and the others on his left, like a shepherd in Jesus' day would separate sheep from goats.

The faithful people will have life forever in heaven with God because they lived good lives and reached out to people in need. This includes feeding someone who was hungry, welcoming a stranger, or taking care of a sick person. At the end of the world, Jesus will reveal the secrets of our hearts and judge each of us in light of our works and the degree to which we accepted his grace or refused it and sinned. Jesus knows what each of us do, just as he knows when we turn to him or turn away from him in our lives.

The kingdom that Jesus talked so much about will come into fullness at the last judgment. As Christ has risen, so will we. Our bodies will be transformed by reuniting with our souls. The righteous will be with Jesus forever and the world will be transformed. Then God will be "all in all."

What do you think about being judged?

What can you do to prepare yourself?

The Works of Mercy The Works of Mercy are ways to respond to Jesus when we see him in the poor and needy. The Corporal Works of Mercy meet people's physical needs, and the **Spiritual Works of Mercy** bring spiritual hope and healing.

Often several Works of Mercy are done together. For instance, if a friend's grandma dies, you're more likely to comfort your friend and pray for her grandma, while somebody else will deliver flowers and other people will speak at her funeral. Jesus is pleased with whatever we do for people in need.

ACTIVITY

LIVE YOUR FAITH Complete the third column with your own ideas.

CORPORAL WORKS OF MERCY	ONE THING YOU CAN DO	SOMETHING I'LL TRY
Feed the hungry.	Donate to a food drive.	
Give drink to the thirsty.	Help Catholic Relief Services.	
Clothe the naked.	Donate your old clothing.	
Shelter the homeless.	Support Habitat for Humanity.	
Visit the sick.	Visit a nursing home.	
Visit those in prison.	Support Jubilee Campaign.	
Bury the dead.	Help clean up a local cemetery.	
SPIRITUAL WORKS OF MERCY		
Counsel the doubtful.	Share God's love with a friend.	
Instruct the ignorant.	Help teach little kids at church.	
Admonish the sinner.	Confront a friend who's sinned.	
Comfort the sorrowful.	Help a friend who's sad.	
Forgive injuries.	Accept someone's apology.	
Bear wrongs patiently.	Give someone a second chance.	
Pray for the living and the dead.	Pray for a loved one by name.	

IN SUMMARY

CATHOLICS BELIEVE

By his death and Resurrection, Jesus makes it possible for believers to have eternal life—life with God forever.

► Christian hope is based upon putting our trust in God and the hope that we will rise one day as Jesus did.

► We will be judged at our death based upon the ways we have accepted and acted on God's grace in our lives; God desires all of us to make the right choices in life, so we can be with him forever in the happiness of heaven.

► Jesus will come at the end of time to judge the living and the dead, and the Kingdom of God will be complete and full in its glory.

PRAYER

PRAYER OF HOPE

Leader: Awesome and loving Father,
who knows our thoughts before we speak them,
who through your Son gave clear instruction,
who through the Spirit sent insight and wisdom,
teach us and show us the joy of your kingdom.

Side 1: Jesus tells us that
"the kingdom of God is like the mustard seed,
the yeast, the narrow door," and more . . .
We hear all who question,
"what must I do to live in your kingdom?"
And every time we pray the Lord's Prayer, we say,
"thy kingdom come, thy will be done."

All: Teach us and show us the joy of your kingdom.

Side 2: We live in a time where seeing is believing,
a world sometimes led by the loudest voice . . .
So often these days fear and anxiety,
power and greed,
boredom and sadness drive the thoughts of our mind.

All: Teach us and show us the joy of your kingdom.

Side 1: Help us, Loving Father, help us right now.
Turn our eyes to you,
bend our ears to hear your voice,
to trust in your word,
to have faith and believe.
Give us the mind of your Son, Jesus,
that we may know the gift that awaits us,
that we may live for a better day,
that we may share in the promise of
your kingdom.

All: Teach us and show us the joy of your kingdom.

Leader: At the Savior's command
and formed by divine teaching,
we dare to say:

All: Our Father, who art in heaven . . .

♪ "Eye Has Not Seen"
Marty Haugen, © 1982, GIA Publications, Inc.

REVIEW

A **Work with Words** Circle the letter of the choice that best completes the sentence.

1. Faith, hope, and charity are _____.
   - **a.** moral virtues
   - **b.** necessary for healing
   - **c.** sacraments
   - **d.** theological virtues

2. In Jesus' parable of the rich man and the beggar, the rich man is sent to _____.
   - **a.** the netherworld
   - **b.** Purgatory
   - **c.** heaven
   - **d.** both a and c

3. At the time of the _____, each person's soul is rewarded with the blessings of heaven, given a time in purgatory, or condemned to hell.
   - **a.** divine judgment
   - **b.** eternal judgment
   - **c.** particular judgment
   - **d.** none of these

4. Purgatory is a process of being _____ before entering heaven.
   - **a.** cleansed
   - **b.** judged
   - **c.** condemned
   - **d.** rewarded

5. In the Gospel of John, when Jesus goes to raise Lazarus from the dead, Jesus says he is _____ and the _____.
   - **a.** forgiveness, salvation
   - **b.** hope, peace
   - **c.** mercy, grace
   - **d.** Resurrection, life

B **Check Understanding** Indicate whether the following statements are true or false. Then rewrite false statements to make them true.

_____ 6. Catholic Tradition defines heaven as the state of being happy with God forever.

_____

_____ 7. Hell is defined as a state where people are separated from God for a short time.

_____

_____ 8. Prayers for the dead help provide the grace needed by souls in hell in order to be welcomed into heaven.

_____

_____ 9. At the second coming of Jesus, the last judgment will take place.

_____

_____ 10. At the last judgment, those who have died in God's good graces will become spirits.

_____

C **Make Connections: Cause and Effect** Write a one-paragraph response to the question below.

Think about the Corporal and Spiritual Works of Mercy. What would happen in your life and in the lives of others if you responded to people's needs with God's love? Give a specific example.

OUR CATHOLIC FAITH

WHAT NOW?

★ Think about who your brothers and sisters are.

★ Consider what their needs are.

★ Act on one of those needs this week.

★ Think about how you can help as you get older.

★ Pray for those who have died.

ACTIVITY

LIVE YOUR FAITH Take the meaning of Christian hope to heart. Change your outlook on troubling issues. Offer hope-filled advice to friends and family. Consider what it really means to trust in God.

▶ Use each of the letters below to name something you can do to become a more hope-filled person.

H _____

_____

O _____

_____

P _____

_____

E _____

_____

GO online Visit www.osvcurriculum.com for more family and community connections.

PRAYER

Lord, help me live simply so that others might simply live.

Saint Peter Claver

In the 1600s and 1700s, when Africans were kidnapped and brought to the Americas as slaves, they had little reason for hope. In many cases, they didn't even know why they were being kidnapped, and could not ask because they didn't know the language of their captors. They were herded into the holds of ships and chained together. They were forced to live in close, squalid quarters with little or no food on a journey across the Atlantic Ocean that took many weeks.

When they got to the Americas and began to understand their captors' plans for them, they had even less reason for hope. They were prisoners in a strange land with unfamiliar language and customs, and they were often treated inhumanely. No one seemed to care whether they lived or died—until Peter Claver came along.

Peter Claver was born in Spain in 1580. He took his vows in 1604, two years after entering the Jesuit novitiate in Tarragona. While studying philosophy on the island of Majorca, Alphonsus Rodriguez (who was later canonized) encouraged Peter Claver to go to the Americas and "save millions of perishing souls," the souls of the captured African slaves.

Landing in Cartagena, New Granada (later Colombia) in 1610, Peter went to work immediately. He boarded ships as they docked and helped feed and clothe the Africans before they disembarked. He brought warmth, medicine, and spiritual remedies. He ministered the Gospel to them. To those who were already dying, he administered the Sacraments and last rites, giving them hope of heaven.

Peter followed the enslaved Africans to the plantations on which they were forced to work. There he and his followers taught them the Gospel. He gave them hope for a glorious afterlife. In many cases, he persuaded their owners to treat them humanely. He spoke out against the evils of the slave trade and founded charitable societies similar to those of St. Vincent de Paul.

Over a forty-year period, Peter Claver was reputed to have saved about 300,000 souls, mostly enslaved Africans, by converting them to Christianity. He died in 1654 and was canonized by Pope Leo XIII in 1888. The Knights of St. Peter Claver is a predominantly African American fraternal order that is named after him. He is also the namesake of predominantly black dioceses in two of the largest cities in Louisiana.

▲ Saint Peter Claver, 1580–1654

GLOBAL DATA

Colombia

- Colombia is in the northwest corner of South America and is the only South American nation bordering on both the Caribbean Sea and the Pacific Ocean.

- Colombia has a population of 44 million, 90 percent of whom are Roman Catholic.

- Colombia was conquered by the Spanish in the 1530s and administered as a part of New Granada, which also included what today is Venezuela, Ecuador, and Panama.

- Colombia won independence from Spain in 1819 and lost Panama in 1903 to rebels who wanted a canal built across it by the Americans.

Faith in Action!
CATHOLIC SOCIAL TEACHING

DISCOVER — Catholic Social Teaching:
Option for the Poor and Vulnerable

IN THIS UNIT you learned about using your time, talents, and things for others and about that important passage in the Gospels—whatever you do to the least of Jesus' brothers and sisters, you do to him.

Option for the Poor

Nothing in the life of Jesus is as clear as his love for the poor and others considered outcasts by society. In fact, the Church says that Jesus had a "preferential love" for these people. Saint Rose of Lima put it this way: "When we serve the poor and the sick, we serve Jesus. We must not fail to help our neighbors, because in them we serve Jesus, (P. Hansen, *Vita mirablis* [Louvain, 1668])." No wonder the Church says that among the options we face when we decide what to do with our time, with our talents, and with our possessions and money, our first option, perhaps after our own family, should be the poor. We should prefer (show "preferential love" for) them more than others.

This may be easy to say, but it is certainly difficult to do. Everyone wants to hang out with their friends and take care of their own needs. Hanging out with those who don't have lots of friends or things, sharing with them, or helping them in some way—that's sacrificial love. But that's our mission—to be the sacrificial love of Jesus for others.

A story might help here. It's about an American soldier during World War II. His unit was marching across an Italian hillside. When they stopped for a break, he wandered into some tall bushes, where he discovered a statue of Jesus, but the hands were missing. He stared at that statue for a long time. Then he took out a piece of paper and wrote these words— "I have no hands but yours." Jesus is saying that to each of us, too. He has no hands but ours.

> **If Jesus is to show the poor who live around you his preferential love for them, how will he do it except through you and others like you?**

294

JESUS CALLS US TO REPOND to injustice with compassion. Let's look at how some students responded.

HUNGER CALLS FORTH COMPASSION

YOUNG PEOPLE RESPOND CREATIVELY

The Caritas Food Shelf in St. Cloud, Minnesota, had recently relocated, and the coordinator was concerned about how "sterile and unwelcoming" the waiting area felt—just rows of chairs and bare white walls. She mentioned this concern to a group of students from an art class at John XXIII Middle School, who had come to the Food Shelf on a field trip. They responded by creating murals to be hung on the walls. Their sense of compassion was clear to Julie Grimsley, their art teacher, who said this was the first time they hadn't asked how they would be graded.

A second group from John XXIII Middle School wanted to go further in their exploration of poverty and hunger. They developed a videotape for Caritas, including an interview with a woman who had experienced poverty, plus a "tour" of the Food Shelf. They also added a packet of classroom materials that could be used with the video. One of the activities was a budgeting exercise. Students received an income similar to that of a low-income household and were asked to work with their parents or guardians to set up a monthly budget. The exercise touched the students deeply. It gave them a real sense of what it's like for poor people and a new sense of respect for the courage of poor people to keep going in the face of such difficult choices. Caritas now uses the video and these other materials as part of its effort to educate the local community on poverty and hunger issues.

What do you think are some of the difficult choices that low-income families have to make each month in budgeting their income?

▼ **Students created murals for the walls of the Caritas Food Shelf.**

...These three remain: Faith, Hope, and Love And the greatest of these is Love

SERVE Your Community

MAKING THE POOR A "PREFERENCE" IN YOUR LIFE

Figure out for yourself how much "free time" you have each month and how you could choose to spend at least one or two hours a month (of it being) with the poor, the sick, or the lonely people around you.

Figure out how much "spending money" you have each month (week) and what 10 percent of that would be. Then decide how best to use that 10 percent on behalf of others who are in need.

FREE TIME

SERVICE

DONATION

USING YOUR TALENTS FOR THE POOR

Discuss with your classmates what groups serving low-income people in your community might be able to use students' artwork for their facilities. Assign a person or team to contact each group and report their findings. Choose which groups you want to work with and then create a plan for providing the artwork.

Project Planning Sheet

What classes to ask to do the artwork

_____

Who else needs to be contacted about this project?

_____

How to publicize the project

_____

Other specific tasks

_____

_____

Your specific task(s)

_____

_____

Calendar for completing the project

_____

_____

Why is it difficult sometimes to give away things we like to others who need them?

_____

_____

_____

Why is it difficult sometimes to hang out with people whom others consider to be inferior?

_____

_____

_____

How does it feel when you give some of your things, money, or time to others in need?

_____

_____

_____

What did you learn about poverty and the poor in each of these actions?

_____

_____

_____

What did you learn about yourself in doing these actions?

_____

_____

_____

What did you learn about Jesus and about your faith in doing these actions?

_____

_____

_____

List one thing that might be different about you after doing this project.

_____

_____

REVIEW

A Work with Words Match the words on the left with the correct definitions or descriptions on the right.

_____ **1.** lay person

_____ **2.** domestic Church

_____ **3.** vocation

_____ **4.** justice

_____ **5.** repent

_____ **6.** Kingdom of God

_____ **7.** solidarity

_____ **8.** theological virtues

_____ **9.** particular judgment

_____ **10.** purgatory

A. virtue that gives God and neighbor what is due to them

B. unity of all people around the world

C. God's rule of love, peace, and justice in our lives and in the world

D. the family as a community of grace and prayer

E. faith, hope, and charity

F. time when souls are rewarded with heaven, required to be cleansed in purgatory, or condemned to hell

G. a baptized member of the Church who shares in Jesus' mission and witnesses to him, especially in their families, workplaces, and civic communities

H. the state of being cleansed before being able to enter heaven

I. a holy calling

J. to be sorry for sin and change behavior

B Check Understanding Indicate whether the following statements are true or false. Then rewrite false statements to make them true.

_____ **11.** The family is the first place to learn about the good within people and discover Christ's love.

_____

_____ **12.** Lay people share in Jesus' priesthood by teaching in parables as he did.

_____

_____ **13.** When you use discernment, you weigh your choices and pray for guidance.

_____

_____ **14.** Jesus taught us that we cannot have the kingdom without justice.

_____

_____ **15.** The Lord's Prayer is often called the perfect prayer because it sums up the message of the Gospels.

_____

_____ **16.** In the Gospel according to John, when Jesus goes to raise Lazarus from the dead, he says he is the Resurrection and life.

_____

_____ **17.** Hell is defined as being apart from the people you love forever.

_____

_____ **18.** At the last judgment, those who have died in God's good graces will be glorified in body and soul.

_____

C **Make Connections** Write a short answer to the questions below.

19. Cause and Effect. Jesus taught that all people deserve to be treated equally. How would your school be different if the Kingdom of God—God's love, peace, and justice—became a reality there?

_____

_____

_____

_____

20. Explain. Imagine you are a reporter at the last judgment. Write about what you see happening there. How are different people responding? What are your reactions as you watch?

_____

_____

_____

_____

CATHOLIC SOURCE BOOK

THE BOOKS OF THE BIBLE

The Catholic Bible contains seventy-three books—forty-six in the Old Testament and twenty-seven in the New Testament.

The Old Testament

The Pentateuch

Genesis	Exodus	Leviticus	Numbers	Deuteronomy

The Historical Books

Joshua	1 Samuel	2 Kings	Ezra	Judith
Judges	2 Samuel	1 Chronicles	Nehemiah	Esther
Ruth	1 Kings	2 Chronicles	Tobit	1 Maccabees
				2 Maccabees

The Wisdom Books

Job	Proverbs	Song of Solomon	Sirach (Ecclesiasticus)
Psalms	Ecclesiastes	Wisdom	

The Prophetic Books

Isaiah	Ezekiel	Amos	Nahum	Haggai
Jeremiah	Daniel	Obadiah	Habakkuk	Zechariah
Lamentations	Hosea	Jonah	Zephaniah	Malachi
Baruch	Joel	Micah		

The New Testament

The Gospels

Matthew	Mark	Luke	John

The Acts of the Apostles

The New Testament Letters

Romans	Ephesians	2 Thessalonians	Philemon	2 Peter
1 Corinthians	Philippians	1 Timothy	Hebrews	1 John
2 Corinthians	Colossians	2 Timothy	James	2 John
Galatians	1 Thessalonians	Titus	1 Peter	3 John
				Jude

Revelation

Creeds

A creed is a summary of the Christian faith. The word *creed* means "I believe." Two examples of creeds are the Apostles' Creed and the Nicene Creed.

The Nicene Creed

I believe in one God,
the Father almighty,
maker of heaven and earth,
of all things visible and invisible.

I believe in one Lord Jesus Christ,
the Only Begotten Son of God,
born of the Father before all ages.
God from God, Light from Light,
true God from true God,
begotten, not made, consubstantial
    with the Father;
through him all things were made.
For us men and for our salvation
he came down from heaven,

*At the words that follow up to and
including* and became man, *all bow.*

and by the Holy Spirit was incarnate of the
    Virgin Mary,
and became man.

For our sake he was crucified under
    Pontius Pilate,

he suffered death and was buried,
and rose again on the third day
in accordance with the Scriptures.
He ascended into heaven
and is seated at the right hand of
    the Father.
He will come again in glory
to judge the living and the dead
and his kingdom will have no end.

I believe in the Holy Spirit, the Lord,
    the giver of life,
who proceeds from the Father and the Son,
who with the Father and the Son is
    adored and glorified,
who has spoken through the prophets.

I believe in one, holy, catholic and
    apostolic Church.
I confess one Baptism for the
    forgiveness of sins
and I look forward to the resurrection
    of the dead
and the life of the world to come. Amen.

The Apostles' Creed

I believe in God,
the Father almighty,
Creator of heaven and earth,
and in Jesus Christ, his only Son,
    our Lord,

At the words that follow, up to and including the
Virgin Mary, *all bow.*

who was conceived by the Holy Spirit,
born of the Virgin Mary,
suffered under Pontius Pilate,
was crucified, died and was buried;
he descended into hell;

on the third day he rose again from
    the dead;
he ascended into heaven,
and is seated at the right hand of God
    the Father almighty;
from there he will come to judge the
    living and the dead.

I believe in the Holy Spirit,
the holy catholic Church,
the communion of saints,
the forgiveness of sins,
the resurrection of the body,
and life everlasting. Amen.

THE CHURCH WORSHIPS

The Sacraments

Sacraments of Initiation: Baptism, Confirmation, Eucharist

Sacraments of Healing: Reconciliation, Anointing of the Sick

Sacraments at the Service of Communion: Matrimony, Holy Orders

The Liturgy of the Hours

The Liturgy of the Hours is the Church's public prayer to mark each day as holy. This liturgy is offered at set times throughout the day and night. In monasteries monks and nuns gather as many as ten times each day and night to pray the Liturgy of the Hours. Parishes that celebrate the Liturgy of the Hours do so less frequently, perhaps once or twice each day. The most common celebrations of the Liturgy of the Hours are Morning Prayer and Evening Prayer.

The Liturgical Year

The liturgical year is the Church's annual cycle of seasons and feasts that celebrates the Paschal mystery. It begins on the First Sunday of Advent and ends on the feast of Christ the King. This feast honors Jesus' reign over all of heaven and earth. It affirms the messianic kingship of Christ who gave his life through his death on the cross.

Advent

In this liturgical season, the Church devotes four weeks for the People of God to prepare to celebrate the coming of Christ at Christmas. The color for this season is violet, as a sign of anticipation and penance. On the third Sunday vestments may be pink, as is the Advent wreath candle. This is in joyful anticipation of the nearness of Christmas.

Christmas

Christmas celebrates the Son of God becoming man, God visible in humankind. This season includes the feast of Epiphany. In the current liturgical calendar, the Churches of the East and the West celebrate the birth of Christ on December 25, with the East also including the adoration of the three wise men.

Ordinary Time

This season actually occurs twice during the Church year. The first, shorter period falls between Christmas and Lent; the second period accounts for the most amount of Sundays in the Church year, starting at the end of Easter Season and ending with the Feast of Christ the King the Sunday before Advent begins. Ordinary Time is a time set apart for the everyday living of a Christian life, to learn more about Jesus' life and teaching as recorded in one of the Gospels. The color during Ordinary Time is green, a symbol of hope and new life.

Lent

The forty days of Lent are a time of fasting, prayer, and almsgiving. Lent begins with Ash Wednesday; ashes are blessed and put on the foreheads of Catholics as a reminder of their sinfulness and of penance. Ashes may be distributed during Mass after the homily or outside of Mass as part of a Liturgy of the Word. Fasting, abstinence, and personal reflection during Lent help prepare Catholics for the celebration of Easter.

Passion Sunday, also known as Palm Sunday, is the day that commemorates Jesus' entrance into Jerusalem, during which he was greeted by people waving palms and saying: Hosanna to the Son of David. Blessed palms are distributed on Passion Sunday. Later in the year, the palms from Palm Sunday are collected, burned, and may be used for the following year's Ash Wednesday liturgy.

The Triduum

The word *Triduum* means, "three days." Triduum starts with the celebration of the Lord's Supper on Holy Thursday. Good Friday is observed with a Liturgy of the Word, Veneration of the Cross, and a Communion service. On Holy Saturday evening the Easter Vigil is celebrated. The Triduum ends with evening prayer on Easter Sunday. Because the Triduum specifically celebrates the Paschal mystery—the life, death, and Resurrection of Jesus—it is the high point of the entire Church year.

Easter Season

Easter, the feast of the Resurrection of Christ, is the greatest feast of the Church year. The Easter Season begins on Easter Sunday and lasts until Pentecost, fifty days later. White is the major color of this season, but gold is used in vestments as well.

DEVOTIONS
Stations of the Cross

The Stations of the Cross commemorate the journey of Christ from the praetorium—where Pilate held court—to Calvary and the tomb. Many crusaders during the Middle Ages retraced this path, and the prayerful reflection many people experienced while retracing these steps was brought back to churches throughout Europe. The Stations of the Cross focus on fourteen scenes of Christ's Passion.

First Station: Jesus is condemned to death on the cross.

Second Station: Jesus accepts his cross.

Third Station: Jesus falls the first time.

Fourth Station: Jesus meets his sorrowful mother.

Fifth Station: Simon of Cyrene helps Jesus carry his cross.

Sixth Station: Veronica wipes the face of Jesus.

Seventh Station: Jesus falls the second time.

Eighth Station: Jesus meets and speaks to the women of Jerusalem.

Ninth Station: Jesus falls the third time.

Tenth Station: Jesus is stripped of his garments.

Eleventh Station: Jesus is nailed to the cross.

Twelfth Station: Jesus dies on the cross.

Thirteenth Station: Jesus is taken down from the cross.

Fourteenth Station: Jesus is placed in the tomb.

The Great Commandment

"You shall love the Lord your God with all your heart, and with all your soul, and with all your strength, and with all your mind; and your neighbor as yourself."

—Luke 10:27

The New Commandment

"I give you a new commandment, that you love one another. Just as I have loved you, you also should love one another."

—John 13:34

The Ten Commandments

1. I am the Lord your God. You shall not have strange gods before me.

2. You shall not take the name of the Lord your God in vain.

3. Remember to keep holy the Lord's day.

4. Honor your father and your mother.

5. You shall not kill.

6. You shall not commit adultery.

7. You shall not steal.

8. You shall not bear false witness against your neighbor.

9. You shall not covet your neighbor's wife.

10. You shall not covet your neighbor's goods.

Precepts of the Church

The following precepts are important duties of all Catholics.

1. Take part in the Mass on Sundays and holy days. Keep these days holy and avoid unnecessary work.

2. Celebrate the Sacrament of Reconciliation at least once a year if there is serious sin.

3. Receive Holy Communion at least once a year during Easter time.

4. Fast and abstain on days of penance.

5. Give your time, gifts, and money to support the Church.

Holy Days of Obligation

Catholics are required to attend Mass on Sunday unless a serious reason prevents them from doing so. Catholics also must go to Mass on certain holy days.

In the United States the holy days of obligation are the feasts of:

▶ Mary the Mother of God
January 1

▶ the Ascension of the Lord
forty days after Easter, or the Sunday nearest the end of the forty-day period

▶ the Assumption of Mary
August 15

▶ All Saints' Day
November 1

▶ the Immaculate Conception of Mary
December 8

▶ Christmas
December 25

Gifts of the Holy Spirit

Wisdom
Understanding
Right judgment (*Counsel*)
Courage (*Fortitude*)
Knowledge
Reverence (*Piety*)
Wonder and awe (*Fear of the Lord*)

Fruits of the Holy Spirit

Charity
Faithfulness
Goodness
Peace
Self-control
Gentleness
Kindness
Joy
Modesty
Generosity
Patience
Chastity

WHERE TO FIND IT

Beatitudes	page 108
Cardinal Virtues	page 202
Theological Virtues	page 201
Works of Mercy	page 151, 289

The Sign of the Cross

In the name of the Father, and of the Son, and of the Holy Spirit.
Amen.

In nomine Patris

In nomine Patris, et Filii, et Spiritus Sancti.
Amen.

The Lord's Prayer

Our Father, who art in heaven,
hallowed be thy name;
thy kingdom come,
thy will be done
on earth as it is in heaven.
Give us this day our daily bread,
and forgive us our trespasses,
as we forgive those who trespass against us;
and lead us not into temptation,
but deliver us from evil.
Amen.

The Magnificat (Mary's Canticle)

My soul proclaims the greatness of the Lord,
   my spirit rejoices in God my Savior;
   for he has looked with favor on his lowly servant.
From this day all generations will call me blessed:
   the Almighty has done great things for me,
   and holy is his name.
He has mercy on those who fear him
   in every generation.
He has shown the strength of his arm,
   he has scattered the proud in their conceit.
He has cast down the mighty from their thrones,
   and has lifted up the lowly.
He has filled the hungry with good things,
   and the rich he has sent away empty.
He has come to the help of his servant Israel
   for he has remembered his promise of mercy,
   the promise he made to our fathers,
   to Abraham and his children for ever.

—See *Luke 1:46–55*

GO online Visit www.osvcurriculum.com for other prayers in Latin.

An Act of Contrition

My God,
  I am sorry for my sins with all my heart.
  In choosing to do wrong
    and failing to do good,
  I have sinned against you
  whom I should love above all things.
  I firmly intend, with your help,
  to do penance,
  to sin no more,
  and to avoid whatever leads me to sin.
  Our Savior Jesus Christ
  suffered and died for us.
  In his name, my God, have mercy.

Memorare

Remember, most loving Virgin Mary,
  never was it heard
  that anyone who turned to you for help
  was left unaided.
  Inspired by this confidence,
  though burdened by my sins,
  I run to your protection
  for you are my mother.
  Mother of the Word of God,
  do not despise my words of pleading
  but be merciful and hear my prayer.
Amen.

WORDS OF FAITH

A

abba The Aramaic word with the English equivalent of "daddy" or "papa." (*34*)

abortion The deliberate termination of a pregnancy by killing an unborn child. It is a grave sin. (*191*)

actual sin A personal thought, word, or deed that violates God's law. (*117*)

Annunciation The visit of the angel Gabriel to Mary to tell her that she would be the Mother of God and give birth to the Savior. (*65*)

Anointing of the Sick One of the Sacraments of Healing for people who are seriously ill, elderly, or in danger of dying. In the sacrament, the person's forehead and hands are anointed with the blessed oil of the sick. (*246*)

Apostles The twelve men Jesus chose to be his closest followers and to share in his work and mission in a special way. (*136*)

B

Baptism The sacrament of new life in Christ through the forgiveness of sins and incorporation into the Church; the first Sacrament of Initiation. (*230*)

GO online Visit www.osvcurriculum.com for a mutimedia faith glossary.

Beatitudes

Beatitudes Jesus' eight teachings about the meaning and path to true happiness; they depict the attitudes and actions that followers of Christ should have and the way to live in God's kingdom today. They describe the way to attain the eternal holiness or blessedness to which God calls all people. (*108*)

Bible God's word written by humans acting under the inspiration of the Holy Spirit. (*20*)

Blessed Trinity The mystery of one God in three divine Persons: Father, Son, and Holy Spirit. (*52*)

C

canon The Church's official collection of inspired books of sacred Scripture. (*20*)

cardinal virtues The four most important moral virtues to which all others are connected: prudence, justice, fortitude, and temperance. (*202*)

chastity A moral virtue that helps individuals maintain the right balance of body and spirit in human sexuality. Chastity helps individuals express their sexuality in the right way for their state of life (married, single, ordained, or consecrated). (*203*)

Church The community of all baptized people who believe in the Blessed Trinity and follow Jesus. (*146*)

Confirmation The Sacrament of Initiation through which the spiritual life received in Baptism is strengthened and the person is sealed with the Gift of the Holy Spirit. (*230*)

conscience The God-given ability that helps individuals know the difference between right and wrong. (*25*)

consecrated life A state of life lived by religious sisters, brothers, and priests in community and characterized by the vows of poverty, chastity, and obedience. (*264*)

contrition True sorrow for disobeying God and the commitment to try to avoid sin in the future. (*243*)

conversion A sincere change of mind, heart, and desire to turn away from sin and evil and turn toward God. (*243*)

Corporal Works of Mercy Actions that care for the physical needs of others. (*151*)

covenant A sacred promise or agreement between humans or between God and humans. (*33*)

discernment The process by which a person reflects, discusses, and prays about how God might be calling him or her to live out a particular vocation. (*263*)

doctrines Official teachings of the Church. (*137*)

domestic Church A term for the Christian family, which is as a holy community where children first learn about God through the love, teaching, and good example of parents and other family members. (*261*)

encyclicals Official letters written by the pope, usually addressed to all Church members. (*137*)

eternal The term that means "God is" and "has always been," even before the beginning of time, and will be forever. (*12*)

Eucharist The Sacrament of Initiation during which the bread and wine become the Body and Blood of Christ and all who receive him in Holy Communion are brought closer to him and one another. (*230*)

euthanasia The deliberate action or non-action which causes the death of someone who is sick, dying, or suffering because of disabilities or a debilitating condition. It is a grave sin. (*191*)

evangelist One of the four authors of the Gospels: Matthew, Mark, Luke, and John. The word is also used for those who actively spread the Christian faith. (*23*)

free will The God-given ability to choose and make decisions on your own without being forced to choose or act in a certain way. (*158*)

grace The free and undeserved gift God gives us of his life so that we can become his adopted children. (*54*)

heaven The state, or experience, of being happy with God forever; eternal life with God. (*286*)

hell The state, or experience, of eternal separation from God. (*286*)

hierarchy The organization of the Church into different levels of leadership and membership. (*146*)

I

Incarnation The mystery that the second Person of the Blessed Trinity, the Son of God, assumed human nature and became man while remaining God; Jesus Christ is both true God and true man. (*63*)

inspiration The process by which the Holy Spirit assisted the human authors in writing the Bible. (*20*)

311

intellect The God-given ability which makes it possible for humans to think, reason, and judge. (*176*)

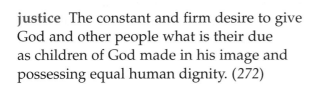

justice The constant and firm desire to give God and other people what is their due as children of God made in his image and possessing equal human dignity. (*272*)

kingdom of God God's rule of love, peace, and justice in our hearts, lives, and world. (*272*)

L

last judgment Christ's judgment of both the living and the dead that will occur at his Second Coming at the end of time. (*288*)

lay person A baptized member of the Church who shares in Jesus' mission and witnesses to him and his message in his or her home, work place, school, and in the broader community. (*261*)

M

miracle A sign or wonder such as a healing, which can take place only through the power of God. (*66*)

modesty A moral virtue that helps individuals respect their sexuality by being discreet and decent in the ways they dress, talk, and act. (*203*)

mortal sin A grave (very serious) sin by which someone turns completely away from God. The conditions of mortal sin are: the matter must be serious, the person must know the sinful action is serious, and the person must freely choose to do it. (*177*)

murder The deliberate killing of another person. It is always gravely sinful because it shows the contempt the murderer has for the dignity of human life as well as for the holiness and goodness of God the creator. (*189*)

mystery A truth of faith that cannot be fully understood but that is believed because God has shown it in Scripture, in the life of Jesus, or in the teachings of the Church. (*9*)

Mystical Body of Christ An image or description for the Church, which unites all believers through the Holy Spirit into one holy people, with Christ as their head and themselves as the body. (*146*)

Nativity The birth of Jesus. (*92*)

natural law God's fatherly instruction that is written on the hearts of all people and understood through intellect. (*36*)

original sin The sin of the first humans that wounded human nature and introduced sin, suffering, and death into the world; all humans are born with original sin and are thus tempted to sin. (*117*)

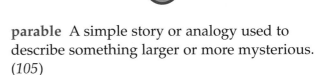

parable A simple story or analogy used to describe something larger or more mysterious. (*105*)

particular judgment The judgment that takes place at the moment of death at which each person's soul is rewarded with the blessings of heaven, given a time of purification in purgatory, or condemned to eternal separation from God in hell. (*286*)

Paschal mystery Christ's work of redemption through his Passion, death, Resurrection, and Ascension. (*121*)

prayer Raising one's mind and heart to God. (*78*)

purgatory A state of purification between death and heaven that removes any remaining personal obstacles to eternal union with God. Purgatory frees the person from the temporal punishment (being deprived of the entrance into heaven for a time) due to sin. (*287*)

Reconciliation The Sacrament of Healing in which, through God's mercy and forgiveness, the sinner is reconciled with God and also with the Church. (*244*)

reparation An attempt to directly or indirectly "repair" the damage done by the sin. (*205*)

sacraments Effective signs of God's grace, established by Jesus and given to his Church, by which God shares his life through the work of the Holy Spirit. (*218*)

scandal The destructive behavior by which a person deliberately leads, through his or her own action or inaction, another person to sin. (*193*)

Sermon on the Mount The well-known section of Matthew's Gospel that gathers many of Jesus' teachings. (*106*)

solidarity A Christian virtue that motivates believers to share their spiritual gifts as well as their material ones. (*277*)

soul The spiritual principle of humans. (*176*)

Spiritual Works of Mercy Actions that care for the spiritual needs of others. (*288*)

spiritualities Ways of praying and living as a disciple. (*138*)

temporal punishment The process of purification after death that is necessary before entering heaven. (*161*)

Ten Commandments The ten fundamental moral laws recorded in the Old Testament and given by God to his people to help them live by the covenant. (*36*)

theological virtues Gifts from God that help us believe in him, trust in his plan for us, and love him as he loves us; they are faith, hope, and love. (*201*)

transubstantiation The process by which, through the power of the Holy Spirit and the words and actions of the priest, the bread and wine are transformed into the Body and Blood of Christ during the Eucharistic Prayer of the Mass. (*235*)

universal A mark of the Church. The Church is for all people at all times and in all places. (*160*)

venial sin A less serious sin that weakens, but does not destroy, a person's relationship with God and other people. (*177*)

virtue A strong habit of doing good that helps people make good moral decisions. (*201*)

Visitation The event of Mary, who was pregnant with Jesus, visiting her cousin Elizabeth, who was pregnant with John the Baptist. (*92*)

vocation A holy calling from our Baptism to love and serve God and others. This vocation can be lived out through the various states of life: a lay person (married or single), a member of the ordained ministry, or a consecrated religious (sister, brother, priest). (*262*)